Abstracts
of the
Inventories
and Accounts
of the
PREROGATIVE COURT
of MARYLAND

Libers 16, 17, 18, 19, 19½A, 19½B

———

1697–1700

Vernon L. Skinner, Jr.

HERITAGE BOOKS
2012

HERITAGE BOOKS
AN IMPRINT OF HERITAGE BOOKS, INC.

Books, CDs, and more—Worldwide

For our listing of thousands of titles see our website
at
www.HeritageBooks.com

Published 2012 by
HERITAGE BOOKS, INC.
Publishing Division
100 Railroad Ave. #104
Westminster, Maryland 21157

Originally published 1992

International Standard Book Numbers
Paperbound: 978-1-58549-244-2
Clothbound: 978-0-7884-9444-4

The probate records of the Prerogative Court of Maryland contain several types of records: testamentary proceedings, wills, administration accounts, inventories, inventories and accounts, and distributions. Each kind of record has value for the genealogist. Prior to 1777, all probate records were required to be filed with the Prerogative Court of Maryland.

The Inventories and Accounts was a separate series of probate records established in 1674 and continued until 1718. At that time, the series was split into two: Inventories; and Accounts. Both series continued until 1777, when the Prerogative Court was abolished. Abstracts of the Inventories series have been published in 17 volumes by Family Line Publications.

The Inventories and Accounts contain the following records:

1. An inventory was performed if the estate had moveable goods. The inventory included a listing of such things as clothes, household items, negroes, occupational tools. (A particular type of inventory cited debts due to the estate.) Items in the inventory reveal a great deal about the decedent and the family, especially his wealth, occupation, and manner of living. As part of the inventory, names of several other persons might be cited: appraiser(s) of the estate, creditors, next of kin (or relations), legatees, and administrators or executors. The abstracts of the inventories cite the following:

    Information about the inventory.
        Name of the decedent.
        Liber and folio reference.
        "I"--indicating that this particular entry in the abstracts is an inventory.
        County. (See the table below for abbreviations.)
        Amount cited in the inventory. The amount will be either in pounds of tobacco (a number preceded by a "#") or in currency specified in pounds, shillings, and pence (a number preceded by "£"). In some cases, the amount cited included part of a pence; this part has been dropped.
        Date of the inventory.
        Date of the approval by the executor/administrator.

    Name(s) of the appraiser(s).
    Name(s) of the creditor(s).
    Name(s) of the next of kin.
    Name(s) of the executor/administrator.
    Name(s) of debtors.
    Name(s) of servants.
    Name(s) of other persons mentioned.

2. An administration account was the reconciliation of the payments against the estate. This included persons to whom money was owed, legatees, payments made for recording the testamentary acts, etc. The abstracts of the accounts cite the following:

    Information about the accounts.
        Name of the decedent.
        Liber and folio reference.
        "A"--indicating that this particular entry in the abstracts is an administration account.
        County. (See the table below for abbreviations.)
        Amount cited in the account for the associated inventory/inventories. The amount will be either in pounds of tobacco (a number preceded by a "#") or in currency specified in pounds, shillings, and pence (a number preceded by "£"). In some cases, the amount cited included part of a pence; this part has been dropped.
        Amount cited in the account for the total amount of payment. The amount will be either in pounds of tobacco (a number preceded by a "#") or in currency specified in pounds, shillings, and pence (a number preceded by "£"). In some cases, the amount cited included part of a pence; this part has been dropped.
        Date of the approval by the executor/administrator.

    Name(s) of the surety(ies).
    Name(s) of additional debtor(s).
    Name(s) of legatee(s).
    Name(s) of persons paid to:
    Name(s) of persons to whom the remainder of the estate was distributed.
    Name(s) of the executor/administrator.

3. In some cases, both an inventory and the administration account appear in the same entry. The abstracts of the these cite the following:

Information about the inventory and account.
    Name of the decedent.
    Liber and folio reference.
    "B"--indicating that this particular entry in the abstracts is both an inventory and an administration account.
    County. (See the table below for abbreviations.)
    Amount cited in the account for the associated inventory/inventories. The amount will be either in pounds of tobacco (a number preceded by a "#") or in currency specified in pounds, shillings, and pence (a number preceded by "£"). In some cases, the amount cited included part of a pence; this part has been dropped.
    Amount cited in the account for the total amount of payment. The amount will be either in pounds of tobacco (a number preceded by a "#") or in currency specified in pounds, shillings, and pence (a number preceded by "£"). In some cases, the amount cited included part of a pence; this part has been dropped.
    Date of the approval by the executor/administrator.

Name(s) of the surety(ies).
Name(s) of the appraiser(s).
Name(s) of the creditor(s).
Name(s) of the next of kin.
Name(s) of debtors.
Name(s) of servants.
Name(s) of legatee(s).
Name(s) of persons paid to:
Name(s) of persons to whom the remainder of the estate was distributed.
Name(s) of the executor/administrator.

4. Some of the wills for Anne Arundel County appear in the Inventories and Accounts. The abstracts of the these wills cite the following:

Information about the wills.
    Name of the decedent.
    Liber and folio reference.
    "W"--indicating that this particular entry in the abstracts is a will.
    County. (See the table below for abbreviations.)
    Date the will was written.
    Date of probate by the executor/administrator.

Name(s) of the legatee(s).
Name(s) of other persons mentioned.
Name(s) of the executor/administrator.

The following table cites the abbreviations used for the counties. The date of establishment for the county is shown in parentheses.

Anne Arundel	AA	(1650)
Baltimore	BA	(1659)
Calvert	CA	(1654)
Cecil	CE	(1674)
Charles	CH	(1658)
Dorchester	DO	(1668)
Kent	KE	(1642)
Kent Island	KI	
Prince George's	PG	(1695)
Queen Anne	QA	(1706)
St. Mary's	SM	(1637)
Somerset	SO	(1666)
Talbot	TA	(1661)

All names are cited in the index; however, a name may appear more than once on a particular page. All efforts have been made to correctly interpret the names. However, sometimes the handwriting was difficult or impossible to read. The reader should refer to the original liber or photo-copy thereof when possible. No attempt has been made to resolve differences in the spelling of names. Entries such as "his Lordship" or "the Secretary", where no specific name was cited, have been omitted. Copies of any particular inventory or inventories can be obtained on microfilm from the library of the Church of Jesus Christ of the Latter Day Saints, or by means of photoduplication from the Maryland State Archives (350 Rowe Boulevard, Annapolis, Maryland 21401).

All dates prior to 14 September 1752 have been recorded in Old Style format. However, the denotation "(OS)" has not been specified. (Thus, the date January 1, 1751/2 will be written as Jan 1 1751.)

David Pew   16.1   I CH   £8.7.4   Jun 21 1698
    Appraisers: John Barker, James Martin.

Mathew Dyke   16.1   I CH   Jun 4 1698
(also Mathew Dike)
    Appraisers: Thomas Davis (also Thomas Dail), Christopher Foorde (also Christopher
        Forde).

William Smith   16.3   I CH   £142.3.6   Jun 27 1698
    Appraisers: John Booker, Lewis Jonns.

John Vickory   16.4   I DO   £9.17.0   Apr 7 1698
    Appraisers: Ph. Prois, Richard Foster.

Ann Brown   16.4   I   £36.0.0   Apr 30 1698
    Servants mentioned: Robert Ferriell.
    Appraisers: John Clement, John Saunders.

Robert Lofton, Jr.   16.5   I CH   Nov 23 1697
    Appraisers: Thomas Craxson, Francis Billary (also Francis Bohary).

Richard Chandler   16.6   I CH   £417.10.5   Nov 4 1697
    Appraisers: William Stone, Thomas Craxon.

Mr. Baker Brook   16.8   I   £317.4.0   May 28 1698
    Appraisers: Luke Guardiner, John Fenwick.

Maj. Henry Tripp   16.9   I   £260.11.6   May 3 1698
    Appraisers: Mr. John Taylor, Mr. Walter Campbell.

John Lewellin   16.11   I SM   £98.0.7   Apr 21 1698
    Appraisers: Anthony Evens, Solomon Jones.
    Administratrix: Audry Llewellin.

John Forest   16.13   I PG   Apr 21 1698
    Appraisers: Charles Beven (also Charles Beaven), John Chittum (also John
        Chittam).

Mrs. Willmott Hill   16.14   I SO   £29.19.4   May 24 1698
    Appraisers: John Weeb, Walter Evens.
    Administrator: William Wouldhave.

Madam Ann Neale   16.15   I CH   £154.2.6   Jun 20 1698
    Appraisers: Gilbert Clarke, Joseph Wilson.
    Legatees: Anthony Neale, James Neale (son of Henry Neale), Mary Neale, Mr. James
        Neale, Elisabeth Neale.

Mrs. Parthenia Burditt   16.18   I CH   £65.19.10   Apr 4 1698
    Appraisers: John Barker, John Bannester.

John Davis   16.20   I SM   £107.6.11   Apr 14 1698
    Appraisers: John Gillem, Richard Southeron.
    Mentions: Mary Davis (girl).
    List of debts: Joseph Edwards, John Ducker.

John Davis   16.21   A   #7834   Jun 27 1698
    Payments to: Mr. Shofell, Mr. Crooke, Mr. Morland, Mr. Capt. Emmes, Mr. Taney,
        Thomas Barrow.
    Administrator: Peter Harris.

Mr. Thomas Burford   16.22   I CH   £166.12.7   Mar 14 1697
    Appraisers: Robert Yates, Capt. Henry Hardy.
    Approvers: Notley Warren, Richard Dodd.
    Executor: Mr. Walter Story.

Hugh Merriton   16.24   I AA   £345.7.7   Jun 27 1698
    Appraisers: Thomas Homewood, Jonathon Neale.
    List of debts: Capt. Grandy, Richard Jonnes.

John Edmonson   16.26   I TA   £387.13.3   Mar 11 1697
    Appraisers: William Catrop, John Swallow.
    List of debts: Johannas Vaughan, Isack Searylen, Edward Green, John Shayl, John
        Hemler, William Dorrington, Anthony Rumball, George Plater, Robert
        Goldsborough, Samuel Whittherd, William Tayler, Thomas Tomco, Nicholas Lurtty.

Richard Burkett   16.28   I   £37.11.10   Mar 12 1698
    Appraisers: John Tant, James Greenal (also James Greewell).

Edward Cocknell   16.29   I CA   £8.12.0   Apr 4 1698
       Appraisers: William Barton, Thomas Howe.
       List of debts: Mr. George Lingan.

Osias Wells   16.29   I   £34.2.0   May 6 1698
The amount of the inventory also included #950.
       Appraisers: Henry Smith, Charles Smith.

Thomas Fairfax   16.30   B CA   #3010   Jun 12 1698
       Payments to: J. Goldsborough, John Broadhurst, Charles Joy, John Mills.
       Administrator: Nathaniell Cooper (also Thomas Cooper).

William Chesum   16.30   I SM   £19.5.0   Jun 4 1698
       Appraisers: Solomon Jonnes, John Maning (also John Manning).

John Miles   16.31   I SM   £15.15.6   May 30 1698
The amount of the inventory also included #2200.
       Appraisers: Payn Turberfeild, Edward Horne.
       List of debts: Edward Perce, Dr. Richardson.

Robert Bayly   16.31   I SM   £10.4.0   Apr 8 1698
       Appraisers: Stephen Gough, John Britte (also John Britt).
       List of debts: Ann Able, John Sheapeard.

Charolus Watts   16.32   I   £9.0.6   May 17 1698
       Appraisers: Thomas Attaway, Henry Poultery (also Henry Pott).

Ester Williams   16.33   I   Jun 12 1697   Jun 15 1698
       Appraisers: Edward Hillerd, Thomas Grace.
       List of debts: Andrew Mograh.

Elias Beach   16.34   I SM   £21.16.0   Feb 17 1697
       Appraisers: William Guyther, Zacharia Vanswaringen.

Mr. James Pattison   16.34   I   £178.17.0   Apr 26 1698
The amount of the inventory also included #9701.
       Appraisers: Henry Smith, Thomas Smith.
       List of debts: Thomas Rose, Mr. John Lewellin, Mr. Rosewell, Mr. Vanswearingen,
         John Dunbarr, Thomas Guither, Thomas Williams (taylor), Daniell Moy, Col.
         John Cood.

John Smith (Irish)   16.36   I AA   £30.8.9   Apr 12 1698
       Appraisers: Mr. John Gadesby, Mr. Richard Sorrell.
       List of debts: John Cousens, Richard Berry, Patrick Yoodall, Patrick Yowdall.

Mary Aldred   16.37   I DO   £36.10.2   Apr 9 1698
       Appraisers: William Douse, Arthur Betty.

Richard Baly   16.38   I PG   £14.13.2   Jan 20 1696   Apr 16 1697
(also Richard Baylye). The amount of the inventory also include #3945.
       Appraisers: Robert Orme, John Smith.
       Administrator: Thomas Kiniston.

Nicholas Beade   16.39   I CH   £30.3.9
       Appraisers: James Fenley, John Booker.

Richard Hadock   16.40   I AA   £4.15.2   Jun 18 1698
       Appraisers: James Methven, John Daviss.
       List of debts: John Radford, James Badcock, Thomas Huse (planter), Robert Stone,
         John Shearbutt, Thomas Hills (joyner), William Hardin, Thomas Watkins, Abraham
         Burkhead, Edmond Evens, William Byars, John Trundle, John Chandler, Mr.
         Robert Brothers (carpenter), John Murphy, George Robinson (subsheriff), Mr.
         Thomas Hust (lawyer), John Stanford, Jeremiah Eldridge, Thomas Daviss, Robert
         Summers, George Lane, Mr. John Cobroth, John Green, Richard Sidell, Henry
         Padgett, John Mortemore, John Russell, John Merriton, Richard Rake, Patrick
         Morely, Edward Harrison, Thomas Martin, Mr. William Taylor, Oliver Cambridge,
         Robert Stone, John May (planter), Thomas Phillips, David Jones, Nicholas
         White, Mr. William Chew, John Nicholson, Joseph Lowe (carpenter), Mr. John
         Thompson (schoolmaster), Dr. Chappell, John Dodson, Mr. Timothy Hickman, Job.
         Barns, Mr. Henry Bonner, Mr. Richard Sands, Mr. James Cranford, John
         Deavour, Peter Timms, James Pashell, John Ford, Mr. Thomas Hinton, John
         Smith, Joseph Saunders, John Walters, John Harris, Mr. John Duckworth, John
         Proutt of Somerset County, William Roads, William Knight (shoemaker), John
         Colle (cooper), John Norris, John Grifine, Henry Fish (smith), John Norris in
         the swamp, Robert Stone.

Thomas Smithick   16.42   I AA   £10.0.9   May 26 1698
The amount of the inventory also included #1600.
       Appraisers: Cornelius Howard.
       List of debts: Edward Rumbly, Samuell Wealdes, George Bird, James Finely.

Cornelius Watkins   16.42   I SM   £55.15.0   Apr 22 1698   Jun 26 1698
The amount of the inventory also included #22380.
     Appraisers: John Gillum, Richard Sothoron.
     Mentions: Mrs. Elisabeth Watkins.
     List of debts: Col. Henry Jowles, Col. Beale, Mr. William Stone, Christopher
         Bane, Jonathon Wilson, John Dunken, Mr. William Dent, Joseph Harrison, Mr.
         Wooton, Mr. Joshua Cecill, Vestry of All Faith's Parish, Peter Divine
         (runaway).

Thomas Booker   16.45   I TA   £61.3.6   Feb 20 1696
     Appraisers: Daniell Walker, Edward Latham.

George & Elisabeth Norman   16.46   I BA   £74.10.0
     Appraisers: James Morray, Jacob Jackson.

John Sawell   16.47   I SM   £103.16.7   May 10 1698
     Appraisers: John Nutthall, Robert Clarke.

James Jackson   16.48   I BA   £56.11.6   May 5 1698   May 25 -----
     Appraisers: James Marry, John Gardi.

Edward Man   16.48   I TA   £68.19.6   Jun 9 1697
     Appraisers: Mr. Robert Grundy, Thomas Delaway (also Thomas Delahay).

Mr. John Cracraaft   16.50   I PG   £1222.1.3   Mar 10 1697
The amount of the inventory also included #14495.
     Appraisers: John Burd, William Smith.
     List of debts: Micajah Perry, Joseph Willson, Samuell Groome, Maj. Barton, James
         Cranford, Jonathon Tench, Thomas Tasker, Joseph Hall, Richard Sandy, Ignatius
         Cracraft, Nicholas Sewall, John Wight, James Downall, Thomas Tinsly, George
         Plater, William Stone, Thomas Johnson, Capt. William Holland, Nicholas
         Sporne, Philip Lynes, Charles Tracey.

Thomas Baker   16.51   I AA   £7.2.8   Jun 10 1698
     Appraisers: Laurence Draper, Jacob Lushy.

Richard Beauman   16.52   I   £156.15.1   Jun 15 1698
     Appraisers: Mr. Anthony Neale, Mr. Gilbert Clarke.
     List of debts: Thomas Dixson, Thomas Simpson, William Foster, Walter Story, Henry
         Hardy, Clement Lomax, D. French, Michaell Webb.

Thomas Morgan   16.53   I BA   £58.3.0   May 25 1698
     Appraisers: John Hayes, John Barrett.
     List of debts: Nicholas Fitzsymond, Robert Parker, Nath. Stinchcome, Alexander
         Lumly, James Morray, Hector Macklane.
     Administrator: Nicholas Fitzsymond.

William Johnson   16.54   I   £26.11.0
     Appraisers: Silvester Welsh, Theophilus Cittor (?).
     Administrator: Francis Johnson.

Gabriell Parrott, Jr.   16.55   I AA   £482.4.3   Jun 23 1698
The amount of the inventory also included #1950.
     Appraisers: Anthony Smith, James Ford.
     List of debts: Capt. Richard Hill, Capt. Anlley, William Burgess, Jonathon
         Tipton, Samuell Thorley, James Ford, Edward Harrison.

Mr. Richard Bayly   16.58   I AA   £471.10.11   Apr 2 1692   Jun 28 1698
     Appraisers: Humphry Boone, Edward Gibbs.
     List of debts: Mrs. Constable, William Mote, Richard Todd.
     Mentions: Capt. Strottan in London.

Thomas Phillman   16.60   I SO   £15.17.7   Apr 20 1698
(also Thomas Hillman)
     Appraisers: John Panter, John Jones.
     Administrator: George Hutchins.

William Boswell   16.60   I SM   £5.2.7   Feb 18 1697
     Appraisers: Thomas (no surname given), Thomas (no surname given).

Mr. Henry Trueman   16.61   I
     List of debts: Samuell Groome, John Hyde, John Burd, James Marline, Richard Keen.

Maj. Thomas Francis   16.61   A   £3.9.4   Mar 16 1697
     Payments to: Charles Whitehead.
     Administratrix: Mary Young, wife of Samuell Young.

Francis Freeman   16.61   I CA   £558.11.7   May 28 1698
     Servants mentioned: William Bardo, John Ferguson, James Morison, Ann Eston.
     Appraisers: John Scott, Francis Maldin.

Arthur Kene   16.62   I SM   £3.15.0   May 21 -----
     Appraisers: Richard Attwood, John Manning.

John Heard   16.63   A SM   £223.11.3   #1620   1698
     List of debts: Samuel Watkins, Arthur Thompson, Symon Pearch.
     Administratrix/Executrix: Susan Heard.

Nathaniel Innis   16.63   A   £136.19.11   Jun 14 1698
     Payments to: ------ Blackstone, Samuell Hopkins, Robert Cade, Hugh Hinson, John
          Webb, John Burdage, James Maynard, Mr. Jenkins, Mr. Eriskin, Maj. Whittington.
     Distribution to: 3 orphans (unnamed).
     Administrator/Executor: William Bittingham.

Roger Bishop   16.63   A   £78.8.8   Jun 28 1698
     Received from: Daniell Palmer.
     Administrator: John Batty.

Robert Downs   16.63   A   £41.0.8   #9139
The amount of the inventory is equivalent to #9848.
     Payments to: Maj. Whittington, Peter Dent, Mr. Jenkins, William Piper, Daniel
          Hast, Roger Barker, Elisabeth Walter, John Hamlin, Gabriell Coper, Richard
          Jefferson, James Wetherly, William Phillips, John Kemp, John Tayler, Edward
          Bennett, Richard Tull, Samuell Wothrinton.
     Mentions: 3 orphans (unnamed).
     Administrator/Executor: John Leverton.

Arthur Pursivall   16.64   A   #1739
     List of debts: Thomas Bruff.
     Administrator: William Hemsley.

John Davis   16.64   A SM   £107.6.11   Jun 28 1698
     Payments to: James Crooke, Jacob Moreland for Mr. Mason, Philip Porish, Thomas
          Taney for Joseph Hartley, William Morris, Joseph Edwards for William Bull.
     Mentions: Mary Davis (daughter, dead), 1 orphan (unnamed).
     Executrix: Mary Harris, wife of Peter Harris.

Michaell Disharoon   16.65   A SO   #5364   #3074   Jun 14 -----
     Payments to: Maj. Whittington, Mr. Jenkins.
     Mentions: 4 orphans (unnamed).
     Administratrix/Executrix: Jone Disharoon.

Stephen Costin   16.65   A SO   £194.12.9   £206.10.9 Jun 20 1698
A second inventory was cited in the amount of £11.18.0.
     Payments to: Teague Linllame, Thomas Jones, William Foxen, George Layfield, Maj.
          Whittington.
     Distribution to: widow, 6 orphans (unnamed).
     Administratrix/Executrix: Comfort Costin (widow).

Mr. Ignatius Cussine   16.66   A CH   £129.16.5   £36.16.1
     Payments to: John Watkins, Samuell Luckett, Thomas Smallwood, John Wathen, Mr.
          Francis Green.
     Executrix: June Reeves (relict), wife of Ugatt Reeves.

John Tillotson   16.66   A   #4834   Apr 12 1698
     Payments to: Edward Swetman, John Hawkins, Robert Norrest for Alexander Campbell,
          Capt. James Smith for administrators of ------ Butler, ------ Lewellin,
          Nicholas Low, Christopher Denney, Stephen Rich, Edward Smith, Patricke Obryan,
          Daniell Toads, Esq. Smith.
     Mentions: 5 children (unnamed).
     Administratrix: Ann Hugh, wife of John Hugh.

Robert Noble   16.67   A   £287.2.2
     Distribution to: widow (unnamed, her thirds).
     Administrator/Executor: William Hemsley.

Mr. Richard Charlett   16.67   A PG   #1753   Jun 28 1698
     Payments to: Charles Tracy, Robert Gates, Mr. Ignatius Cracraft, Mr. Josias
          Willson.
     Administrator: Mr. Thomas Greenfield.

Col. Blackiston   16.67   A   #1800   Apr 12 1698
     Received from: estate of Daniell Longman.
     Mentions: daughter (unnamed, dead).
     Administratrix: ------ (name not given).

Thomas Hillman   16.67   A   #1581   Jun 16 1698
     Payments to: John Winsor, Margarett Little, Charles Williams.
     Administrator/Executor: George Hutchins.

David Floyd   16.68   A   £2.12.2   #960   Mar 20 1697
The amount of the inventory is equivalent to #1034.
        Received from: Daniell Pope.
        Payments to: Esq. Cheseldyne, Joshua Cæcill.
        Administratrix: Mary Floydd, wife of Henry Gutridge.

Dennis Smith   16.68   A   £2.17.2   #1966   Mar 20 1697
He is also known as "Deaf Dennis".
        Payments to: James Moore, Joshua Cecill.
        Administrator: Thomas Clarke.

John Rowell   16.69   A AA £27.18.6   #5014   Apr 18 1698
        Payments to: Ann Hammon, John Meriton, George Vestall, Ralph Basell.
        Mentions: family of 8 people (unnamed).
        Executrix: Elisabeth Walters, wife of Christopher Walters.

John Howell   16.69   A   Apr 14 1698
        Payments to: Stephen Collman, Thomas Jones, Abraham Wilde, Richard Edmonds,
            Nathaniel Howell, Joseph Hopkins.
        Administratrix: Mary Pope (Quaker).

Mr. Edward Pinder   16.70   I   #22201
        List of debts: John Pope, Robert Brumell, Henry Grifeth.

Richard Baly   16.70   A AA £470.10.11   £21.19.8
        Payments to: Dr. Moore, William Mitchell on account of his wife (unnamed), Edward
            Saunders, William Smith, William Coventry, Jacob Goy, Edward Gibbs, Joseph
            Pettibone, Richard Todd, Stephen Blatchfoord.
        Legatees: wife (unnamed), William Smith, Edward Gibbs.
        Executor: Joshua Meriken.

Thomas Barnett   16.71   A PG £100.7.9   #12169   Apr 4 1698
The amount of the inventory is equivalent to #23978.
        Payments to: Mr. David Small.
        Mentions: 2 orphans (unnamed).
        Executrix: Sabina Wickam, wife of Nicholas Wickam.

Thomas Meech   16.72   A SM £10.13.0   £33.14.5   Mar 15 1697
The accounts are also filed for Somerset County.
        Received from: Col. David Browne.
        Payments to: Philip Clarke, Mr. Robert Mason.
        List of debts: Philip Clarke, Mr. John Lowe, William Johnson.
        Approvers: Mr. Thomas Beale, Mr. Richard Benton.
        Administrators: Robert Mason, Philip Clarke.

Francis Higham   16.73   A   #3938   Apr 11 1698
        Payments to: James Martin, Mary Hall, William Dawkins.
        Administratrix: Elisabeth Gill, wife of William Gill.

John Brasseur   16.73   A CA £97.12.0   #1761   Mar 10 1697
        Payments to: Thomas Nicholls due to John Bussell, Benjamin Arnold, James
            Maclanell.
        Executrix: Ann Lansly, wife of Charles Lansly.

Roger Bishop   16.74   A   £78.8.8   £57.0.5
        Received from: Daniell Palmer.
        Payments to: Nehemiah Burbett.
        Mentions: 3 children (unnamed).

Robert Doyne   16.74   A
        Received from: Mr. Cleborne Lomax, Cornelius Butwell.
        Payments to: Mr. William Hutchins, Mr. William Stone.
        Executrix: Ann Plater, wife of George Plater.

John Curry   16.75   A   Jan 22 1697
        Appraisers: Edward Cole, James French.
        Payments to: Mr. Hubbart, Charles Brooks, Francis Knott, Cornelius Brannocke.

Edward Man   16.75   A TA £68.19.6   Apr 15 1698
        Payments to: Joseph Leech, Solomon Wright, Sebaston Mason, William Edmondson.
        Administratrix: Luce Sherwood, wife of John Sherwood.

Peter Godard   16.76   A   #376   Jan 4 1697
        Administrator: Mr. James Heigh.

Daniell Sherwood   16.76   B   £7.5.0   £2.4.2   Nov 1697
The amount of the inventory also included #400. The amount of the accounts also
included #1450.
        Sureties: John Groves, Esq. Cheseldyne, William Woodward.
        Appraisers: Thomas How, John Mouall.

Col. George Robotham   16.77   I TA   £706.14.11   Apr 20 1698
    Appraisers: John Emerson, William Clark.
    Mentions: Capt. Anthony Slatton, Maj. Thomas Smithson.

John Robins   16.85   I TA   £94.11.10   Oct 6 1697
    Appraisers: Thomas Robins, Jr., William Curtis.
    List of debts: Thomas Johnings, Mr. Thomas Bruff, Robert Brodaway, John Loyd,
        Daniell Waker, Richard Parnes, William Morrison, John Wyles, William Hynson,
        John Briggs, Thomas Beckles, Mr. John Viner, Mr. Samuell Withers, Henry
        Adcock, William Jones (planter), Mr. John Cape, Timothy Dunnevant, John Davis
        (planter), John Duckworth, Charles Hollensworth, Richard Bruff, John Dine, Mr.
        John Lane, John Pattison, Henry Fox, Joseph Vickers, John Lee, Mr. Robert
        Smith, Edmund Norris, John Hiring, Samuell Brodaway, Edward Pond, Moses
        Sherry, Murtah Harvey, John Burnham, John Blak, Richard Taylor, Robert
        Caswell, Henrick Johnson, Edgar Webb, John Freeman, Thomas Sandland, Mr.
        Lawrence Knowles, Mr. Andrew Tonnard, Jeffery Barlow, Abraham Hurlock,
        William Berry, Robert Devenish, George Hutchison, Daniell O'Delly, Richard
        Mirex, Capt. James Murphy, Allexander Moore, Richard Haman, James Davy,
        Christopher Pinder, Thomas Alcock, Robert Robertson, Roger Baddy, Mrs. Mary
        Royston, Thomas Booker, John Roads, William Snelling, Jr., Robert Betts,
        George Smith, James Williams, George Willson, James Seward, John Glandenring,
        James Bishop, William Hopper, Mathew Jenkins, Robert Marley, Ollivar
        Millington, William Watts, Peter Watts, Andrew Price, George Hadaway, Francis
        Lates, John Richards, Robert Ratcliffe, Mr. Thomas Anderson, John Baynard,
        Mr. John Sides, Thomas Camper, David Mills, John Pooley, David Rogers,
        William Boullon, Mr. Jacob Seth, Mr. William Hatfeild, Michaell Deane,
        William Anderson, Richard Harrington, Robert Bishop, Thomas Clements, Richard
        Dudley, Jacob Gibson, Mr. John Hawkins, Obadiah Judkin, Col. Vincent Lowe,
        Arthur Emery, Jr., Robert Morton, John Newnham, Jr., Mr. Samuell Newton,
        Patrick O'Bryan, Mr. Anthony Rumball, Mr. John Vallient, Solomon Jones,
        Richard Purnell, Mr. John Lowe, Mr. James Moony, Mr. Daniell Sherwood for
        Joseph Spell, Arthur Emery, Sr., Mr. Andrew Follen, Christopher Spry, Harman
        Fulk, William Brown, Samuell Wersley, John Faulkner, William Howgood, Richard
        Hynson, Peter Watkins, Henry Lynes, Robert Waters.

James Dunkan   16.88   A SO   £88.12.0   £95.5.4   May 27 1698
    Payments to: John Godin, Robert Perrie, Christian Harmonson, Thomas Scott, John
        Webb, John Henry, Francis Heap, Adam Spence, James Round, James Stanfeild,
        Frances Allexander, Edward Green, John Pope, Mr. Andrew Davis, John Edgar,
        William Hinderson, John Dryden, Thomas Roberts, Archbell Holines, Allexander
        McColluck, Charles Godferry, Mr. Francis Jenkins, William Shanland, Adam
        Spence by Jonathon Towers, George Noble, Bryan Pearl, Martin Curtis, Morgan
        Patten, Maj. William Whittington, Col. Darnall, Mr. Carroll, Thomas Ocford,
        Nicholas White.
    Executrix: Elisabeth Dunkan.

Richard Rawlings   16.89   A   £89.17.6   £27.8.7   May 28 1698
    Payments to: Thomas Bland, Col. Henry Ridgly.
    Executors: Phillip Griffith, Jane Rawlings.

Richard Rawling   16.89   I   #790
    List of debts: John Carter, James Cheiffers, Edward Foster, John Norwood.
    Executrix: Jane Griffin (late Jane Rawling).

Francis Meeke   16.89   A CH   Jun 27 1698
    Payments to: William Bishop, Richard Harrison.
    Administratrix: Mary Meek.

Peter Bodkin   16.90   A SO   #4342   #8304   May 21 1698
    Received from: William Henery, Allen Ross, John Henderson, Anne Bishop (widow),
        Charles Williams.
    Payments to: Anne Bishop (widow).
    Executors: John Henery, William Robison.

Mr. Daniell Selby   16.90   A SO   £228.8.3   £228.8.3   May 28 1698
    Payments to: Mr. Robert Cade, Elisabeth Parker (widow), Mr. George Leyfeild,
        Maj. William Whittington, Samuell Hopkins, Jr., Mr. John Wise, Hope Taylor,
        John Watts, William Faucitt, John Henry, William Noble, Sr., Samuell
        Worthington, John Edgar (merchant), Donock Dennis, Jr., Mr. Thomas Jones.
    Distribution to: executors as 2 of the orphans, 2 brethren (unnamed) and 1 sister
        (unnamed).
    Executors: Parker Selby, Daniell Selby.

Phillip Cooksey   16.91   A CH   £30.8.8   £29.8.5   Jun 28 1697
    Payments to: Joseph Hearsly, Richard Evenes, Jonas Parker, Charles Walson, Thomas
        Hutchinson, Capt. John Bayne.
    Administratrix: Sarah Cooksey.

Dr. William Hall   16.92   I CH £32.16.0   May 13 1697
    Servants mentioned: William Bradbury.
    Appraisers: Mr. John Godshall, Ralph Shaw.

William Hall (chirurgeon)   16.93   A CH £32.16.0   Jun 2 1698
    Received from: Mr. William Hutchinson, Thomas Hargest, Patrick Magetee.
    Payments to: Ignatius Wheeler, Robert Price, Mrs. Anne Fouke, John Wilkeson,
        Thomas Mitchell, David Pew, Col. Madocks, Mr. James Smallwood, Mr. Henry
        Hawkins, Maj. Dent upon account of Anne Fouke.
    Executrix: Mary Hall.

Obadia Evans   16.94   A CA £109.3.6   £109.3.6   Mar 11 1697
    Payments to: Christopher Bayne, John Turner.
    Distribution to: widow (unnamed), orphans (unnamed).
    Executrix: relict (unnamed), wife of Darby Henly.

Rouland Thornbourgh   16.94   A BA £81.8.0   £81.8.0   Mar 10 1697
    Payments to: Mr. Henry Land paid to John Spink (merchant) in England, Mr.
        Boothby, Thomas Weekes.
    Distribution to: widow, 5 children (unnamed)>
    Executrix: Anne Royston (relict), wife of John Royston.

John Hambleton   16.95   A   £29.2.6   £31.8.0   Jan 17 1697
    Payments to: John Macmamy, Samuell Watkins, Ellinor Parslow, Francis Pattee,
        Joseph Edloe, Samuell Holdsworth for use of Robert Carvile, Samuell Watkins
        for use of Charles Carroll, William Parker, Thomas Purnell, Col. Jowles, Sir
        Thomas Lawrence, Col. Beale, John Griggs, Samuell Watkins for William Cooper.
    Executor: William Braborne.

Maurice Hooper   16.96   A KI £4.15.7   £5.15.2   Jun 11 1698
    Payments to: Mr. John Coppedge.
    Administrator: Lewis DeRocheborne.

Richard Beaumount   16.96   A CH £43.14.0   #19244   Jul 11 1695
    Payments to: Dr. Kingsbery, William Hatch, Col. Blakiston, Col. Warren, Capt.
        Hardidge, William Simmons, Gilbert Clark, John Turling, Mrs. Anne Neale,
        Thomas Clark, James Neale.
    Administratrix: Mary Burgess (relict).

Capt. Samuell Bourne   16.97   A   Jan 17 1697
    Payments to: William Dent, William Herring, Kenelm Cheseldyne, Nathan Dare, Capt.
        William Eaton, Robert Stratton, Samuell Watkins, Henry Fernly, Sir Thomas
        Lawrence, John Llewellin, William Parker, Michaell Taney, Capt. Claget on
        account for Israell Morgan, William Stone, Col. Jowles, Col. Beale, Henry
        Henington.
    Legatees: Thomas Billingsly, Sarah Roberts, Mary Pollard, Samuell Bourne, Robert
        Roberts for his wife Sarah that left by her father ------ Billingsly.
    Executrix: Mrs. Elisabeth Bourne.

William Moss   16.98   A CA £47.9.3   £50.6.5   Aug 17 1698
A second inventory was cited in the amount of £2.17.2.
    Payments to: William Feild, James Cobb, John Manning, executrix of Henry Truman,
        Joshua Cecill.
    Distribution to: executor.
    Executor: Michaell Taney.

Mr. Richard Charles   16.98   A PG £241.2.6   #6663   Jul 9 1698
    Payments to: Mr. Gilbert Clarke upon Mr. Arthur Camwell paid to Mr. James
        Browne, George Plater, Esq., William Phillip Allen, Mr. Henry Lowe, Mr.
        Jacob Moreland.
    Administrator: Mr. Thomas Greenfeild.

Mr. Joseph Ferry (gentleman) 16.99 A CA £35.15.0   £40.12.0   Aug 5 1698
The amount of the inventory also included #14888.
    Payments to: Thomas Tench, Esq., Col. Henry Mitchell, John Dorman, Edward Evans,
        Richard Sands, Henry Fernely, Mr. James Cranford, Mr. William Parks, Thomas
        Hinton, Ambros Gardiner, Mr. Cheseldyn per George Lingan, William Williams.
    Administrator: Thomas Nichols.

Amos Persons   16.100 I   £4.19.6   Jul 3 1698
    Appraisers: Richard Tull, William Wallace.

John Williams   16.101 A SO   £45.3.3   Jul 7 1698
    Payments to: Mr. Francis Jenkins, Maj. William Whittington, John Broadhurst,
        Katherine Tomlinson (widow), William Brittingham, Allexander Maddox, John
        Cornish.
    Distribution to: 7 children (unnamed).
    Administrator/Executor: Henry Rich.

Sarah Cocke   16.101   I   £93.5.11   May 25 1698   Jun 20 1698
        Appraisers: Mathew Howard, Richard Moss.

Thomas Fisher   16.103   I KI   £67.13.6   Jul 4 1698
        Appraisers: William Elliott, John Winchester.
        List of debts: John Winchester.

Thomas Hyde   16.105   I   £49.12.3   Jun 15 1698
        Appraisers: Bartholomew Goff, Joseph Addison.

Charles Hay   16.105   I PG   £21.7.2   May 14 1693
        Appraisers: Thomas Sprigg, Daniell Donellson.

Henry Jones   16.106   I PG   £5.9.9   May 7 1698
        Appraisers: John Josling, Thomas Nellson.

Martin Falkner   16.107   I PG   £26.16.0   Jun 25 1698
        Appraisers: Thomas Sprigg, Edward Dawson.

Joseph Morley   16.107   I TA   £76.16.5   Jul 3 1698
        Appraisers: George Vincent (also George Vinson), Richard Kempston.
        List of debts: Winefred Harvey, Michaell Miller, Phill. Copedge, George Vincent.

Mr. Thomas Blanford   16.108   I   £118.19.2
        Appraisers: Samuell Magruder, John Pottenger.

John Lawrence   16.109   I   £58.9.0   Jul 20 1698
        Appraisers: John Hunt, Henry Cox.
        List of debts: John Hyde, Joseph Jackson.

Alice Smith   16.110   I CA   £210.4.3   Jul 28 1698
        Appraisers: George Coale (also George Cole), Richard Evans (also Richard Evens).
        Mentions: Mr. Joseph Jackson.

Tymothy Guntor   16.111   I CA   £47.17.0
        Appraisers: George Spicer, Thomas Kingcart.

Thomas Danvas   16.112   I AA   £11.11.0   Jun 27 1698
        Appraisers: Thomas Hughs, Zachariah Cadle.

John Bouye   16.113   I   £5.7.9   Aug 6 1698
        Appraisers: Charles Kilburne, Robert Phillips.

Robert Cooper   16.113   I TA   £10.19.6   May 27 1698
        Appraisers: John Copedge, Thomas Marsh.

Mr. William Dorrington   16.114   A   £210.11.0   £99.9.8   Sep 9 1698
        Payments to: Mr. Morrice Mathewes, Mr. Phillip Pitt, John Dickingson, Allice
        Wheeler, Christopher Short, Mrs. Anne Hunt, Obadiah King, Anthony Thompson,
        Sarah Wheeler, Mr. Walter Campbell, John Rickards, Thomas Martin, William
        Wattson, Mr. John Taylor, Nicholas Phillips, Cornelius Arrington, Mr. John
        Rawlings, Gervas Cuttler, Maj. William Dent, George Plater, Esq., Sir John
        Dudlestone, Allice Kennerly, Mr. John Snelson, Mr. Daniell Clarke, Capt.
        Richard Smith, Mr. Francis Taylor, Mr. William Sharp, Mrs. Allice Wheeler,
        William Stephens.
        Administrator: Charles Powell.

Henry Aldridge   16.115   A DO   £36.10.2   £40.2.2   Jun 8 1698
The amount of the accounts also included #9626.
        Payments to: James Heartly, Sir Thomas Lawrence, Anthony Thompson, William
        Mackeill, Richard Kilburne.
        Administrator: Walter Campbell administrator of Mary Aldridge (executrix of
        deceased).

Capt. Benjamin Hunt   16.115   I DO   £212.10.11   Apr 26 ----
        Appraisers: John Kirke, Charles Powell.

George Ladmore   16.117   I DO   £74.11.5   Jun 20 1698
        Appraisers: John Nicolls, Matthyes Allford.

Robert Washfell   16.117   I DO   £21.4.2   Jul 20 1698
(also Robert Washfeild)
        Appraisers: John Nicolls, John Wade.

Thomas Nicholson   16.118   A CE   £43.2.2   £55.15.5   Jul 20 1698
        Payments to: Kenelm Cheseldyn, Esq. paid to Col. William Pearce, Col. William
        Pearce, John Thompson, James Barbott (merchant), Maj. John Donaldson.
        Executrix: Elisabeth Brockson (relict), wife of William Brockson.

Ezeakeall Jackson   16.119   A CE   #7527   #7538   Sep 2 1698
     Payments to: Mr. Charles Bass, Mr. John Carvile, Edward Bathurst for Micajah
        Perry & Co., Mr. William Harry.
     Mentions: 2 children (unnamed).
     Administrator: William Thoms.

John Gilders   16.120   I   £33.14.0
The amount of the inventory also included #2980.
     Appraisers: Richard Franklin, Thomas Parker.
     List of debts: William Oldfeild, Joseph Bornham, James Gore, Lawrence Mounce,
        William Love.
     Administrator/Executor: Charles Dermot.

John Gilders   16.121   A   #2112
     Payments to: Cornelius Pears and Mathias Freeman, Robert Hancock, Col. John
        Thompson, Jeffry Peterson, Thomas Tenesse, Daniell Smith.
     Administrator/Executor: Charles Dermot.

Mr. Charles James   16.121   I   £213.14.9   Jun 17 1698
     Appraisers: Robert Gibbson (also Robert Gibson), Richard Kennard.
     List of debts: Joseph Trulock, Richard Bowden, Col. William Pearce, Hugh Jones,
        Patrick Davison, Dennis Cormack, Thomas Thackstone.

Thomas Linsey   16.124   I   £43.10.10
     Appraisers: Thomas Terry, Mathias Hendrixson.

James Taylor   16.125   I   £28.12.8
     Appraisers: Cornelius Nuckin, Thomas Parker.

John Morris   16.126   A CE   £32.6.6   £32.6.6   Jun 27 1698
     Payments to: Col. William Peerce for use of Kenelme Cheseldyne, Esq., Mr.
        Edward Blay, Gideon Gundry, John Thompson, Col. William Pearce, Jane
        Whetherell, Edward Crew, James Frisby, Kenelme Cheseldyne, John Thomson.
     Distribution to: widow, 4 orphans (unnamed).
     Administratrix: Margarett Redgrave (relict), wife of Abraham Redgrave.

Abraham Hollins   16.127   A CE   £16.1.4   £16.4.0   Jul 26 1698
     Payments to: Kenelm Cheseldyne, Esq. paid to Col. William Pearce, John Thompson,
        Mathias Vanderhyden, Edward Johnson, Isack Vigore paid to John Thompson.
     Administrator: Owen Hewes executor of Edward Johnson (administrator of deceased).

William Groves   16.128   A   #4867   Aug 29 1698
     Mentions: 2 children (unnamed).

William Sutton   16.129   A AA   Sep 12 1698
     Payments to: John Gadsby, Maj. John Hammond.
     Executrix: Mary Crouch by her grandfather Maurice Baker.

David Steward   16.129   A AA   £46.8.8   £46.8.8   Aug 30 1698
     Payments to: Dr. Moore, John Walls, Mordica Moore for use of Benjamin Scrivener,
        Capt. Isacc Wilde per Charles Telley, Capt. Edward Burfford per James Lewis.
     Distribution to: executrix.
     Executrix: Margarett Steward.

Edward Harrison   16.130   I   £16.12.10   Aug 29 1698
Items at the house of Richard Chesher.
     Appraisers: Richard Goott, John Blackmore.

John Cozens   16.130   I AA   £13.15.8   Jul 18 1698
     Appraisers: Abraham Wild, Henry Right.
     List of debts: William Sutton.

William Grove   16.131   I AA   £53.4.11
     Appraisers: Thomas Hughs, John Trundle.

Mr. William Burges   16.132   I   £603.14.7
     Appraisers: Mr. John Baldwin, Mr. Thomas Odell.

Samuell Austin   16.135   A AA   £65.15.0   £102.0.10   Aug 31 1698
A second inventory was cited in the amount of £15.0.0.
     Payments to: Robert Smith, Esq., Dr. Moore, Humphry Jarvis per his note and
        Thomas Baker, Capt. James Braine, Otho Holland, William Biddott, David
        Mackelfish, Nicholas Roades, Richard Jones, Gabriell Parrett, Thomas Bale per
        Richard Jones, Michaell Temple per Jacob Harness, John Attaway, John Port per
        Mr. John Merriton, John Merriton, Jeremiah Deable.
     Administratrix: Alice Collier.

Edward Owan   16.136   A KE £13.2.2   #4494   Jun 29 1698
    Payments to: Elisabeth Macgregory per William Williams, Mathew Eareckson,
        Michaell Miller, George Martin, Charles Bass, Allexander Walters and Lewis
        Merideth.
    Administratrix: Hannah Osborn, wife of William Osborn.

Peter Clark   16.136   I KE £8.14.6   Aug 26 1698
The amount of the inventory also included #2174.
    Appraisers: John Chaiers, George Smith.
    List of debts: Richard Sweatnam, John Forsler, Thomas Hindsley.

William Hedges   16.137   I KE £42.13.11   Aug 17 1698
    Appraisers: Charles Hipison, William Glanvill.

John Percifull   16.138   I KE .£26.8.8
    Appraisers: Walter Tolley, Sr. (also Walter Toley), Michaell Miller, Jr.

Mr. Thomas Gant   16.139   A   Apr 22 1698
    Payments to: William Bayly.
    Executrix: Anne Wight, wife of John Wight.

John Dunkin   16.139   I   £21.15.6   Aug 9 1698
    Appraisers: John Josling, John Robeson.
    Administratrix: Sarah Dunkin.

Charles Tracy   16.140   I PG   £66.13.0   May 30 1698
    Appraisers: James Stoddart, Joshua Hall.

John Edmondson   16.142   I TA   £386.11.3   Aug 26 1698   Aug 27 1698
    Appraisers: Nicholas Lowe, John Dawson.
    Creditors: William Sharp, Abraham Morgan.

Jacobus Seth   16.145   I TA   £266.13.7   Apr 19 1698
    Servants mentioned: Edmond Fitzgerrald, Francis Ozen, Dennis Redman, Mary
        Stewart, Richard Greene.
    Appraisers: William Hemsley, Arthur Emery.
    List of debts: Mr. John Salter, Richard Hammond, Robert Walters, John
        Hetherington, Roger Gill, William Coursey, Richard Skinner, George Hadaway,
        Richard Price, Richard Tilghman, William Hemsley, Thomas Lewis, Charles Blake,
        Henry Green, William Griffith, John Valliant, Morris Lane, Robert Broadway,
        Arthur Emery, William Scott, Thomas Jackson, Henry Everett, Robert Smith for
        John Kelly, Thomas Thomas, Richard Jones, Jr., Zorobabell Wells, David Deau,
        Vincent Hemsley, John Worley, John Sargent, Edward Lloyd, Col. Peter Sayer,
        Andrew Imbert, Mr. Thomas Heath, Thomas Evans, Darby Meran, John Hawkins,
        Robert Smith, Robert Macklin, John Salter, Anne Watkins, James Merue, Nicholas
        Milburne, Mr. Charles Blake, John Sides, Thomas Ward, John Hacker,
        Christopher Denny, Dennis Councill, Elias Nutwell, William Prosser, Hugh
        Paxton, John Edmondson, Robert Bell, John Gill.

Capt. Richard Sweatnam   16.149   I TA   £660.13.11   Aug 6 1697
    Appraisers: Thomas Smithson, William Coursey.
    Mentions: James Downs.

Samuell Farmer   16.162   I TA   £25.19.0   Jul 16 1698
    Appraisers: John Swallow, John Gloves.

John Wright   16.163   I   £19.13.9   Jun 30 1698
    Appraisers: John Nunam, Thomas Eubanks.

Obadiah Judkins   16.163   I TA   £145.11.7   Jul 25 1698
    Appraisers: Thomas Hopkins, Thomas Ewbanks.
    List of debts: Capt. James Neale, David Mills.

John Gibson   16.165   A TA   £33.17.6   £34.10.0   Aug 9 1698
    Payments to: Mr. William Hemsley, Capt. James Smith, John Sides, Richard
        Carter, John Hacker, Mr. John Salter, Thomas Bruff, John Roce.
    List of debts: Thomas Bruff, William Smith (runaway), John Rose.
    Mentions: wife (dead), child (unnamed).
    Appraisers: Jacob Seth, Robert Robinson.
    Administrator: John Sargent. Accounts were signed by William Sargent.

Mr. Thomas Blackader   16.167   I TA   £26.19.4   Jun 28 1698
The amount of the inventory also included #13212.
    Appraisers: Thomas Smithson, William Coursey.
    List of debts: Nicholas Clouds, Robert Norrest & Sollomon Wright, Robert Master,
        Mr. Simon Wilmer, Mr. Robert Macklin, Richard Jones, Jr., Col. Henry
        Coursey, Daniell Morris, William Gibson, Mr. Robert Smith, estate of Mr.
        William Carpenter, Samuell Maxwell, George Heyes, Robert Porter, John Burrill,
        Richard Taylor & Francis Morris.

John Swaine   16.168   I TA   £23.10.0   Oct 14 1697
    Appraisers: M. Earle, Christopher Denny.

John Swaine   16.168   I TA   £11.2.2   Jun 26 1698   Sep 2 1698
    Appraisers: M. Earle, Christopher Denny.
    Administrator/Executor: Mr. Richard Tilghman.

Daniell Towes   16.169   A KE   £1009.14.9   Sep 2 1698
The amount of the accounts also included #6674.
    Payments to: John Hick, Thomas Thackston, Jossias Wainewright, Lord Baltimore per
        S. Willmer, Lord Baltimore paid to Ralph Moone, Ralph Moone paid to Robert
        Smith, Esq., Mr. John Daviden per Mr. Hennage Robinson, Thomas Harman & Co.,
        Michaell Turbett per Edward Dyer, Nicholas Lowe, Dr. Imbert, George Ellitt,
        Richard Sweatnam, John Primrose, John Curtis, John Valliant, Thomas
        Thackstone, Robert Ashton (administrator of Isaac Derow), John Jones, James
        Frisby, James King for levies in Pennsylvania, William Harry, Charles Bass,
        Mr. William Dent.
    Executor: Daniell Toas (Quaker).

John Edmondson   16.171   A TA   £386.11.3   £470.4.1   Sep 1 1698
    Payments to: Lidy Bryant, Dr. Andrew Imbert, Nicholas Milburne, George Plater,
        Richard Bennett, John Woolfe, Thomas Robins, Phill. Hemsly, Col. Bayard, John
        Dorson, John Hawkins, John Bayne paid to Nicholas Lowe, Benjamin Peck.
    Executor: Mr. William Edmondson (Quaker), et. al.

Allan Smith   16.171   A KE   £192.3.0   Sep 2 1698
    Payments to: Thomas Joce, Mr. Michaell Miller, Morris Hooper, William Rickards,
        Anthony Workman, Zachariah Allen, Thomas Beall, Richard Sweatnam, Richard
        Sweatnam on note in favor of Benjamin Smith, Richard Sweatnam paid to Edward
        Sweatnam, Tobias Wells, John Wells, Richard Pullin, Robert Gouldesborough,
        Benjamin Smith, John Bennett (runaway), Robert Sadler (runaway), Mr. Thomas
        Joce.
    Executrix: Mary Copedge (relict), wife of John Copedge of Talbot County.

John Boone   16.173   A   £15.13.6   #4551   Sep 5 1698
The amount of the inventory is equivalent to #3762.
    Payments to: Mr. Gouldesboroug, James Smith, Mr. William Hemsley, Samuell
        Withers.
    Administratrix: Jane Boone (widow).

George Robins   16.174   A TA   £286.10.6   £53.12.8   Sep 2 1698
    George Plater, Esq., Mr. Robert Carvile, Maj. Smithson, Francis Sutton, Thomas
        Delehay, Mr. John Salter, Mr. John Pope, Mr. Samuell Weathers, Mr. John
        Edmondson, Mr. Richard Macklin, Dr. Andrew Imbert, John Carver, James Rayle,
        Dr. Benson, widow Catterson, William Jones, Mr.
    Executor: Thomas Robins.

Edward Ruth   16.174   A   £13.6.8   £16.13.8   Apr 19 1698
    Mentions: widow (unnamed) who married Edward Colestack.
    Administrator: John Hacker.

Sarah Bartlett   16.175   A TA   £32.0.0   £28.12.5   Aug 31 1698
    Payments to: James Sandford, Thomas Delehay.
    Administrator: John Bartlett (under age).

Jocob Abrahams   16.176   A TA   £81.13.10   £59.13.1
    Payments to: John Davis, Robert Gouldesborough, Nicholas Lowe, Samuell Stavies,
        Mr. Richard Carter, Rebecca Anderson (executrix of Thomas Anderson), Francis
        Anderson paid to Mary wife and administratrix of Francis Anderson and sister
        of the deceased, Sir Thomas Lawrence, James Benson, Daniell Sherwood.
    Mentions: 2 orphans (Isaac, Elisabeth).
    Administratrix: Elisabeth Hopkins (relict), wife of Thomas Hopkins, Jr.

Joseph Wiggott   16.177   A TA   £70.10.2   £63.12.11   Sep 2 1698
    Payments to: Thomas Delehay, Mr. Gouldesborough, John Salter, Nicholas Low, John
        Price, Dr. John Mannatt, Thomas Martin.
    Legatees: Rebecca Clemence, Daniell Mullakin, Ann Tiley, Ann Withington.
    Executor: William Carr.

Col. George Robotham   16.178   A TA   £706.14.11   Sep 7 1698
    Appraisers: John Emerson, William Clayton.
    Payments to: Nicholas Lowe an assignee of Capt. James Smith, Nicholas Milbourne,
        Benjamin Peck, John Baynard, Patrick Higgin, Edward Sweatnam, (executor of
        Richard Sweatnam), John Pitts, Mr. Richard Kilburne, Mr. James Frisby,
        Charles Hemsley.
    Legatees: William Wrench, Jr., John Lane, John Errington, Fra. Holmes, Roger
        Baddy, Edward Satterfatt, William Wrench, Sr., Margrett Pemberton, Walter
        Quinton, John Pemberton, Thomas Smithson, Edward Loyd.
    Executors: John Pemberton, Edward Lloyd, Thomas Smithson.

Thomas Cooke   16.179   A TA   £87.17.5   £44.16.2   Sep 7 1698
        Payments to: John Lane, Naiomy Berry, Michael Earle, widow Inchboard, Francis
        Vickers, James Ridley.
        Administrator: John Pitt (attorney).

John Estall   16.180   A TA   £103.3.10   £103.17.6   Sep 7 1698
        Payments to: James Smith, Robert Grundy, Michaell Earle, Francis Willis, John
        Pemberton, John Lane, Cornelius the sadler, Jon & David Arey, Jonathon Wells.
        Mentions: widow (unnamed), child (unnamed).
        Administrator/Executor: John Pitt (Quaker).

Henry Boston   16.181   A TA   £18.0.6   £29.9.7   Aug 21 1697
        Payments to: Stephen Burdin, Moses Harris, John Salter, Benjamin Pecke.
        Administrator: John Glover.

Clement Hopkins   16.182   A TA   £124.6.10
        Payments to: Capt. Johnson, Edward Edwards, William Hopkins, James Hopkins, Sir
        Thomas Lawrence, Mr. Mann, Robert Webb part of bill due Mr. William Comebes,
        Robert Hopkins, Clement Sayles for Gilbert Liverley, Richard Hopkins & Mary
        Hopkins, Henry Johnson & William Jones.
        Mentions: James Butler (dead), Thomas Turner.
        List of debts: George Hughs, Samuell Millson, John Luisey.
        Administrator: Thomas Hopkins, Sr.

Samuell Abell   16.183   A SM   £57.9.0   Jul 25 1698
The amount of the inventory also included #1600.
        Payments to: Robert Mason, Jonathon Mathews, Mr. Thomas Hatto.
        Mentions: widow (unnamed), 6 children (unnamed).
        Executrix: Anne Abell.

Robert Large   16.184   A SM   #1441   Jul 29 1698
        Payments to: Thomas Haddock, William Guider upon account of Thomas Grunwin,
        Elisabeth Blumfeild, William Brayday, Arthur Delahay, Edward Miller.
        Mentions: 4 children (unnamed).
        Administratrix: Elisabeth Morgan, wife of William Morgan.

John Powell   16.184   A SM   £64.2.5   £64.2.5   Aug 6 1698
        Payments to: Thomas Hutchinson, Jacob Moreland, James Keech, Mrs. Katherine
        Brooke, Mr. Thomas Hutchinson, Mr. Robert Mason, John Shepard, William
        Dacres, George Gray.
        Mentions: 1 orphan (unnamed).

John Crooke   16.185   A SM   £100.0.0   #4689   Aug 8 1698
        Payments to: Mr. James Crooke, Mr. Jacob Moreland, Robert Stourton, Richard
        Maplington, Thomas Hutchinson, James Crooke assigned from Thomas Wilson.
        Mentions: 3 orphans (unnamed).
        Administratrix/Executrix: Sarah Crooke (widow).

Nicholas Cole   16.185   A   £27.4.0   #8697   Aug 30 1698
The amount of the inventory is equivalent to #6528.
        Payments to: Thomas Gwither, Dr. William Lowrey, Richard Benton, Mr. William
        Dent, William Taylard.
        Executor: Thomas Gwither by William Gwither.

Sollomon Rottee   16.186   I SM   £25.9.4   Jun 18 1698
        Appraisers: Richard Attwood, Thomas Haddock.

Samuell Abell   16.187   I SM   £57.9.0   Apr 12 1698
The amount of the inventory also included #1600.
        Servants mentioned: James Gray.
        Appraisers: John Fenwick, Richard Newman.

John Jones   16.188   I SM   £4.16.0]$tab Apr 6 1698
        Appraisers: John Gawdard, Cornelius Dunevas.

Thomas Keirkly   16.188   I SM   £62.10.0   Mar 26 1698
        Appraisers: Stephen Gough, James Greenwell.

William Knight   16.189   I SM   £56.3.0   Aug 8 1698
        Appraisers: Richard Newman, Christopher Sorrill.
        Approvers: Mr. Richard Vowell, Mr. John Daish.

Elisabeth Brimmer   16.190   I SM   £19.19.0   Jun 6 1698
daughter of James Brimmer.
        Appraisers: Thomas Reeves, Abraham Brookbanke.

John Bayle   16.191   I SM   £13.17.0   Dec 11 1698
        Appraisers: Thomas Kerkly (deceased when inventory filed), Richard Vowles.

Thomas Shankes (planter)   16.191   I SM   £7.3.0   May 12 1698
       Appraisers: Samuell Chamberlain, David Parsons.

John Miles   16.192   I SM   £75.8.2   Apr 4 1698
       Appraisers: Ro. Clarke, John Fenwick.

Richard Walker   16.193   I SM   £49.16.6   Jul 20 1698
The amount of the inventory also included #5127.
       Appraisers: Henry Spink, William Sheircliffe.
       List of debts: Martin Yates, Edward Clark, William Bannister.

John Murphey   16.193   I SM   £2.7.0   Jul 27 1698
The amount of the inventory also included #5707.
       Appraisers: John Gawdard, Lewis Hazlon.
       List of debts: Timothy Mohoone.

Thomas Tole   16.194   I SM   #2996
       Appraisers: John Cowly, William Hellen.

Walter Taylor   16.194   I SM   £24.18.0   May 16 1698
       Appraisers: John Miller, Daniell Bell.
       List of debts: William Taylor.

William Spinke   16.195   I SM   £29.16.6   Jun 20 1698
       Appraisers: Richard Newman, John Jorboe.

Folio 196 does not exist.

William Medly   16.197   I SM   £28.18.0   Mar 17 1697
       Appraisers: Stephen Gough, John Tant.

Francis Swailes   16.197   I SM   £45.0.0   Jul 23 1698
       Appraisers: John Smith, Joshua Holdsworth.

Thomas Warren   16.198   I SM   £53.12.0   Jun 25 1698
       Appraisers: Henry Spink, Richard Newman.

Adam Head   16.199   I   £67.8.0   Jul 14 1698
       Appraisers: Joshua Guibert, James French.

John Sissell   16.200   I SM   £75.11.0   Jul 26 1698
(also John Sessill)
       Appraisers: Henry Spink, James French.

Christopher Gwinn   16.201   I SM   £23.10.0   Jun 4 1698
       Appraisers: Solomon Jones (also Sollomon Jones), William Morgan.

Thomas Barker (mariner)   16.201   I SM   £100.12.6   Apr 25 1698
The amount of the inventory also included #13456.
       Appraisers: Henry Lowe, Richard Southorn, Sr. (also Richard Sothoron).
       List of debts: James Crooke, Capt. James Keech, widow Watkinson, Joseph Edwards,
          Charles Tracy, John Gillam, John Davis, John Burroughs, Francis Knott, Henry
          Norris, James Bigger, Jacob Moreland, Henry Toll, Jr., William Groome, Thomas
          Beach.

Peter Jorboe   16.203   I SM   £20.19.7   Apr 13 1698
       Appraisers: Stephen Gough, James Greenwell.

William Heunton   16.204   I SM   £30.3.6   Jun 25 1698
       Appraisers: John Nutthall, Sr., John Nutthall, Jr.
       Approvers: Thomas Cooke, Robert Coomes.

John Powell   16.204   I SM   £64.2.4   Apr 19 1698
       Appraisers: Nathaniel Vivers, George Aketh.

Capt. Thomas Peace   16.205   I SM   £14.0.0   May 16 1698
(also Thomas Pace)
       Appraisers: Thomas Hebb, Edward Halerd.

William Mason   16.206   I SM   £20.10.6   Jun 20 1698
(also William Mecens)
       Appraisers: Richard Newman, Henry Spinke.

John Crooke   16.206   I   £99.16.9
       Appraisers: Thomas Hall, George Keeth.

Bartholomew Merry   16.207   I   £1.15.6   Apr 30 1698
(also Bartholomew Murry). The amount of the inventory also included #3295.
       Appraisers: Peter Peake, William Bannister.
       List of debts: Charles Dart, Thomas Kerkley.

Jane Long   16.208   A BA   £166.14.6   £62.4.3   Aug 31 1698
     Payments to: Mr. Edward Boothby, Luke Raven, Mathew Bellamy, John Wilkinson,
        John Hall.
     Legatees: Belitha King, Jane Baker, Catherine Peake (grandchild), George Peake
        (grandson), Pennellophia Skidmore, Susannah Robinson, Joseph Peake, John
        Wilkinson, John Hedge, Jr. (executor of Thomas Hedge, Sr.), Joseph Wells.
     Executrix: Jane Peake, wife of Joseph Peake.

Francis Watkins   16.209   A BA   £169.11.4   £39.2.8   Sep 5 1698
     Received from: Isaack Millner per Dr. Moore.
     Payments to: Luke Raven.
     Administratrix: Mary Barker, wife of ------ Barker. (The page is torn here.)

Thomas Morgan   16.210   A   £58.3.6   Sep 5 1698
     Administrator/Executor: Nicholas Fitzsymons.

Thomas Hedge   16.210   I BA   £689.12.8   May 16 1698
     Appraisers: Daniell Sicklemore, Thomas Smith.
     List of debts: (see page 57.)

Richard & Ann Thomson   16.216   I BA   £50.19.2   Jun 30 1698
     Servants mentioned: Alic Sutton.
     Appraisers: Joseph Strawbridge, John Coall (also John Coale).

William Wallase, Sr.   16.218   I SO   £36.11.0   Jul 25 1698
     Appraisers: John Gray, James Caldwell.

John Attkins   16.218   I   £10.0.0   Jun 28 1698
     Appraisers: William Coulbourne, John Roach, Sr.

Mr. John Hewitt (minister)   16.219   I   £122.0.4   Jun 29 ----
     Appraisers: James Dashiell, Nicholas Evans.

William Vanibles   16.220   I   £60.3.6   May 28 1698
     Appraisers: Benjamin Collman, Thomas Horseman.

Col. David Browne   16.221   I   £1117.7.1   Nov 14 1697   Aug 9 1698
     Appraisers: Richard Chambers, Samuell Worthington.

Capt. John King   16.223   I SO   £474.6.9
     Executor: John West.

John Booth   16.228   I SO   £77.18.11
     Appraisers: Benjamin Collman, Thomas Horsman.

James Dashiell   16.229   A SO   £130.10.7   £130.10.7   Aug 10 1698
     Distribution to: widow (unnamed), George Dashiell, Robert Dashiell, William
        Jones, Robert Collier, Thomas Dashiell, John Smith, accountant.
     Executor: James Dashiell.

William Head   16.230   A   #11393
     Payments to: Peter Paggen & Co., Clarke Skinner to William Dent, Thomas Tarry
        (administrator of ------ Truman).
     Administrator/Executor: John Bigger.

Mordica Hunton   16.230   A CA   £339.13.9   £139.11.7   Aug 31 1698
The amount of the inventory also included #20728.
     Sureties: Hugh Ellis.
     Executrix: Ruth Maning (relict of Hugh Ellis), wife of John Maning. Executor was
        Hugh Ellis who married Elizabeth Hunton (executrix of deceased).

Mr. John Edwards   16.230   A   £129.2.10   #6379   1697
The amount of the inventory also included #2000. The probate section cites the name
of the deceased as Mr. Joseph Edwards.
     Payments to: Richard Keene, Richard Smith.
     Administratrix: wife (unnamed) of Mr. Aron Hall.

Walter Gellett   16.231   A CA   £13.1.6   Aug 31 1698
     Payments to: Robert Skinner, Mathew Hutchins.
     Legatees: John Lashland.
     Executor: Peter Sewell.

John Holloway   16.231   I   £198.5.9   Nov 4 1698
     Appraisers: Samuell Scott, William Hutchins.

William Harris   16.233   I   Jul 23 1698
     Appraisers: John Leech, Jr., James Heighes.

Hugh Ellis   16.234   I CA   £163.15.0   Aug 29 1698
The amount of the inventory also included #5248.
        Appraisers: John Maning, Robert Skinner.

Dr. Jochem Keirsted   16.236   I CA   £496.8.0   Aug 15 1698
        Appraisers: John Taney, Peter Sewell.
        Mentions: Mrs. Keirsted.

Robert Fisher   16.238   I   £34.11.6   Apr 25 1698
        Appraisers: Edward Wenman, Thomas Edmans.

William Head   16.239   I CA   £60.8.6   Jun 15 1698
        Appraisers: John Godsgrace, Robert Skinner.
        List of debts: John Hedges, Col. John Bigger, Mrs. Elisabeth Hutchins, Mrs.
        Margarett Kersted, Thomas Edmans, Richard Jackson.

Richard Sandys   16.240   I CA   £33.6.5   Jun 8 1698
        Appraisers: William Derumple (also William Derrumple), John Forde (also John
            Ford).
        List of debts: Samuell Heiger, John Bigger, William Derumple, John Norrington,
        Mathew Parrett, Thomas Hinton, Aron Cobreth, Col. Henry Jowles, William
        Nicholls, William Parker, Abra. Clark, John King, Thomas Hill, James Badcock.

Edward Dickerson   16.241   I CA   £9.0.4   Aug 6 1698
        Appraisers: Henry Esterlin, Evan Rice.

Daniell Symons   16.242   I   £54.10.7   May 14 1698
        Appraisers: Robert Shephard, William Hutchins.
        List of debts: Jonathon Mathew.

John Joannes   16.242   A SM   £4.16.0   #2097
        Payments to: Col. Henry Lowe, John Gawdred, Cornelius Dunevan, William Moore,
            Lewis Haezlon.
        Mentions: 3 small children (unnamed).
        Administratrix: Elisabeth Joans (relict).

Robert Doyne   16.243   I   #22546   1695
        List of debts: Thomas Whichaley, Mrs. Delaroach, Capt. Rando. Brandt, Richard
        Wae, Madam Neale, John Harrison, Francis Lurting, Joseph Cooper, Jo. Gooch,
        Richard Ashman, B. Burroughs, William Timothy, George Newman, Jos. Russell,
        Jo. Duglass (cooper), Thomas Taylor, William Bournam, Robert Wider, William
        Marshall, Nicho. Bellamie, William Thompson, William Hungerfoot, Fra. Mason,
        Domingo Agambre, Michell Minooke, Henry Hawkins, John Butcher, Edward Guile,
        John Wood, John Wilkinson, Edward Saunders, John Godshall, John Clarke, John
        Clements, Mark Lampton, Robert Robins, Richard Garworth, John Hamond, Thomas
        Lewis, Thomas Lewis per Richard Hubbard, James Baker, Thomas Rigg, Mr. John
        Wheeler, Philip Hoskins, John Maning, Henry Hexon, John Gray, Ja. Hemsley,
        Richard Price, Ja. Marting, Edward Maingt (?), John Wright, Abra. Sapsole,
        William Thomas, Edward Rookewood, Cuth. Musgrave, Charles Hanson, George
        Miller, Math. Sannds, William Boyden, Fra. Chumble, John BearCroft, Law
        Ratchford, William Holland, George Parke, Capt. William Barton, George
        Langham, Charles Ashton in Virginia.

William Tailor   16.245   A CH   Nov 20 1697
        Administratrix: Magdalene Tailor.

Andrew Ogden   16.245   A CH   £19.3.6   Jun 28 1697
        Payments to: Thomas Hutchison.
        Administratrix: Elisabeth Ogden.

Nathaniell Button   16.246   A   £14.15.6   #1370   Sep 1 1698
        Payments to: Mr. Richard Sothoron, Thomas Williams, John Brookes, Richard
            Hanford.
        Administrator: Christopher Williamson.

James Regon   16.247   A CH   £3.6.0   Apr 1 1698
        Administratrix: Joan Regon, wife of John Wood.

Edmond Duyer   17.1   I CE   £38.12.0   Sep 18 1698
        Appraisers: Thomas Blackwell, Thomas Orrell.
        List of debts: Daniell Goafe (?).

Charles Watts   17.1   I   £40.19.8   Apr 8 1698
        Appraisers: Thomas Lawson, Thomas Price.

John Ward   17.3   I CH   Max 15 1698
        Appraisers: Henry Moore, John Clement.

James Boules   17.4   I CH   £13.18.2   Aug 9 1698
        Appraisers: Joshua Doyne, Math. Barnes.
        List of debts: George Godfrey.

Thomas Dowman   17.5   I   Jun 30 1698
        Appraisers: Christopher Ford, John Banester.

Charles Allison   17.6   I   £11.12.0   Jul 19 ----
        Appraisers: John Gray, Peter Mackmillion.

John Stone   17.6   I CH   £58.18.4
        Appraisers: Thomas Lawson, Thomas Prise.

Mr. Richard Ashman   17.8   I CH   £45.14.4   Jun 22 1698
        Appraisers: Walter Story, Edward Philpott.
        Administratrix: Ann Ashman.

Mr. John Stone   17.11   I CH   Dec 16 1697
        Servants mentioned: Peter Bellman (boy), Mary Pilkton, Edward Lewis.
        Appraisers: John Addison, John Hanson.

Dennis Doyne   17.18   I CH   £149.7.10   Jun 4 1698
        Servants mentioned: Thomas Sheers (boy), Elisabeth Sheers (girl).
        Appraisers: Richard Harrison, William Thompson.

Johanna Hudson   17.20   I CH   £12.1.0   Aug 1 1698
        Appraisers: John Godfrey, Ignatius Wheeler.

Sarah Cooksey   17.22   I   £19.4.0   Apr 26 1698
        Appraisers: Thomas Price, John Hunt.

William Marshall   17.23   I CH   £112.1.2   Aug 2 1698
        Appraisers: Walter Story, Edward Philpot.

Mr. Robert Gates   17.26   I CH   £118.4.2   Jul 18 1698
        Appraisers: William Boarman, Jr., William Norris.
        Approvers: Giles Willson, Edmond Nugent.

Phillip Joanes   17.31   I CH   £2.16.6   Aug 1 1698
        Appraisers: George Godfrey, Ignatius Wheeler.

William Whitom   17.31   I CH   £14.11.4
        Appraisers: William Smith, William Norris.

Phillip Davis   17.33   A KE   £180.10.0   £153.2.11   Oct 1 1698
A second inventory was filed in the amount of £2.12.0.
        Payments to: George Foxon, Amos Chadburne bequeathed by John Wedge, Geoffery
            Power, Charles Hinson, John Wade, Samuell Glew, Charles Tilden, Nicholas
            Clouds, John Cooke, Elias King.
        Executrix: Susannah Wallwin (relict), wife of Edward Wallwin.

Henry Hosier   17.34   A KE   £168.15.3   £109.15.4 Nov 1 1698
        Payments to: Edward Sweatnam, Mr. Max Robinson, John Lawrence, Mr. Michaell
            Miller, Thomas Joce, Phillip Everett, Philip & Anne Sutton, John Lyle, Jeffrey
            Power, Mr. Elias King, Mr. William Cannon, Mr. Charles James, Daniell
            Kelly, Richard Litton, James Upperdine per Charles Tilden, James Barber, John
            Nicholls per John Walden, Charles Tilden, Charles Tilden per Elias King,
            Charles Hollingsworth, Morgan Jones, John Salter, Thomas Steevens, John
            Boules, Cornelius Comegys, John Shaw, Thomas Hicks, Mr. Harris.
        Executor: Henry Hosier.

Col. Casparus Harman   17.37   I CE   £1375.5.6
        Appraisers: Mr. Edward Laremore, Mr. Thomas Killen.
        Mentions: Andrew's wife & 2 children, Boson & wife.

Samuell Vuderhay   17.42   I   £5.0.6   Nov 20 1695
        Appraisers: Robert Randall, Hugh Douch.

Thomas Moore   17.43   I CA   £30.10.3   Jul 29 1698
        Appraisers: William Parce, John Jonson.

Mr. Edward Jones   17.44A I   £420.9.8
There are two folios 44 and 45; for convenience, they are noted (and occur in this
order) as 44A, 45A, 44B, and 45B. The amount of the inventory also included #13533.
        Appraisers: John Vesey, Owen Hughs.
        List of debts: Henry Pennington, Thomas Messer, John Boder, William Elmes, Mr.
            Powell, Daniel Makneale, Richard Franklyn, Mr. Carvile, Mr. Dorrell, Thomas
            Yeoman, William Stevens, William Morgan, John Reade, Felex Furbey, James
            Morgan, Col. William Stevens, Owen Hewes, Mr. John Thompson.

Henry Francis   17.51   I AA   £21.13.6   May 7 1698
     Appraisers: Edward Fuller, William Penington.

Morgan Cooke   17.52   I   £4.13.6   Nov 17 1698
     Appraisers: Henry Chapell, Thomas Rider.

Morgan Cooke   17.53   A AA   £4.13.6   £7.12.2   Nov 19 1698
     Administrator: Lewis Jones.

Col. Nicholas Greenbery   17.54   I AA   £682.2.11   Jun 13 1698
     Appraisers: Roger Newman, Humfry Boone.

John Gassaway   17.60   I AA   £58.14.6
     Appraisers: John Chappell, John Gaile.

Lewis Garman (planter)   17.61   I BA   £8.18.4   Sep 17 1698
     Appraisers: Roger Mathews, Henry Jackson.
     List of debts: Mr. Benjamin Wells, Symon Jackson, Henry Jackson, Samuell Brown.

Thomas Heath   17.62   I BA   Jun 18 1698
     Appraisers: Graves Dellahide, William Howe.
     List of debts: Robert Smith, Edmond Hansley, Robert Parker, Thomas Browne
        assigned to Thomas Howe.

Jane Long   17.65   A BA   Jul 20 1698
     Payments to: Robert Carvile, Phillip Clarke, James Browne, Samuell Watkins,
        Edward Boothby, Mr. Cheseldyne, estate of Col. Blakiston, Luke Raven, Daniell
        Palmer for Mathew Bellamy.
     Executrix: Jane Peake, wife of Joseph Peake.

Mrs. Jane Long   17.67   A BA   £116.14.0   £73.1.9   Oct 26 1698
     Payments to: Mr. Phillip Clark (attorney), Mr. Thomas Hedge, Dr. Moore.
     Legatees: Susannah Robertson, James Todd.
     Executrix: Jane Peake, wife of Joseph Peake.

John Nicholson   17.68   A BA   £48.12.6   £52.0.10
     Payments to: Mr. Philip Gibson, George Smith, Marke Richardson.
     Administrators: Thomas Staley and Robert Olesee (administrators of Mary Warfoot
        (late Mary Nicholson) (executrix of the deceased)).

John Guyatt   17.70   A CA   £97.4.7   £81.15.11   Aug 31 1698
The amount of the inventory also included #20376.
     Payments to: Robert Read, W. Farie, Thomas Cornwell, John Holloway, Allexander
        Lewis, Benjamin Hammon, John Smith, Edward Batson, Simon Wotton, John Bigger
        administrator of Simon Wotton by James Dawkins, John Astin, Joshua Cecill,
        James Cobb, William Shettell, Richard Wally, James Cranford.
     Mentions: 2 children (unnamed).
     Administrator: Michaell Higgons.

John Abington   17.72   A   £142.5.10   Nov 12 1698
     Mentions: Ann Hill, Mr. Greenfield, Col. Jowles.
     Payments to: James Baker, Mr. Henry Denton, Mr. Phillip Clarke for Capt.
        Langley, John Elsey, Robert Biggs, Mr. Walter Smith, Robert Carvile.
     Administrator: George Lingan.

Charles Harrington   17.74   A CA   £65.3.9   £44.9.8
     Payments to: Henry Fernely, Jockem Kersted, Henry Truman, Mr. Samuell Constable,
        Mr. William Parker, William Coale, Mr. John Maning.
     Mentions: 3 children (unnamed).
     Administratrix: Dorothy Tucker (relict), wife of Seaborne Tucker.

John Sunderland   17.75   A CA   £117.6.2   £123.18.11   Nov 10 1698
     Payments to: John Smith, Thomas Tench, Thomas Hughs.
     Administratrix: Margaret Sumner, wife of Robert Sumner.

Mortough Horney   17.77   I TA   £16.15.0   Aug 29 1698
     Appraisers: Samuell Hambleton, Robert Voss.

Col. Peter Sayer   17.78   I TA   Mar 9 1697
     Servants mentioned: John Brazia (Irishman), Robert Johnson (plowman), Jeremia
        Manson.
     Appraisers: William Coursey, Lawrence Knowles.
     List of judgments: Mr. Edward Man, Mr. Stephen Wheelwright of Storton, John
        Davis, William Jackson, Christopher Denny, John Jones, Daniell Walker, William
        Coursey, George Impey, Richard Lock.

Richard Ewebank   17.92   I TA   £27.4.3   Oct 19 1698
     Appraisers: Samuell Hambleton, Daniell Newman.
     Mentions: William Swift.

William Anderson   17.94   A TA   £104.14.10   £104.14.10   Nov 16 1698
        Payments to: David Mills, Nicholas Lowe, John Salter, John Pattison, William
            Sharp, Thomas Robins (administrator of John Robins), John Newman.
        Mentions: 3 children (unnamed).
        Administratrix: Sarah Gwinn, wife of William Gwinn.

Thomas Fisher   17.96   A KI   £67.13.6
in Talbot County.   Nov 16 1698
        Payments to: Phillip Lynes, William Ealen, Jos. Collman for use of Phillip Lynes.
        Administratrix: Anne Fisher.

Capt. Joshua Doyne   17.97   I SM   Aug 16 1698   Nov 12 1698
Also cites items in Charles County.
        Appraisers: Joshua Guibert, Nicholas Power.
        Approvers: John Hillen (neighbor), Peter Johnson (neighbor).

John Askins   17.103   I SM   Mar 4 1697
        Appraisers: John Doxey, John Manning.

Joseph Hartley   17.104   I SM   Apr 25 1698
        Appraisers: Nathaniel Owen, Thomas Hall.
        Mentions: Ann Hartley (widow).
        List of debts: Mr. Tanny, Thomas Goslin, Nathaniell Ureers, Thomas Hall, James
            Keech.

Edward Sissary   17.106   I SM   Apr 9 1697
        Appraisers: Edward Morgan, John Woodward.

Ignatius Warren   17.107   A   £25.17.9   £23.7.8
        Administrator: John Tant.

John Grubb   17.108   I SM   £47.11.8   Mar 4 1697
        Appraisers: John Slye, Francis Swailes.

Thomas Taylor (planter)   17.110   I CH   £91.8.2   Oct 15 1698
        Appraisers: William Timothy, Thomas Dixon.
        Administratrix: Ann Taylor.

Andrew Clark   17.112   A CH   £49.0.0   £73.7.9   Oct 31 ----
        Payments to: James Lyle, Richard Evans, James Stoddard, Mr. Francis Green, Mr.
            David Small, Christopher Thompson, Dorothy Musgrove, Nathaniell Ramsheire,
            James Turner.
        Administrator: James Tompson.

Richard Hobart (gentleman)   17.114   I   £49.9.8
        Appraisers: John Bowling, Richard Edelen.
        Approvers: William Boarman, John Higton.

Henry Kee   17.116   I CH   £21.19.6   Aug 30 1698
        Appraisers: Ignatius Wheeler, Mathew Barnes.

Matthew Stone   17.117   I   £5.14.0
        Appraisers: John Wood, Garrett Sinnett.

Thomas Coffer   17.118   I CH   £20.7.8   Sep 4 1698
        Appraisers: Henry Barnes, John Allen.

John Booth   17.119   A SO   £42.6.6   Oct 29 1698
        Payments to: Levin Denwood, Thomas Dashiell, Thomas Willson, Daniell Heast, Maj.
            Whittington, Peter Parsly, William Phillips, James Spence.
        Mentions: 2 orphans (unnamed).
        Executor: John Booth.

Henry Layton   17.120   A SO   £186.9.11   £219.6.8   Oct 28 1698
        Payments to: Maj. Whittington, Levin Denwood, John Winsor, John Phillips, Richard
            Samuell, John White, Samuell Hopkins.
        Mentions: 2 children (unnamed).
        Administratrix: Margrett Layton.

John Lawes   17.121   A   £53.8.2   £53.8.2   Oct 26 1698
        Payments to: Maj. Whittington, Robert Polk, John Nelson, William Tompson, Levin
            Denwood, George Betts.
        Mentions: 6 orphans (unnamed).
        Administratrix: Katherine Lawes.

Richard Whorton   17.122   I   £37.4.6   Aug 17 1698   Aug 31 1698
        Appraisers: Francis Thorowgood, Peirce Bray.
        Administrator: Mr. Francis Jenkins.

David Richardson   17.125   A   £106.10.11   £106.10.11   John   Edger
     Payments to: Col. David Brown (dead), Capt. Thomas Pointer,   John   Edger
        (merchant), Mr. Layfield, John Helm & Co., Maj. Whittington.
     Distribution to: executor.
     Administrator/Executor: William Richardson.

James Pearll   17.126   I DO   £22.7.1   Sep 30 1698
     Appraisers: Mr. Richard Tubman, Mr. John Phillips.
     List of debts: Peter Adams, Robert Johnson, Mr. Henry Hooper, John Leigh, Arthur
        Whitely (also Arthur Wheatly), William Thomas, Jr.,   John Wheightler
        (administrator of Alice Wheightler of Dorchester County).
     Witnesses: William Mitchew, John Stuart.

Alice Wheeler   17.129   I DO   £88.2.7   Aug 15 1698
     Appraisers: John Draper, Henry Davis.

Roger Trougton   17.130   A DO   £16.16.6   £15.14.8   Oct 18 1698
     Payments to: Mrs. Ann Hunt, Mr. Andrew Parker, Arthur Wright, Charles Powell.
     Administratrix: Elisabeth Troughton.

Henry Carpent   17.130   A DO   £20.9.0   £10.17.11   Oct 18 1698
     Payments to: Charles Powell, Stephen Bess, Ruben Ross.
        Mentions: no orphans.
     Administratrix: Mabell Ross.

Christopher Bettson   17.130   A TA   £13.10.6   £11.11.11   Sep 10 1698
     Payments to: James Smith, Samuell Abbot, Dr. Corrigan, Mr. Gouldsbrough, Thomas
        Smithson.
     Administratrix: Hannah Moore (relict), wife of William Moore.

Amos Parsons   17.131   A SO   £15.14.7   £2.5.8   Oct 29 1698
     Payments to: Mr. Jenkins, William Owens, Roger Truckam, Randoll Revell, widow
        King.
     Administrator: John MacKnitt.

John Townsend, Sr.   17.131   I So   £32.18.0   1698
     Appraisers: John Porter, John Wotton (also John Wroughton).
     Approvers: Hugh Porter, Donock Dennis, Jr.

Richard Davis   17.132   A SO   £121.1.2   £121.1.2   Oct 9 1698
These accounts appear on the upper half of folios 132 and 133.
     Payments to: Maj. Whittington, William Foxon, John Davis.
     Legatees: mother-in-law (unnamed) and 2 children (unnamed) living with her,
        brother Charles Hall and his wife (executor's sister, unnamed) and 2 children
        living with him, executor, 2 children (unnamed).
     Distribution to: widow (unnamed), 8 children (unnamed).
     Executor: Richard Davis (son).

Thomas Hillman   17.132   A   £10.10.0   £10.10.2
     Payments to: administrator of George Hutchins, George Numan, Katherine Laws, John
        Tompson, Thomas Dashield.
     List of debts: George Hutchins.
     Administrator/Executor: Isaac Horsley.

John Emmett   17.133   I   £122.12.8   Jan 30 1698
     Appraisers: Daniell Ellett, William Tannyhill.

James Gamblin   17.135   I PG   £139.11.4   Nov 20 1698
     Appraisers: George Natler, Robert Done.

Katherine Wattkins   17.137   I PG   £50.6.6   Nov 7 1698
     Appraisers: Daniell Connill, Phillip Levin.

Mary Darnall   17.138   A   £87.2.4   £88.6.6   Nov 10 1698
     Administrator/Executor: Henry Darnall.

James Williams   17.139   I   £43.18.9   Oct 14 1698   Nov 17 1698
     Appraisers: Mathew Ogbey, John Joyce.
     Mentions: "my father's estate".

James Williams   17.140   A PG   £43.18.9   Nov 17 1698
     Payments to: Mr. David Small, James Mullikin, Joseph Towgood, Christopher
        Tompson, Col. Darnall, Walter Evans, John Demall, W. Lane.
     Executor: John Chapman.

Jonathon Willson   17.142   I   £62.6.3   Oct 7 1698
     Appraisers: Robert Bradley, James Stoddard.
     Mentions: Mr. Thomas Holliday, Mr. Richard Spourne, widow (unnamed).

Henry Brent   17.144   A CA   £289.1.0   Nov 10 1698
The amount of the inventory also included #166033.
      Payments to: Maj. William Dent, Rudolph Owen.
      Administratrix: Ann Marsham (relict), wife of Richard Marsham.

Thomas Edmondson (merchant) 17.146   I PG   £50.17.5   Oct 17 1698
      Appraisers: Francis Collier, Abraham Clarke.

John Browne   17.147   I TA   £133.6.6   Nov 6 1698
      Appraisers: John Emerson, Danid Blany.

Henry Hanslap   17.149   I AA   £207.11.8   Jan 26 1698
      Appraisers: James Saunders, John Gressam.

William Marke   17.151   I AA   £16.13.6   Oct 8 1698
      Appraisers: William Lewis, Henry Merryday.

Nicholas Terrett   17.152   A AA   £150.13.1   £43.15.5   Jan 4 1698
      Payments to: Mr. Robert Bradley, Mr. Hugh Jones per Capt. William Holland, Dr.
         Allexander Chappell per Capt. Holland, John Morton, Mr. David Small, William
         King, William Powell (taylor), Thomas Box, Henry Bonner, Dr. Hugh Fergason,
         Capt. Thomas Emms.
      Administratrix: Jane Luddall, wife of William Luddall.

Humphrey Jarvice   17.153   I AA   £8.5.4   Dec 12 1698
      Appraisers: Edward Burges, Benjamin Bond.

Mathew Bellamy   17.154   I AA   £2.6.0   Nov 30 1698
      Appraisers: Lenerd Wayman, Walter Phelps.

Mr. Samuell Newton   17.154   I TA   £33.11.1   Nov 22 1698
(gentleman).
      Appraisers: Benjamin Pecke, Anthony Rumball.
      List of debts: Charles Murphy, Mr. Robert Grundy, Mr. William Hemsley.
      Administrator: Mr. John Salter.

William Richardson   17.156   I AA   £655.8.3   Oct 21 1698
      Appraisers: John Chappell, John Merriton.
      List of debts: Mrs. Sarah Groome (administratrix of Samuell Groome).

Robert Gott   17.158   A AA   £118.1.10   £45.13.0   Dec 16 1698
The amount of the inventory also included #8963.
      Payments to: John Sollers, Michaell Yoakeley, Thomas Chandler (executor for his
         father's estate), Mathew Clarke, Christopher Vernon, John Tompson, Samuell
         Groome.
      Legatees: Florence Gott, Rebecca Gott.
      Executrix: Alice Smith (relict), wife of William Smith.

Robert Gresham (merchant)   17.160   A TA   £169.2.6   £158.8.0   Jan 9 1698
      Payments to: Mr. Richard Bennett, Joseph Tonnard, William Troth.
      Administratrix: Mary Gresham by Mr. William Sharpe (Quaker).

Robert Day   17.162   I CA   £219.5.8   Jun 9 1698
      Appraisers: Thomas Clagett, Nathaniell Dare.

Robert Grason   17.167   I   £109.2.6   Dec 15 1698
of Stockton in England.
      Appraisers: John Dawson, William Scott.
      Administratrix: Mary Grason.

George Johnson   17.169   A CA   £35.19.0   £8.6.0   Jan 20 1698
      Payments to: William Shettle, Francis Hutchins & William Feiles, Edward Battson,
         action vs. Jane Truman (administratrix of H. Truman).
      Administratrix: Ann Southern (relict), wife of Henry Southern.

Obediah Jenkins   17.170   A TA   £145.11.0   £142.12.9   Jan 9 1698
      Payments to: John Newman, Thomas Robins, Maj. Thomas Smithson.
      Distribution to: widow Jenkins, Thomas Taylor on behalf of Rachell Jenkins a
         granddaughter of deceased.
      Executor: William Sharpe (Quaker).

Robert Harvy   17.171   I TA   £86.15.0   Jul 20 1698
      Appraisers: Mathew Arackson, George Vinson.

William Meers   17.172   I CA   £189.1.10   Nov 18 1698
(also William Mears)
      Appraisers: Robert Shippard, William Hoskins.

Robert Proctor   17.176   A AA   £365.4.0   £155.11.9   Feb 6 1698
The amount of the inventory also included #42277, which is equivalent to £176.3.1.
    Payments to: William Hopkins, Col. Henry Ridgley, Sr., Mr. Thomas Grunwin per
      Mr. Henry Denton, Mr. Charles Carroll (administrator of Anthony Underwood),
      Mr. Philip Lynes, Mr. James Frisby & Mr. John Molls, Peter Paggan & Co. &
      Henry Ridgely, Jr., Thomas Baker, John Graf, Esq., Christopher Daniell &
      Andrew Underwood, Ephraim Willson.
    Administratrix: Rachell Proctor (also Mrs. Rachell Kilbourne).

Henry Trueman   17.177   A CA   £71.19.2
    Payments to: Samuell Groome, John Hyde, John Burd, James Mortin, Richard Keen.
    Administrator: Thomas Taney.

John Perry   17.177   I   £21.6.6   Nov 14 1698
    Appraisers: George Jackson, Thomas Grunwyn.
    Approvers: Orlando Greenslade.

John Taylor   18.1   I CA £23.16.6   Jan 3 1698
    Appraisers: John Jinking, George Odaham.

Nathaniell Cranford   18.2   I CA £5.13.0   May 6 1698
    Appraisers: William Williams, Sr., Joseph Baker.

Mr. John Short   18.2   I CA £233.17.0   Aug 26 1698
    Appraisers: George Cole, Edward Ball.
    List of debts: Joseph Hall, Richard Sandsberry, William Restall.

Edward Armstrong   18.6   I CA £25.7.0   Jan 14 1698
The amount of the inventory also included #2528.
    Appraisers: Thomas Stone, Thomas Arterby.
    List of debts: Christopher Bateman, David Hillen, Richard White, William Gilley.

Thomas Dickson   18.8   I CA £30.1.8
    Appraisers: Thomas Kingcart, George Spicer.

Mr. Francis Hutchins   18.9   I   £813.17.3   Sep 27 1698
    Appraisers: John Leach, Jr., Mr. Robert Skinner.

William Howard   18.11   I   £4.16.3   Jan 16 1698
    Appraisers: Daniel Sherdue, Ignatius Sinett.

Newman Barber   18.12   I   £45.11.6
    Appraisers: John Loyde, Nicholas Fountaine.
    Mentions: William Grinall.

William Martin   18.13   I AA £25.7.0   Nov 11 1698
    Appraisers: Richard Moss, Joseph Connoway.

Richard Jackson   18.14   I CA £111.16.0   Mar 1698
    Appraisers: Richard Perry, Hugh Hinton.

Robert Blinkhorne   18.15   I   £55.4.0   Feb 13 ----
    Appraisers: David Bole, John Mackdowell.

Cornelius Walkinson   18.16   A SM £55.15.0   £55.4.0   Mar 1 1698
    Servants mentioned: Mary Compton.
    Payments to: Mr. Samuell Watkins, Capt. James Keetch, Col. Henry Jowles,
      William Stone, W. Groome, Thomas Collier, John Guillam, George Gray, Elisabeth
      Jury, Phillip Clarke per Mr. Lecount, Mr. Richard Southerne, Capt. Timothy
      Keyser, Mr. Crooke.
    Legatees: James Keech.
    Executrix: Elisabeth Walkinson.

Ignatius Mathews   18.17   I CH £166.15.10   Aug 16 1698
    Appraisers: John Sanders, Jese Doyne.

Edward Whealock   18.20   I BA £48.14.0   Mar 13 1698
    Appraisers: James Smallwood, John Peasly.

John Noble   18.21A   I SM £5.11.0   Apr 12 1698
There are two folios numbered 21; for convenience, the first is cited as 21A; the
second, as 21B.
    Appraisers: Lawrence Tattershoall, Thomas Deakins.

John Johnson   18.21B   I SM £24.2.0   Nov 3 1698
There are two folios numbered 21; for convenience, the first is cited as 21A; the
second, as 21B.
    Appraisers: Thomas Nicholes, William Maddox.

William Chandler   18.23   I CH   £77.8.6
      Appraisers: James Smallwood, John Hanson.

Robert Foster   18.23   I SM   £13.3.0   Mar 26 1698
      Appraisers: John Smith, Notly Maddox.

Robert Sly   18.24   I CH   £25.18.6   Oct 18 1698
      Appraisers: James Swan, Robert Rose.

Daniell Moy   18.25   I SM   £10.18.0   Dec 3 1698
The amount of the inventory also included #5590.
      Appraisers: William Aisquith, John Horne.
      List of debts: Capt. Thomas Waughop, Mr. Philip Linés, John Shankes, James
          Thompson, Mr. Robert Mason.

William Hodgson   18.26   I SM   £120.14.6   Oct 29 1698
      Appraisers: Ralph Foster, John Smith.

Charles Brooke   18.29   I SM   Oct 5 1698
      Appraisers: Francis Knott, Edward Cole.
      Approvers: Nathaniell Erner, Stephen Bambrick.

John Nicholson   18.31   I   £136.19.8   Mar 18 1698
      Appraisers: Thomas Bison, Edward Fuillor.

Abraham Bird   18.35   I CA   £30.5.2   Feb 22 1698
The amount of the inventory also included #5670.
      Appraisers: Richard Sandsberry, Derby Sherrevan.
      List of debts: Col. Hollyday, James Wilson, John Ratford, Michael Askew, John
          Griffin, Nathaniell Smith, Darby Sherrevan, widow Bowen, Edward Ball, Robert
          Sykes, Samuell Lyles, Timothy Sewell, Daniell Buckmaster, Will Johnson, Jenkin
          Wells, widow Leaf, Daniell Armiger, William Harbourne.

Katherine Constable   18.38   I AA   £1073.13.3   Jun 10 1698
      Appraisers: Roger Newman, Humphry Boone.

William Willson   18.51   I PG   £26.8.9   Dec 15 1698
      Appraisers: John Josling, Phillip Tattersall.

William Atchyson   18.53   I PG   £22.12.0   Sep 26 1698
      Appraisers: Daniell Elliott, William Tannehill.

Gawin Hamilton   18.54   I PG   £74.1.0
      Appraisers: Daniell Elliott, Michael Ashford.

Michaell Kerry   18.56   I PG   £5.15.10   Nov 21 1698
(also Michaell Kary)
      Appraisers: Thomas Dickson, William Hunter.

Francis Buttery   18.57   I   Jul 17 1698
      Appraisers: John Willeson, Michaell Ratcliff.

Stephen Mankin   18.58   I CH   £32.18.8   Jul 22 1698
      Servants mentioned: Lawrence Lary.
      Appraisers: John Wood, John Wilkison.
      List of debts: Mr. William Thompson.

James Bile   18.59   A CH   £13.18.2   Nov 6 1698
      Administrator: Philip Hoskins.

Phillip Allen   18.60   I   £20.14.0   Aug 24 1698
      Appraisers: Thomas Lorson, Thomas Hagan.

John Clarke   18.61   I CH   £51.17.7   Oct 20 1698
      Appraisers: Ralph Shaw, John Barron.

Francis Adams   18.64   I CH   £19.0.0   Dec 22 1698
      Appraisers: George Godfry, John Paine.

Henry Brawner   18.65   I CH   £43.16.0   Apr 23 1698
      Appraisers: Francis Frampton, Thomas Plunkett.

Sarah Till   18.65   I CH   £15.17.8
      Appraisers: George Brett, Francis Frampton.

Robert Smallpage   18.66   I CH   £34.0.0   Jul 5 1698
The amount of the inventory also included #7865.
      Appraisers: Mathew Saunders, William Ellitt.

Thomas Hutchinson   18.67   I CH   £287.13.11   Sep 23 1698
(also Thomas Hutchyson) (merchant)
        Appraisers: Jacob Moreland, John Sotheron.

Sarah Till   18.72   A CH   £15.17.8   Nov 5 1699
relict of Edward Till.
        Payments to: William Barber, George Brett, Francis Frampton, John Eldor, Capt.
            Phillip Hoskins.
        Administrator: Thomas Craxon.

Robert Loxton, Jr.   18.74   A CH   Sep 30 1698
There are two folios numbered 75; for convenience, the first is cited as 75A; the
second, as 75B. This inventory includes folio 75A.
        Payments to: Capt. Nicholas March, Cleborne Lomax.
        Administrator: Robert Benson.

John Gourley   18.75B   A CH   Oct 1 1698
There are two folios numbered 75; for convenience, the first is cited as 75A; the
second, as 75B.
        Received from: Richard Linwcomb, Susannah Savoy.
        Payments to: Mr. William Hunter, Maj. William Dent & Col. Hum. Warren, Mr.
            Henry Hawkins, Maj. John Stone, Thomas Davis, Edward Chapman, Francis
            Buttery, Mr. Richard Harrison.
        Administratrix: Barbary Gourley.

John Cornish   18.76   A CH   Nov 19 1698
        Received from: William Barton, one of the sons (unnamed) of Edward Minges.
        Payments to: Capt. John Bayne, George Brett, Peter Mackmillion.
        Executrix: Martha Cornish (relict).

Robert Hill   18.78   A CH   £16.9.0   Oct 1 1698
        Payments to: John Lecount, Capt. John Bayne, Col. Darnall.
        Administratrix: Mary Watson (relict, now dead), formerly the wife of John Watson.

John Knight   18.79   A CH   Oct 11 1698
        Payments to: Maj. James Smallwood, Robert Benson.
        Administratrix: Jennett Boy (relict), wife of John Boy.

Col. Nehemiah Blakeston   18.81   A SM   #39585   Mar 21 1698
        Payments to: Mr. Charles Carroll, Mr. William Turner, Mr. Boothby, Mr. Phillip
            Clarke, Mr. Joshua Guybert, Elisha Adams, Mr. Henry Denton, Mr. Garrett
            Vansweringen.
        Administrator: Nehemiah Adaneron (?).

Jarvis Morgan   18.82   I   £170.14.10   Feb 15 1698
        Appraisers: Leonard Wayman, Richard Snowden, Jr.

Robert Grason   18.83   I TA   £191.12.7   1699
        Mentions: George Allen.
        Administratrix: Mary Grason.

John Smith   18.84   I   £54.0.11   Aug 2 1698
The amount of the inventory also included #8499.
        Appraisers: John Turner, Davis Hellen.
        List of debts: Morris Davis, William Dawkins, Mr. John Cranford, Barett Booth &
            John Elsey, Edward Blackbourne, William Breed.

John Stone   18.88   A CH   £58.18.4   £27.2.0   Mar 21 1698
        Payments to: Capt. Peter Pagan & Co. of London (merchants).
        Mentions: 7 children (unnamed).
        Administratrix: Dorothy Stone (widow).

William Burges, Esq.   18.89   I AA   Oct 11 1687
        Appraisers: Thomas Knighton, Maren Devall, Henry Ridgley.
        List of debts: Maj. Nicholas Sewell, Col. Vincent Lowe, Elisabeth Larkins,
            Francis Downes, Madam Calvert, Robert Proctor, Nicholas Nicholson, George
            Burges, Col. Edward Pye, John Merriton, Gerrard Vansweringain, Job Evans,
            Maj. Peter Sawyer, Benjamin Lawrence, Phillip Lynes, Henry Linch, Capt.
            Thomas Everard, Capt. Hune, James Neale, George Cornish (merchant) at London,
            Dr. Benjamin Arnatt, Henry Exon, Joseph Storey, John Longman, Thomas Ivery,
            John Stone, Capt. Jonathon Francis, George Parker, John Spicer (gentleman) of
            London, Charles Willmare, Jacob Delahay, Chr. Mettley, William Bison, Thomas
            Hollandworth, George Yates, Benjamin Caple, Merren Duvall, John Fairbrother,
            John Harberdine, James Lewis, Leonard Wayman, Walter Phelps, John Howard, Sr.,
            Thomas Sutton, Robert Wade, John Jacobs, John Simpson, John Lineam, Robert
            Wade, John Walters, Richard Gott, Mark Richardson, John Willobey, William
            Yeildhall, Robert Conant, Robert Lockwood, Peter Impey, Thomas Hooker, Chr.
            Moate, Wolfran Hunt, Anthony Holland, John Brewer, Madam Jane Calvert, Richard
            Cheney, Sr., Mathias Haws, Alexander Macfarland, Col. Pye, John Gyles, William
            James, James Powell, Thomas Pratt, John Nicholson, Edward Burges, Walter Carr,

Gerd Hopkins, Mathew Hawkins, Richard Cheney, Jr., lawrence Draper, John Gressam, Thomas Guillock, Thomas Lunn, Richard Beard, Joseph Nailer, Province of Maryland, Henry Bonner, Thomas Pattison, George Ogg, John Gray, John Robinson, Robert Gott, James Maxfeild, Thomas Edwards, John Larkin, Thomas Standbank, Nicholas Aldridge, Dr. Moore, Abraham Childe, Henry Welch, William Elvn (?), John Harris, Henry Hanslap, Margarett Holland, John Heatchoct, Austin Hawkins, Mathew Elliston, John Hawkins, Col. Darnall, Wharles Whitehead, James Stafford, John Smith, Sr., Robert Gover, Chr. Tully, Thomas Hedge, John Purdey, John Talbot, Jacob Hooker, John Martin, Samuell Garland, Richard Royston, John Seiffin, Chr. Foster, Peter Barnett, Samuell Withers, John Morgan, Samuell Gray, James Mills, William Harris, John Griffin, Robert Watts, George Parker, Richard Webb, John Guile, John Spencer, Mathew Jones, John Brookes, John Stone, Francis Sandry, John Fletcher, Chr. Bayley, Robert Hooper.

William Burges, Esq.   18.108   A   £2198.8.5   Mar 30 1698
The amount of the inventory also included #447169.
     Payments to: Col. Taylor, Col. Elliott, John Larkin, widow Parker, Job Evans, Robert Carvile, Kenelm Cheseldyn, William Dent, Thomas Tourford (?), Phillip Lines, John Edwards, Thomas Sparrow and his wife Ann Burges.
     Legatees: Maj. Sewell and his wife (unnamed) and children (unnamed), George Burgess, Edward Burgess, Maj. Gassaway, Capt. Hanslap, William Burges.
     Executrix: Ursula Moore, wife of Mr. Mordecay Moore.

John Lewellin   18.110   A SM   £98.1.0   #58458   May 19 1699
The amount of the inventory is equivalent to #19906.
     Received from: estate of Nehemiah Blackiston, Thomas Tench, Esq.
     Payments to: Capt. Cleggett, Mr. Robert Mason, judgement to Mr. Samuell Watkins, judgement to John Dudlestone, Capt. Richard Smith attorney of Joseph Stevens, Mr. Edward Sweatnam (administrator of Richard Sweatnam), William Taylard.
     Administratrix: Audrey Lewellin by Mr. William Taylard.

John Bennett   18.114   A AA   £5.18.0   May 26 1699
     Payments to: Joseph Connoway, John Nurn (?).
     Administratrix: Elisabeth Bennett.

Thomas Plummer   18.115   A AA   £110.15.0   £152.11.2   Apr 28 1699
The amount of the inventory also included #10034.
     Payments to: John Edwards, John Beacher former administrator of Joseph Williams and paid to now administrator Benjamin Williams, estate of Richard Tull, David Poole, Henry Bonner, Benjamin Williams, George Burges, Capt. Nicholas Gassaway, Capt. Abraham Wilde & Co., George Bruce, Henry Hanslap.
     Executrix: Elisabeth Plumer.

Thomas Plumer   18.116   I AA   £35.15.0
     Appraisers (on March 12, 1694): Robert Kirkland, William Goodman.
     Appraisers (on September 16 1695): William Goodman, Mark Richardson.
     List of debts: Robert Kirkland, Thomas Plummer, Jr., George Burges.

Hugh Merrikin   18.118   A AA   £345.7.7   £345.7.7   May 3 1699
     Payments to: Phillip Conner, Mr. William Blades.
     Distribution to: widow (unnamed), 2 orphans (unnamed).
     Administrator: Mr. Joshua Merrikin.

John North   18.120   I   £46.15.3   Mar 25 1699
     Appraisers: William Freman, Thomas Knightsmith.

Richard Sandifer   18.122   A CA   £33.6.5   £29.15.0   May 17 1698
     Payments to: William Cole, Mr. Craycroft, Thomas Blake.
     Administrator: William Nicholls.

Thomas Shanks   18.123   A SM   £7.5.6   £7.15.11   Mar 10 1698
     Payments to: Mr. Joshua Guybert, Mr. Tompson.
     Administratrix: Margarett Shanks.

Thomas Ennis   18.124   A SM   £22.8.4   £13.1.6   Mar 15 1698
     Payments to: Enoch Comes, Robert Clarke, William Combes, John Nutthall, Andrew Foy.
     Administratrix: Ann Ennis.

William Boswell   18.125   A SM   #1334   Mar 8 1699
     Payments to: ------ Grissett, Mr. Richard Clouds.
     Legatees: Mr. Hall.
     Administrator: Nicholas Poore.

Thomas Miles   18.126   A SM   £158.17.6   Dec 1 1698
The amount of the inventory also included #2885.
     Payments to: Capt. Lanham, Dr. Richardson, William Aisquith.
     Administratrix: Susannah Miles.

Mr. Thomas Mudd   18.126   A CH   Dec 15 1698
    Payments to: Anthony Simms, Walter Storey, Mr. Gilbert Clarke, Mr. Thomas
        Hussey, Maj. William Dent, David White, Dr. George Burch, Mr. Charles
        Cornwell, Mr. Jacob Moreland, Mr. Thomas Clarke, Capt. John Beane, Capt.
        John Rymer, Edward Newgatte, John Allerd, Mr. Richard Hubbard, Mr. Richard
        Boughton, John Tenniston, Mr. James Bouling, Mr. John Sirelson, J. Wallice,
        Thomas Simson.
    Executors: Thomas Mudd, Ann Hoskins (widow), wife of Phillip Hoskins.

Elias Beech   18.128   A SM   £21.16.8   £13.17.8   Feb 1 1698
    Payments to: Mrs. Sarah Bouton, Mr. Thomas Beale, William Tompson, Richard
        Griffin, William Guither, John Dunbarr, Thomas Haddocks, Mr. James Browne,
        Mr. Charles Egerton, Dr. Richardson.
    Mentions: 2 children (unnamed).
    Administrator: Henry Smith.

Col. Edward Pye   18.128   A
    Received from: John Clement, Richard Edlin, Mr. Thomas Jenkins, Mr. Robert
        Tompson, Mr. Richard Hubbard, Mr. John Smith, Moyses Jones, Mr. Benjamin
        Hall on account of Mr. William Boreman, Moses Jones, Maj. James Smallwood,
        Mr. Roger Brook, Jr., Dr. George Burch, Mr. Thomas Smoote.
    Payments to: John Bayne, Capt. George Brent from Allerton Issaack, Esq., Mr.
        Thomas Browne, Moses Jones, Mr. Richard Marsham, John Knight, Mr. William
        Stone, Capt. Bane, Mr. Thomas Beale on account of Capt. John Bayne, George
        Plater, Esq., Thomas Mitchell, Capt. Joshua Doyne, John Crackson on account
        of Capt. John Bayne, Mr. Phillip Clarke, Capt. John Baine, Madam Elisabeth
        Blakiston on account of Capt. John Baine.
    Administrator: Notley Rosier (gentleman).

John Cooney   18.131   A SM   £40.9.8   £40.5.6
    Payments to: Mr. Phillip Clarke, W. Bladen, Mr. Jacob Moreland, John Fenwick &
        Thomas Dillon, Mr. William Parker, Mr. Elzey, Mr. Robert Mason.
    Administrators: Edward Cole, James French.

Arthur Keefe   18.132   A SM   £13.0.0   #4403
    Payments to: John Shurley, Thomas Grace, Ann Chessam, Martin Kirk, Mr. Robert
        Mason, John Rallow, John Manning, Thomas Haddock, Mr. William Addison
        (merchant), Mrs. Twisdeal (midwife).
    Mentions: widow (unnamed).
    Administrator: Isaack Paine.

Thomas Cole   18.133   A SM   #2996   #2480   May 8 1698
    Payments to: Guillian Powell.
    Administrator: Luke Gardner.

Patience Burkett (widow)   18.134   I SM   £40.11.1   Nov 4 1698
    Appraisers: John Brill, Lawrence Tettersall (also Lawrence Tetersham).

Patience Burrell   18.137   A   £40.11.1   #3360   Feb 14 1698
The amount of the inventory also included #1650.
    Payments to: Mr. Briscoe, Thomas Lowe, Margarett Manly from Richard Burkett.
    Executor: Joseph Walters.

Thomas Cole   18.x138   I SM   #2996
    Appraisers: John Cooley, William Hellen.

Robert Bayley   18.138   A   £11.6.0   £25.19.10 Feb 16 1698
    Payments to: Mr. Robert Mason.
    Administrators/Executors: Joseph Walters, Margarett Bayley.

Mr. Thomas Mudd   18.139   I CH   #23343
    List of debts: Edward Newgent, William Wells, George Short, John Dickinson.

Thomas Mooney   18.139   A SM   £20.19.10 £32.13.9
    Payments to: Col. Henry Darnall.
    Administratrix: Rose Mooney (relict).

John Noble, Sr.   18.140   A   #810   Dec 26 1698
    Payments to: Mr. William Husband.
    Administrator/Executor: John Noble, Jr.

John Bennett   18.141   I   £5.18.0   May 13 1699
    Appraisers: John Hurst, Joseph Connoway.

Thomas Pennington   18.141   A   £29.2.0   £4.7.8
    Payments to: Edmond Duncalfe.
    Administratrix: Alce Gardner.

Edmond Duncalfe   18.142   I AA   £80.8.6   Mar 24 1698
    Appraisers: John Hurst, Ralph Moss.

Hugh Ellis   18.143   A CA   £143.15.2   May 12 1699
    Payments to: Symon Wooten, Col. John Bigger, executor of William Moss, Mr.
       George Lingan, Mr. William Turner, Mr. Hugh Jones, Jonathon Willson assigned
       to John Maccall, John Siennett, Mr. Thomas Greenfield, Mr. Jones for funeral
       sermon for a child (unnamed) of the deceased.
    Distribution to: Ignatius Sewell who married a daughter (unnamed), Thomas Goslin
       who married a daughter (unnamed), Charles Fowler who married a daughter
       (unnamed) of Mordecai Hinton.
    Executrix: Ruth Manning, wife of John Manning.

Walter Powell   18.144   I SO   £62.0.11   Mar 13 1696
    Appraisers: John Cornish, Peter Dent.
    List of debts: Maj. Whittington, Daniell Cox, Mr. Samuell Hopkins, Sr., Capt.
       John Cornish, Mr. Peter Dent, Thomas Kelly.

John Dynes   18.145   I TA   £48.19.0   May 1 1699
    Appraisers: Valentine Carter, Mathew Errickson,
    List of debts: Thomas Turner, estate of William Ricketts, John Oulden, Benjamin
       Peck, Valentine Sotheron, Robert Ipling.

Laurence Garey   18.146   I AA   £3.0.8   May 1 1699
    Appraisers: Richard Jones, Sr., William Jelfes.
    Approvers: John Scantey, N. Heatham.

Maj. Henry Trippe   18.147   A DO   £260.11.6   #15718   May 14 1699
A second inventory was cited, in the amount of £25.0.0.
    Payments to: Charles Powell, Ann Markerly, John Rickward, William Arrundell, John
       Sneyon (?), Mr. John Taylor, Mr. William Dent.
    Mentions: children (unnamed).
    Administrator: Richard Owen.

William Rabitts   18.148   I TA   £80.0.4   May 5 1699
    Appraisers: Mathew Erickson, Francis Stephens.

Symon Wooten   18.149   A   £428.14.9   £436.15.9 May 11 1699
    Payments to: Mr. Edward Buttler, Joshua Wilson, Mr. Richard Keen, Mr. John
       Elsey, Peter Pagan, William Philmore (runaway), John Fisher, Nathaniell Dare
       per Martin Morgan, James Martin, John Scott, Col. Henry Mitchell per Robert
       Reynolds, William Wadsworth, Mr. Walter Smith, Mr. Charles Carroll, David
       Small, Thomas Blake, John Bigger, Robert Hobbs.
    Administrator: John Fisher. Estate unadministered by John Bigger.

Michaell Taylor   18.151   A AA   #400
    Received from: William Griffin.
    Administrator: Charles Stevens.

Michaell Taylor   18.151   A AA   #650   May 12 1699
    Payments to: Mr. John Boye.
    Administrator: Charles Stephens.

Robert Phillips   18.152   I AA   £11.10.4   May 8 1699
    Appraisers: John Waters, John Willoughby.

Col. Nehemiah Blakiston   18.152   I SM   #42884   May 11 1699
    List of debts: Benjamin Scrivener, Henry Smith, Daniell Moy, William Hardage,
       Choptico Indians, Humphrey Warren, Stephen Gough, Col. Ninian Beall, John
       Conant, Mr. William Dent.

Col. Nehemiah Blackiston   18.153   I SM   £681.17.9
He is also cited as Col. Nehemiah Blackiston, Esq.
    List of debts: Samuell Watkins due from Madam Bourne, Mr. William Harris, Mr.
       John Scott, Robert Smith, Esq. on account of Capt. Harris, Gou. Nicholson,
       Esq., Mr. Thomas Tench on account of Miles Barrop, Mr. Thomas Tench on
       account of William Cole of Anne Arundel County, George Plater, Esq.

Ralph Smith   18.154   I CH   £334.6.9   Mar 10 1693
    Appraisers: Cleborne Lomax, Walter Storey.
    Executrix: Sarah Smith (relict).

William Groves (cooper)   18.158   A AA   £53.4.11   #9124   May 20 1699
A second inventory was filed in the amount of £2.9.6.
    Payments to: Mr. Brecher, Capt. Holland, William Hollyday, Mr. Samuell Chew,
       Mathias Clarke, Esq. Tench, Roger Roberts, Dr. Kingsbury, Thomas Symons,
       Morgan Jones, John Thompson.
    Administrators/Executors: Thomas Heifford, James Wood, Esq.

John Evans   18.160   A CA £175.17.0   £40.8.6   May 18 1699
The inventory also included #10737, which is equivalent to £44.14.9.
    Payments to: Mr. Thomas Beall, William Taylor.
    Legatees: Guy White.
    Administratrix: Sarah Collyer, wife of Francis Collyer.

Robert Cooper   18.161   A TA £10.19.6   £11.16.6   May 13 1698
    Payments to: Mr. Edward James, Maj. Thomas Smithson.
    Administrator: Robert Blunt.

Stephen Ownbey   18.162   A   £152.0.7   May 11 1699
    Payments to: Edward Carlton & Co., Capt. Keyser, Mr. Jacob Moorland, Thomas
        Emerson.
    Mentions: 1 orphan (unnamed).
    Administratrix/Executrix: Elisabeth Watts, wife of James Watts.

John Edmondson   18.162   A TA   £683.16.3   May 13 1699
    Payments to: Col. John Addison, Sir Thomas Lawrence, ------ Bourne, Nicholas
        Lowe, Robert Goldsburrough, Clerk of Dorchester County.
    Executor: William Edmondson.

Dennis Doyne   18.163   A   £53.10.0
    Payments to: Mr. Prooke Preist (?), Sarah Kee, Mr. George Tubman, Ignatius
        Wheeler, David Dueer, Gerrard Slye, Capt. John Baynes.
    Legatees: William Doyne, Ethelbert Doyne.

Col. Nehemiah Blackiston, Esq.   18.164   I   SM   £156.6.8
    List of debts: (see page 58.)

Thomas Dinew   18.170   I TA £43.11.8   Mar 13 1698
    Appraisers: Mathew Ereckson, Francis Stephens.

Richard Charlett   18.172   A PG   #7140
    Payments to: Mr. John Wight, Thomas Collier.
    Administrator: Mr. Thomas Grenfeild.

William Kenerly   18.172   A DO £322.5.6   £322.5.6   May 10 1699
    Payments to: Walter Cambell.
    Mentions: 2 orphans (unnamed).
    Administratrix: Alice Kenerly.

Robert Grason   18.173   A TA £191.2.7
    Mentions: George Allen, Robert Grason & Co., Mathew Flumbsteed.
    Administratrix: Mary Grason.

Samuel Withers   18.173   I TA £261.14.6   Jan 26 1698
    Appraisers: Laurence Knowles, Ralph Dawson.
    List of debts: (see page 59.)

Alexander Toulson   18.180   I TA £41.8.6   May 18 1699
    Appraisers: Isaack Winchester, Thomas Marsh.
    List of debts: William Starter, Thomas Marsh, Augustin Fane, William Gumey,
        William Shores.

Thomas Durbin   18.182   A BA £60.2.8   £60.2.8   May 11 1699
    Payments to: John Smith of Beddeford, Capt. Dean Cock & Co., Roger Newman,
        Thomas Thomas, Maj. Maxwell, John Hall.
    Mentions: wife (unnamed, dead).
    Administrator: Roger Newman.

Henry Tripp   18.183   I DO £47.2.9   May 16 1699
    Administrator: Richard Owen.

Mareen Duvall   18.183   A AA   #7178   May 15 1699
    Payments to: Charles Chyney, Abell Browne, Col. Ninian Beall, Thomas Boudle,
        Capt. Hall, Henry Hanslapp, Capt. Isaack Lild (?).
    Executrix: Mary Ridgley, wife of Col. Henry Ridgley, Sr.

Col. Phillomen Loyd   18.185   A   £4672.18.8   Apr 19 1699
    Legatees: Richard Bennett (executor of Madam Henrietta Maria Loyd) by his
        father's (unnamed) will (deceased married the widow).

John Cornelius   18.186   I   £17.18.0   Aug 3 1699
    Appraisers: John Turner, David Hellen.
    List of debts: Christopher Bealman.

Thomas Gant   18.186   A PG £40.1.6   Mar 19 1699
    Payments to: Mr. Michaell Taney, Mr. Samuell Groome (merchant in London).
    Executrix: Ann Wight, wife of John Wight.

Henry Pratt   18.187   A TA   £67.13.6   £76.0.4   May 10 1699
    Payments to: Nicholas Lowe.
    Administratrix/Executrix: Seth Ingerson, wife of Daniell Ingerson (also Daniell Ingram).

John Smart   18.188   A AA   £36.15.0   £12.9.6   Mar 9 1699
    Payments to: Abell Browne, Richard Bankes, Richard Bayley, William Hammond, Edward Gibbs, Humphrey Boone.
    Administrator: William Mort.

John Hume   18.189   I CA   £43.16.6   May 1 1699
    Appraisers: John Scott, James Heigh.

Jacob Kellett   18.190   A AA   £46.7.9   £46.7.9   May 9 1699
    Executor: William Clarke.

Benjamin Hunt   18.191   A DO
    Payments to: Sir Thomas Lawrence, William Abbott, John Swoins, Alice Kennerly, Richard Meekins, Capt. Elisha James, Mr. Charles Powell, Joseph Goutey, Capt. Richard Smith, John Foster, Mr. Daniell Clarke, Maj. William Dent, Rubian Ross.
    Mentions: 1 child (unnamed).
    Administratrix: Ann Hunt, wife of William Mockdell.

Stephen Onsby   18.192   I PG   £152.0.7   Jul 21 1698
    Servants mentioned: Richard Sumy (?), William Barnard.
    Appraisers: Thomas Brigell (also Thomas Bridge), Charles Bevin (signed William Cougley).
    List of debts: Col. Arnol.

Christopher Rowles   18.194   A AA   £45.14.6   £45.14.6   May 30 1699
    Payments to: Capt. William Harris.
    Administratrix: Elisabeth Hawkins (relict), wife of Joseph Hawkins.

Nathaniell Dolton   18.195   I AA   £13.1.1   Mar 16 1698
    Appraisers: Charles Stephens, Thomas Browne.

                       18.196   I CH   Jun 28 1698
This is a list of bills and receipts for the estates of Benjamin Rosier and Edward Pye, Esq.
    Appraisers: Clement Hill, Joshua Guibert. (Both of St. Mary's County).
    Receipts: (see page 60.)

Richard Thornton   18.220   I CE   £14.8.10   Jan 8 1697
    Appraisers: Thomas Windle, Peter Cole.

Mr. Thomas Thaxton   18.221   I CE   £373.16.0   Aug 12 1698
    Appraisers: Robert Gibson, Richard Kinwood.
    Mentions: Walter Rawlegh.

James Taylor   18.224   A CE   £28.12.8   £27.3.7   Apr 9 1699
    Payments to: Kenelm Cheseldyn, Esq., John Thompson, Owen Hues paid to Mr. James Charbott, Mr. James Charbott, Col. William Pearce paid to Mr. James Charbott, Thomas Parker & Cornelius Harkin, Richard Barker, Col. Casparus Harman paid to Katherine Harman (his administratrix), Col. John Thompson.
    Administratrix/Executrix: Jane Taylor (relict), wife of George Beston.

Peter Jefferson   18.226   I CE   £38.2.0   Dec 12 1698
    Appraisers: Henry Adesley, John Stoop.

Richard Thornton   18.227   A CE   £44.8.10   £31.13.10
    Approvers: Thomas Windall, Peter Cole.
    Payments to: Kenelm Cheseldyn, Esq., Mr. George Warner, Col. William Pearce, Capt. William Lurtin & Co., John Thompson.
    Administrator: Col. William Pearce.

Robert Scrivneright   18.229   I CE   £55.8.3
    Appraisers: Alexander Cambell, James Grey.
    List of debts: Mrs. Katherine Herman, John Buswell, Jane Hiland, John Hardin, John Neales, George Cousin, John Vesey, Abraham Willett, Benjamin Wells, Hugh Foutch, Capt. Rappe, Samuell Hues, Walter Scott.
    Administrator: James Cannon.

Thomas Moore   18.231   A CE   £30.10.3   £30.10.3   May 1 1699
    Payments to: Hon. Kenelm Cheseldyn, Esq., John Thompson, Charles Bass, Robert Smith, Esq., estate of Mathias Mathiason, William Sander.
    Distribution to: widow (unnamed), 2 orphans (unnamed).
    Administratrix: Bridget Brockson, wife of John Brockson.

John Sergent   18.233   I TA   £169.14.0   Nov 30 1698
The amount of the inventory also included #5543.
     List of debts: William Laott, Bryan Cowley, Owen Lallyvan, Thomas Yewell, John
        Hogin, William Smith, John Caves, Thomas Bruff, William Coursey, Vincent
        Hemsley.

Mr. Richard Pott   18.238   I TA   £18.8.6   Dec 2 1698
     Appraisers: Anthony Brumball, Andrew Kinemont.
     List of debts: Capt. Nicholas Lowe, Mr. Alexander Forubss.
     Administrator: Mr. William Scott.

Thomas Barnet   18.238   I AA   £11.8.2   Mar 17 1698
     Appraisers: Robert Eagle, Jonathon Neall.

Christopher Betson   18.239   I   £13.10.6   Feb 6 1696   Jul 22 1697
     Appraisers: John Cave.

Peter Hadway   18.240   I TA   £106.15.3
     Appraisers: John Lowe, William Webb.
     List of debts: William Fisbourne, Richard Clarke, Capt. James Murphey.

George Robinson   18.242   I AA   Mar 5 1698   Jun 20 1699
     Appraisers: Edward Gibbs, Samuell Smith.

John Winsmore   18.246   I DO   £49.15.6   Jan 15 1698
     Appraisers: Thomas Vickers, Peter Stoakes.

Phillip Pitt   18.247   I DO   £88.5.4   --- 2 1698
     Appraisers: Francis Hayward, Edward Stevens.

John Russell   18.250   I   £30.17.0   Jan 19 1699
     Appraisers: Anguish Morrow, William Fisher.
     Administratrix: widow Russell.

Clew Gay   18.252   I   £17.7.0   Jan 19 ----
     Appraisers: John Hazelwood, Humphrey Hubert.

William Dorington   18.253   I DO   £4.9.6   Nov 8 1698
     Appraisers: John Hazelwood, John Richardson.
     Mentions: Cornelius Arrundell.

John Southey   18.254   A   £39.0.0   £3.4.4   Jan 3 1698
     Payments to: Peter Stoakes, Anthony Thompson.
     Executrix: Elenor Ennalls, wife of John Ennalls.

Col. Nehemiah Blakiston   18.254   A   May 11 1699
     Payments to: Mr. James Browne, Josiah Willson, Col. Jowles, Michaell
        Butterworth, William Bladen, Col. Henry Lowe, William Aisquith, Thomas Blake,
        Mr. Curtis, Mr. Robert Mason, Mr. Dent, Mr. Carbery & Mr. Anthony Neall,
        George Plater, Esq.
     Administrators: Madam Elisabeth Blakiston, Ralph Rymer.

Thomas Boudle   19.1   I TA   £240.10.2   Dec 2 1698
Items at the house of Phoebe Boudle.
     Appraisers: Joseph James, Richard Moore.

Stephen Benson   19.2   I TA   £80.2.0   Dec 30 1698
     Appraisers: John Lowe, Thomas Lurkey.

John Pritchard   19.3   I TA   £11.18.7   Apr 20 1699
     Appraisers: John Pargdan, Edward Tourlin.

Richard Harris   19.4   I TA   £5.2.1
     Appraisers: William Webb, John Lowe.

John Smith   19.4   I   £3.6.1   Dec 1 1697
     Appraisers: William Hatfeild, Thomas Evans.

Moses Groome   19.5   I BA   £105.14.7   Jan 10 1698
     Servants mentioned: John Makensee.
     Appraisers: Thomas Staley, William Pickett.

Thomas Smith   19.7   I BA   £166.0.3   Jan 17 1699
     Appraisers: John Rawlings, Samuell Standifor.
     List of debts: Thomas Heath, Abraham Taylor, William Gudgoon, Michaell Gudgoon,
        Col. John Thomas, Francis Whitehead, John Cutter, Dr. Gerardus Wissells, Mr.
        John Hall, Mr. George Smith, George Morgan, John Wright, Edward Jones, John
        Ewings, Anthony Drewe, George Hopham, Thomas Hedge, Sr., Katherine Lomax,
        Peter Norton, William Yorke, Ralph Guillam, Robert Drisdall, Symon Pursor,
        Margarett Marke, John Copin, Richard Allion, Samuell Jackson, Josias Bridges,

Page 29

Mr. Colegate, Samuell Standefer, Mr. Francis Smith, Sarah Teale, Phillip Roper, Daniell Daney, Samuell Sicklemore, Thomas Preston, Maj. James Maxwell, Robert Parker, Charles Addams, William Lenox, Thomas Blackwell, Cornelius Harrington, John Taylor, Thomas Stone, Michaell Cannady, Charles Howell, Mr. Thomas Hedge, Sr., William Beck, William Slade, Francis Robinson, Benjamin Wells, John Scott, Benjamin Nensley (?), Moses Groome, Mrs. Elisabeth Gibson, John Hazelewood, Josias White, Cornelius Boyce, John Boone, Mr. Henry Wriothsley, John Devigh, Amos Evans, William Chirne, George Norman, Symon Jackson, Peter Fucale, John Miles, Alexander Dimosa, Dr. John Roberts, Walter Halock, Richard Bright, John Watson, Samuell Baker, John Wright, William Robertson, Francis Whitehead to George Morgan, George Smith, John Biven, John Wells, James Mazzard, William Pickett.

Francis Robinson   19.11   I BA   £59.18.6
    Appraisers: John Gay, Josias Bridge.

Patrick Davison   19.12   I   £8.2.0
    Appraisers: William Elder, John Webster.

Humphrey Day   19.12   I BA   £35.0.2
    Appraisers: John Ferry, Roebuck Linch.

Isaack Mashett   19.13   I   £17.5.10   Nov 6 1698
    Appraisers: William Farfar, Daniell Swindall.

Joseph Gallion   19.14   A BA   £17.16.0   £17.16.0   Mar 9 1699
The amount of the accounts also included #1734.
    Payments to: Sarah Hensley, William Lenox, Peter Pagan & Co., Thomas Heath, Lt.
        Col. Thomas Richardson.
    Administrator: William Peckett.

Anthony Phillips   19.15   I BA   £100.11.10   Mar 4 1698
    Appraisers: George Smith, Samuell Chaine.

Stephen Walton   19.16   A SM   £10.1.11   £16.5.8   Apr 15 1699
    Payments to: David Vaughan, Isaack Cuson, Mr. Thomas Jameson, James Thompson,
        Sollomon Jones, Capt. Greenhalf, John Manning, Mr. James Cullen, Mr.
        Benjamin Sumer, Mr. John Hall, John Weeks.
    Mentions: 3 children (unnamed).
    Executor: Thomas Haddock.

John Duckworth   19.17   I SM   £44.9.3   Mar 29 1699
    Appraisers: John Wiseman, William Aisquith.

James Browne   19.18   I   £417.4.10   Dec 23 1698
    Servants mentioned: John Browne (runaway), James Welsh (shoemaker), William
        Moriot (carpenter), John Luke (taylor), Dennis Tommy, John Dinaho (plowman),
        Gillian his wife and Eleanor his daughter, Thomas Magar (tanner), Peter
        Knowles (runaway), William Benton.
    Appraisers: Charles Egerton, John Evans.
    Mentions: Luke Gardner, Cornelius Brunnon.

Stephen Walton   19.20   I SM   £10.1.11   Mar 4 1698   Mar 31 1698
    Appraisers: John Doxey, John Manning.

William Shrine   19.21   I   £42.3.6   Apr 30 1698
    Appraisers: William Herbert, William Bradley.

John Pearce   19.22   A CA   £6.5.4   £7.15.0   Feb 28 1698
    Payments to: John Turner and David Hillen, Mr. Richard Smith.
    Administratrix: Mary Pearce.

John Taylor   19.23   A CA   £23.16.6   £15.11.4   Mar 27 1699
    Payments to: Mr. Lingan, Mr. Joseph Jackson & Co., Dunkin Micollum, David
        Morgan, William Parker, James Martin.
    Administratrix: Mary Taylor.

James Gardner   19.24   A CA   £39.18.0   Mar 3 1698
    Payments to: Daniell Sherwood, William Williams, Sr., James Martin, John Bigger
        on account of Peter Paggan & Co., John Godcross.
    Cites: no orphans.
    Administrator: Mathew Gardner.

Nathan Cranford   19.25   A CA   £6.0.0   £7.0.0   Jan 2 1698
    Payments to: Mr. Parker, Mr. Lingan, William Turner.
    Mentions: 1 orphan (unnamed).
    Administratrix: Martha Cranford.

George Bruce   19.25   I   £166.0.0   Apr 22 1699
    Appraisers: John Gather, Leonard Wayman.

Charles Watson   19.27   A CH   Mar 17 1698
     Payments to: Thomas Hutchinson, Thomas Greenfeild, David Murphey, Jonathon
     Prather, Margarett Swift, William Wilkinson, John Edmyfeild, Dorothy Stone.
     Mentions: widow (unnamed, dead).
     Administrator: John Kelley.

Mr. Randolph Hinson   19.29   I CH   £189.15.7   May 5 1699

Capt. Randolph Brand   19.31   I   £241.4.8   May 11 1699
     Appraisers: Anthony Neale, William Hawton, Sr.

Thomas Harrison   19.34   A CH   £3.14.0   Jan 4 1698
     Payments to: Robert Clarke, Maj. William Dent, William Sergeant, Edward
     Millstead.
     Administrator: Francis Harrison.

Stephen Mankin   19.35   A CH   £32.18.8   May 24 1699
     Payments to: Phillip Lines & Cleborne Lomax.
     Administratrix: Mary Howard, wife of Thomas Howard.

Henry Brawner   19.36   A CH   May 3 1699
     Payments to: Francis Frampton, Thomas Bowling, James Smallwood, Hugh Fergeson.
     Executrix: Mary Brawner.

George Delahay   19.37   I CH   £44.0.7   Apr 22 1699
     Appraisers: Richard Harrison, Joseph Harrison.

Edward Fitzgerrald   19.39   I   £7.5.3   May 11 1699
     Appraisers: William Hawton, Sr., Anthony Neale.

John Ward   19.39   A CH   Apr 28 1699
     Payments to: Maj. William Dent for advice against William Legcam.
     Administrator: John Ward.

John Martin   19.40   I CH   £21.8.6   Oct 29 1698   Nov 2 1698
     Appraisers: John Godshall, Robert Benson.

Sarah Till   19.41   I   Jun 19 1699
(executrix of Edward Till)
     Appraisers: John Watton (?), Robert Tailor.
     Administrator: Thomas Craxon.

Henry Tompson   19.41   I   £20.6.6   Apr 21 1699
     Appraisers: Mathew Saunders, Edward Roockwood.

John Nelson   19.42   I   £14.6.10   Apr 21 1699

Francis Buttery   19.43   A CH   Jun 20 1699
     Payments to: John Allen, Richard Harrison, Emanuell Ratcliff, James Courett,
     Thomas Hussey, Thomas Chapman, George Godfrey, Joakim Kirsteed, Michaell
     Martin.
     Executors: John Wood, Michaell Martin.

Henry Key   19.44   A CH   £31.19.6   Jun 9 1699
(also Henry Kee)
     Payments to: Elisabeth Hawkins, William Serjant, William Stone, Hugh Ramstopp,
     Capt. John Bayne, William Summers, John Paine, Thomas Jenkins, Capt. Phillip
     Hoskins, Benony Thomas & Ignatius Wheeler.
     Administratrix: Sarah Kee.

John Martin   19.46   A CH   £21.8.6   May 25 1699
     Payments to: Capt. John Sherriff.
     Administratrix: Mary Martin.

Francis Adams   19.47   A   Jun 7 1699
     Administratrix: Grace Adams.

Henry Brawner   19.48   A   Jun 20 1699
     Received from: John Turner, Henry Brice, Capt. John Bayne.
     Executrix: Mary Brawner.

John Rockhold   19.48   I AA   £56.6.0
The amount of the inventory also included #1710.
     Appraisers: John Howard, Thomas Blackwell.
     List of debts: John Smith, William Jones, Robert Rogers.

Charles Egerton   19.51   I SM   £425.4.10   May 29 1699
The amount of the inventory also included #36200.
     Appraisers: John Evans, Thomas Haddock.

William Knight   19.53   I SM   £1.17.0   May 30 1699
     Appraisers: Richard Newman, Christopher Horrell.

William Knight   19.53   I SM   #874   Jun 14 1699
     List of debts: William Heyden, John Bayley, John Glass.

Richard Wallis (cooper)   19.53   I KE   £6.9.0   Jun 7 1699
     Appraisers: Richard Duncells, Benjamin Bond.
     Approvers: William Price, George Lumley.

Robert Davenish (planter)   19.54   I KE   £56.4.0   Jun 16 1699
The amount of the inventory also included #1350.
     Appraisers: William Smith, Thomas Tolley.
     Approvers: Charles Smith, James Smith.

Thomas Kinningston   19.55   I PG   £226.8.9   May 4 1699
     Appraisers: Thomas Greenfeild, Robert Orme.
     List of debts: ------ Walker, William Barton.

William Knight   19.56   A SM   £56.6.0   £65.3.2   Jun 14 1699
A second inventory was cited at £1.17.0; a third inventory was cited at £4.7.5.
     Payments to: Mr. Robert Mason, Mr. Anthony Neale, Mr. Clement Hill, Elisabeth
          Phillips, John Glass, John Bayley, Thomas Ashman, William Howell.
     Mentions: wife (unnamed, dead), son (unnamed), son (unnamed, aged 6).
     Executor: James Martin.

John Sewell   19.58   A SM   £28.0.0   £19.1.10   Jun 14 1699
     Payments to: Mr. Robert Mason per Arthur Thompson, Mr. John Hance per James
          Sewell, William Norris, John Wad, Capt. Holland per Ignatius Sewell, Thomas
          Blackman.
     Mentions: 5 orphans (unnamed).
     Administratrix: Ann Head (relict), wife of Adam Head.

John Powell   19.59   A SM   £26.11.3   £25.6.6
     Payments to: John Gosling, Capt. Timothy Keysey & Co. per Charles Carless,
          James Keetch, Jacob Mooreland & Co., Mr. Thomas Crabb per John Sothern,
          Joseph Hartley, Edward Batson.
     Administratrix: Susanna Whitter (widow), wife of William Whitter.

Thomas Barker   19.59   A SM   £100.12.6   £156.12.2   Jul 5 1699
A second inventory cited an amount of #55.19.8.
     Payments to: Mrs. Elisabeth Watkinson, John Baker, Capt. James Keetch, Edward
          Hunt, Jacob Moorland, Mr. Abraham Dill, Mr. Samuell Watkins, James Crooke,
          George Plater, Esq. & Mr. Amos Garrett attorney for Mary Barker (widow) in
          England, Capt. Thomas Wharton paid to Mr. Benjamin Brame.
     Administrator: Jacob Moorland.

William Douland   19.61   I TA   £515.13.4   Jun 2 1699
     Appraisers: Edward Brown, John Wells.
     List of debts: John Hall, John Mason, William Slaughter, John Reynolds, widow
          Pindor.

Maj. Robert King (gentleman) 19.62   I   £629.0.10   Jul 1 1699
     Appraisers: Peter Dent, Ephraim Willson.

Samuell Greenwood   19.64   A BA   £33.16.11   £39.1.5
The amount of the inventory also included #2416.
     Payments to: Maj. James Maxwell, William Paultry, Thomas Hedge.
     Mentions: 1 orphan (unnamed).
     Administrator: Roebuck Lynch.

Col. Nicholas Greenbury   19.64   I AA   £163.12.4   Jun 16 1699
     Appraisers: Humphrey Boone, Roger Newman.
     List of debts: Mr. Peter Paggen (merchant) in London, Mr. Isaack Millner
          (merchant) in London.

Col. John Winder   19.65   I SO   £107.19.3   Feb 23 1698
     Appraisers: Ja. Dasheill, Thomas Dasheill.

John Conner   19.66   A   £13.14.0   £12.8.0   Mar 29 1699
The amount of the inventory also included #424.
     Received from: Levin Denwood.
     Payments to: Charles Ballard, Nehemiah Covington.
     Administrator/Executor: Levin Denwood, Jr.

Thomas Lewis   19.67   A PG   £55.10.0   £55.10.0   Jul 3 1699
     Payments to: Robert Clarke, Mr. Greenfeild, John Redman, Daniell Counell, John
          Tompson, Dr. Ferguson, Alexander Harbert.
     Distribution to: widow, 5 orphans (unnamed).
     Administratrix: Katherine Watkins (widow), wife of John Watkins.

Edward Wooland   19.68   A DO   £16.2.2   £25.7.1   Jun 10 1699
    Payments to: Mr. William Robson, David Mackall, Henry Davis.
    Administratrix: Jane Wooland.

John Weals   19.69   I   May 1 1699
    Appraisers: William Wilkinson, Roebuck Lynch.
    List of debts: John Bays, John Ferry, Joseph Peake, James Todd, Joseph Weales.

Thomas Johnson   19.69   I SO   £16.18.0   May 6 1699
    Appraisers: Samuell Flewelling, Nicholas Evans.

Mr. William Burgis   19.70   I   £456.16.7
    Appraisers: Mr. James Rigbey, Mr. John Baldwyn.

John Hamon   19.73   A   £47.13.0   £47.13.0   Apr 25 1699
    List of debts: Maj. Whittington, Dr. Davis, George Truitt, Capt. Hamon, Thomas
        Purnell, Francis Heap, Mr. James Round, William Richardson, Samuell
        Worthington, Samuell Hopkins, Sr.
    Distribution to: widow (unnamed), 6 orphans (unnamed).
    Administratrix: Elisabeth Hammon.

Mary Clio   19.73   I BA   £40.14.6   Jan 30 1698
    Appraisers: Lawrence Taylor (also Lawrence Tailor), George Smith.
    Administrators: John Hall, Marke Richardson.

John Sharp   19.74   I DO   £19.2.3   Apr 3 1699
    Appraisers: William Gray, Thomas Gray.
    List of debts: William Edmondson.

John Comber   19.75   I AA   £20.17.6
    Appraisers: William Lewis, Jonathon Neale.

John Mockguyer   19.75   I TA   £8.2.10   Apr 24 1699
    Appraisers: Anthony Rumball, William Scott.
    Mentions: estate of William Garey.
    Administrator: John Jones (brazier).

Richard Chaffee   19.76   I TA   May 17 1699
    Appraisers: Richard Jones, Sr., John Johnson.

Mortogh Horney   19.76   I   £24.5.10   Feb 20 1698
    Appraisers: Robert ------ (surname unreadable), Samuell Hamilton.
    Mentions: John Newman.
    Administrator: ------ (name not given).

John Sides   19.77   I TA   £40.8.6   Mar 31 1699
    Servants mentioned: Dennis Swine (boy).
    Appraisers: John Salter, Da. Blaney.

Daniell Glover   19.78   I TA   £64.7.5   Jun 13 1699
    Appraisers: William Hynson, John Davis.

William Carsey   19.79   I TA   £9.9.3   Dec 29 1698
    Appraisers: Henry Frith, Robert Harrison.

Thomas Mason   19.80   I TA   £31.16.2   May 10 1699
    Appraisers: Henry Frith, John Hunt.

David Rogers   19.82   I   £117.10.7   Jun 21 1699
    Appraisers: Thomas Emerson, William Hatfeild.

James Harintun   19.85   I   £7.13.0   May 15 1699
    Appraisers: Frances Mead, Thomas Vorson.

Capt. Thomas Harman   19.85   I KE   £1.5.0
    List of debts: Robert Smith, Esq., John Norrest, Mr. John Hamer, Thomas Hyndes.

Capt. Thomas Harman   19.85   A KE   £7.5.0   £25.17.10   Jul 20 1699
The amount of the inventory included the balance from previous accounts as £44.1.6.
    Payments to: William Hemesley, Capt. James Smith, Mr. Charles Carroll.
    Administratrix: Henage Robinson.

Stephen Francis (mariner)   19.86   I AA   £320.14.6   Jul 18 1699   Jul 26 1699
    Appraisers: John Freeman, Thomas Hutchins.
    List of debts: Recampens Stanbrough to Samuell Watkins & Robert Mason per James
        Fowler (merchant) in London, Henry Sutton paid to Samuell Watkins on Thomas
        Sands (merchant) in London, John Norwood on Micajah Perry & Co. (merchant) in
        London, William Wilkinson on Edward & Dudley Carleton (merchants) in London
        paid John Perry per Sarah Perry, Robert Mason on Mr. Isaac Milner (merchant)
        in London paid Thomas Blackwell, Peter Paggen (merchant) in London paid John

Freeman per George Plater, John Hall on Anthony Strutton (merchant) in London, Samuell Chew on Samuell Groome (merchant) in London paid George Slacom, Samuell Chew on John Hyde (merchant) in London, Andrew Norwood on John Taylor (merchant) in London, Dean Cock (merchant) in London, Samuell Howard on Mr. John Taylor (merchant) in London, Richard Beard on David Dennis (merchant) in London, Philip & Samuell Norwood on Micajah Perry & Thomas Lane (merchants) in London paid to Lancelot Todd (merchant) in London, Philip & Samuell Norwood on Micajah Perry & Co., Richard Gallaway on Robert Ridle & Benjamin Doroline (merchants) in London paid Stephen Francis & George Slacum, Abell Brown on Robert Redle (merchant) in London, Thomas Ennalls on Capt. Jonathon Searth (merchant) in London paid Edward Dorsey, John Hamilton on Robert Blacklock (merchant) in Whitehaven, Cumberland paid Anthony Bowles, John Garner on John Taylor (merchant) in London, Edward Taylor of Dorchester County, George Slacomb, Samuell Manthorp, Abel Browne, Henry Bonner, Matthias Elliston, Capt. Richard Hill, Sr., Thomas Blackwell, Lancelot Tod, Mr. Thomas Stayley.
    List of desperate debts: Samuell Scot (servant) in Philadelphia, Samuell Norwood, John Norwood.
    Administrator: Mannus Devoren.

William Owens   19.92   I   SO   £61.14.6   Apr 28 1699
    Appraisers: Richard Chambers, Ephraim Willson.

William Wheatle   19.93   I   £1.1.4   Feb 20 1698
    Appraisers: Robert Givan, John Winder.
    Administratrix: Mary Whitle.

Richard Minckin   19.94   I   SM   £60.0.0   Apr 29 1699
    Appraisers: Charles Smith, James Tomson.

Alexander Price   19.95   I   £96.11.9
    Appraisers: Nicholas Evans, Thomas Horseman.

Mathew Selby   19.96   I   AA   £98.8.8   May 23 1699
    Appraisers: John Chappell, Christopher Milby.

Joseph & Sarah Strawbridge   19.97   I   BA   £86.1.4   Jul 7 1699
The amount of the inventory also included #5626.
    Appraisers: Mr. William Wilkison, Mr. Robuck Linch.

Capt. Nicholas Gassaway   19.98   I   AA   £339.11.6   Jun 13 ----
    Appraisers: James Lewis, John Baldwin.
    Administratrix: Ann Gassaway.

Mary Hall   19.100   I   CH   £11.17.0   Jun 17 1699
    Appraisers: George Britt, Richard Nelson.

William Battes   19.101   I   AA   £17.7.7   Nov 12 1696   Aug 1 1699
    Appraisers: Frances Mead, Matthew Howard.

Bryan Omaley   19.102   I   TA   £264.19.0   Jun 21 1699
(also Bryan Omely)
    Appraisers: James Benson, Daniell Sherwood.
    List of debts: Mr. Ralph Fishbourn, Mr. John Edmondson, Mr. William Sharpe, Mr. William Dixon, Mr. Abraham Morgan.

Timothy Hickman   19.103   I   £87.6.3   Apr 10 1699
    Appraisers: John Hunt, Richard Fidoe.
    List of debts: John Hyde (merchant), Thomas Wharton (merchant).

Joseph Pettybone   19.104   I   AA   £261.12.9   May 13 1699
    Appraisers: Robert Eagle, Humfrey Boone.

Charles Tracey   19.106   I   PG   £23.0.0   Jul 9 1699
    Appraisers: James Stoddert, Joshua Keen.
    Mentions: Richard Groome. Also a description of the land.

John Bennet   19.107   I   AA   £807.8.10
    Appraisers: Robert Eagle, Humfrey Boone.

Edward Watters   19.111   I   £121.12.10   Jun 10 1699
    Appraisers: John Hast, Francis Mead.

Elisabeth Young   19.113   A   CH   £10.2.6   £46.16.6   Jun 1699
    Legatees: Mr. Robert Yates, Mr. Hunter & Mr. Hall, Mr. Richard Hubbard, James Tiers, Bowles Tyers.
    Executor: William Boreman.

Mr. Robert Roberts   19.114   I   £107.8.9   May 6 1699
    Appraisers: Isack Baker, William Marston.

Gillburt Pattisson   19.115   I   £45.5.6   Jul 4 1699
        Appraisers: Lennord Wayman, Robert Hopper.

Thomas Hooke   19.116   I   £43.9.4   Jun 8 1699
        Appraisers: Joseph Harrenson, James Watts.

Thomas Parker   19.117   I KE   £10.4.6   Aug 29 1696
        Appraisers: Thomas Pinner, John Wade.

Charles Whitehead   19.117   I AA   £38.16.6   Jun 28 1699
        Appraisers: Jacob Harris, Richard Garrett.

Samuell Showell   19.118   I   £35.9.6   Nov 15 1698
        Appraisers: Thomas Powell, Thomas Morris.

William Carvort   19.119   I   £68.0.0   Apr 22 1699
        Appraisers: Edward Tench, Anguish Marow.

George Leek   19.120   I CH   £19.17.0   Apr 21 1699   May 7 1699
        Appraisers: John Thopson, Richard Edgar.
        Mentions: widow (unnamed).

John Blackister   19.121   I   £61.1.6
        Appraisers: Thomas Hinton, William Meade.
        Creditors: John Eves, Samuell Turner.

Capt. Edward Greenhalgh   19.122   I SM   £96.15.1   May 28 1699
        Appraisers: William Harburt, Henry Smith.

John Dobbs   19.124   I TA   £79.11.2   Aug 5 1699
        Appraisers: Matt. Eareckson, James Ringgold.
        List of debts: Thomas & Roger Baxter, Elly Benton, William Willson, Christopher
            Granger, John Jones, Thomas Ward, James Ringold, George Vinson.

Daniell Palmer   19.125   I BA   £5.16.11   May 3 1699
The amount of the inventory also included #13160.
        Appraisers: William Hollis, Henry Jackson.
        List of debts: ------ Todd, Charles Meryman, Mr. Thomas Stayly, Andrew Anderson,
            Anthony Johnson, William Wilkisson, Samuell Smith, Robert Parker, Aquila
            Peacke, Mr. John Hall, Mr. Marke Richardson, Richard Parker, William Lofton,
            James Ive, Thomas Tribell, Nathaniell Anderson, John Ferry, John Wright,
            Samuell Baker, John Evens, John Haselwood, Edmund Hersley, William Prichard,
            William Osburne, Joseph Peack.
        Administrator: Mr. Anthony Drew.

Henry Hawkins   19.127   I CH   £327.18.8   May 29 1699
Cites items in the possession of Elisabeth Hawkins (relict).
        Servants mentioned: Francis Crumton (boy), Robert GillCross (boy), John Lory
            (boy), Ann Tanner, John Tippon, Francis Gyard, Francis Crandell, Daniell
            Mockyfelt (boy), Thomas Martin, Joan Brett, David Southerland (boy).
        Appraisers: William Barton, Cleborne Lomax.

Edward Wooland   19.131   I DO   £16.2.2   May 17 1699
        Appraisers: William Robson, Jr., David Mackeall.

Jonas Bowen   19.132   I BA   May 13 1699
        Appraisers: George Ashman, William Wilkinson.
        List of debts: Mr. Merryman, Edward Rutledge.

Arthur Emory   19.135   I TA   £23.15.4   May 5 1699
        Appraisers: Thomas Evans, John Simmons (also John Simons).

Edward Day   19.136   I   £147.10.3
        Appraisers: Thomas Horseman, Benjamin Cattnell.

William Wright   19.137   I   £24.6.6   Jun 17 1699
        Appraisers: John Jones, John Panter.

William Powell   19.137   I AA   £144.4.3   Nov 28 1696
        Appraisers: John Denner, Thomas Hughs.

Thomas Shepard   19.139   I PG   £3.2.8   Mar 16 1698   Apr 6 1699
        Appraisers: Thomas Sprigg, William Affotts.
        List of debts: James Beale.
        Administrator: James Beale.

Ann Pitt   19.139   I DO   £61.0.0   Mar 10 1698
        Appraisers: William Meshew, Petter Stokes.

Joseph Hinett   19.141   I CA   £18.7.6   Apr 4 1699
     Appraisers: John Meads, Joseph Berry.

Daniell Buckmaster   19.141   I CA   £40.16.0   Jun 7 1699
The amount of the inventory also included #2420.
     Appraisers: Clarke Skinner, Thomas Harvey.
     List of debts: Thomas Layne, William Carter, John Ball.

Obadiah King   19.142   I DO   £60.18.4   Jul 1 1699
     Appraisers: Henry Eccleston, Hezekiah Makey.

William Smith   19.143   I CA   £19.0.0   Jul 6 1699
     Appraisers: Henry Boteler, Robert Summers.

John Ricketts   19.144   I   £91.8.10   Nov 5 1698
     Appraisers: Edward Becke, John Willis.
     List of debts: George Fater (?).

Francis Leafe   19.145   I   £42.1.8   Jun 6 1698   Apr 6 1699
     Appraisers: Jeremiah Eldridge, John Underwood.

John Hedger   19.146   I CA   £94.8.0   Feb 6 1698
There are two folios numbered 147; for convenience, the first is cited as 147A, the
second as 147B.
     Appraisers: Thomas Arnold (also Thomas Arnall), John Grover.

Thomas Sedgwick   19.147B I CA   £106.13.1   Mar 4 1698
There are two folios numbered 147; for convenience, the first is cited as 147A, the
second as 147B.
     Appraisers: George Young, Sr., Hezekiah Bussey.

Mary Russell   19.148   I   £175.19.10   Jun 14 1699
     Appraisers: William Margent, Roger Furley.

John Wheeler   19.150   I   £41.11.9   Nov 26 1698
     Appraisers: John Atkison, Phill. Holleger.

Sutton Quincy   19.153   I CE   £239.5.0   Sep 28 1698
     Appraisers: William Harris, John Carvill.
     List of debts: Mr. Edward Basboury, John Fitzgarrett, John Greene, Michaell
     James.

Jonathon Willson   19.155   A PG   £55.1.3   £66.2.8   Jul 14 1699
     Payments to: Richard Marsham and his wife Ann (administrators of Henry Brent),
     Col. John Bigger for judgment vs. Samuell Goosy in Charles County, James
     Kingsbury, Joseph Cacill paid to Mr. William Dent & William Bladen.
     Executors: Katherine Willson, Joseph Cacill.

Elisabeth Young   19.156   A CH   £10.2.6   Jun 1699
     Legatees: Mr. Robert Yates, Mr. Hunter & Mr. Hall, Mr. Richard Hubbard, James
     Tyers & Bowles Tyers.
     Executor: William Boreman.

Thomas Bagg   19.156   A TA   £90.10.8   £90.10.8   Jul 11 1699
     Payments to: Edward Combes.
     Distribution to: widow, 1 orphan (unnamed).
     Administratrix: Mary Bagg.

William Anderson   19.157   A TA   £104.14.10   £5.19.9   Jul 13 1699
     Payments to: Mr. Goldsborough, Mr. Lowe.
     Executrix: Sarah Gwyn, wife of William Gwyn.

Archibald Vauhop   19.158   A CH   £61.1.0   #3671   Jul 24 1699
     Payments to: Capt. Phillip Hoskins by order of Thomas Lowe son of William Lowe.
     Executor: Cleborne Lomax (surviving executor of Elisabeth Smith (executrix of
     deceased)).

William Richardson   19.158   A AA   £655.8.5   Jul 27 1699
     Payments to: Edward, John, and Elisabeth Talbott paid to Elisabeth Talbott (their
     mother).
     Distribution to: Daniell Richardson, Joseph Richardson, Thomas Sparrow for his
     wife Sophia Richardson (daughter), Elisabeth Richardson (her thirds),
     accountant (one-quarter of two-thirds).
     Executor: William Richardson (Quaker).

Col. Nehemia Blackiston   19.159   A SM   #14850   Jun 20 1699
     Payments to: suit by ------ Bareorgh, suit by ------ King, suit by ------ Harris,
     John Lewellin, Capt. Holland, Mr. Freeman for Mr. Tench.
     Administratrix: Elisabeth Rymer, wife of Mr. Ralph Rymer.

John Crooke   19.159   A SM £23.8.11   £12.10.8   Jul 13 1699
     Payments to: Jacob Moreland, Robert Clarke, Thomas Crabb.
     Mentions: 3 orphans (unnamed).
     Administratrix: Sarah Warren, wife of Samuell Warren.

Henry Brent   19.160   A CA £239.1.0   £478.18.8   Jul 18 1699
The amount of the inventory also included #166033.
     Received from: Jonathon Wilson.
     Payments to: Mr. William Lane paid to Mr. John Wight, Mr. Baker Brooke per
          order of Mr. George Plowden.
     Administratrix: Ann Marsham, wife of Richard Marsham.

Jonah Winfeild (planter)   19.161   A CA £69.0.9   £125.8.2
     Payments to: Joshua Hollingmead, Michaell Tauney, Dr. Symon Wooten, Henry
          Nueman, Henry Orton, Cecill Butler, Mary Ashcombe per Arthur Young, Nathan
          Veitch, William Jaggard, Nicholas Sporne, Col. Darnall & Col. Diggs, John
          Lydiatt, George Plater per Baruck Williams, Henry Fernely, Thomas Tasker, John
          Askey, James Cranford.
     List of debts: David Evans (dead).
     Administratrix: Sarah Hall, wife of Edward Hall.

Col. Edward Pye   19.163   A CH £1150.13.6   £1199.6.0   Jul 17 1699
     Payments to: Notley Rosier his share of his father's (unnamed) estate.
     Administrator Notley Rosier.

Col. Benjamin Rosier   19.164   A   £867.3.6   £1983.16.10 Jul 17 1699
     Received from: William Deal.
     Distribution to: Madam Ann Rosier, Notley Rosier (son).
     Administrator: Mr. Notley Rosier (administrator of Col. Edward Pye
          (administrator of deceased)).

Thomas Parker   19.164   A KE £292.10.7   £55.18.6   Jul 20 1699
     Sureties: Dr. Gerardus Weasells, Thomas Pinner & John Wade, Charles Tilden,
          George Smith, Mr. William Harris, James Watson on behalf of his children
          (unnamed), Edward Dowlin.
     Legatees: Edward Denton, Edward Ruth on behalf of his wife (unnamed), William
          Sheild.
     Executors: William Harris, Elisabeth Smith.

William Lisle   19.165   A CA £108.0.10   £108.0.10   Jul 11 1699
     Distribution to: Samuell Lisle, Robert Lisle, Michaell Askew who married
          Elisabeth (daughter), 1 orphan (unnamed).
     Administratrix: Pricilla Ball, wife of Edward Ball.

Henry Dukes   19.166   A CA £244.1.8   £36.3.8   Jul 12 1699
     Mentions: no children.
     Administratrix: Pricilla Ball, wife of Edward Ball.

John Askin   19.167   A   £11.12.6   #4134   Jun 14 1699
     Received from: Michaell Pent, John Ogleby.
     Payments to: Edward Miller, Mr. Robert Mason, Mr. Mason, Isaack Bradley, Gregory
          Suckpale, William Harbert, Mr. John Hall, Thomas Haddock & Arthur Delahay.
     Executor: James Thompson.

John Swatewell   19.168   A CH £47.9.7   £86.0.8   Jul 10 1699
     Received from: Francis Feesley, Ralph Worrell, George Miller.
     Payments to: Mr. William Huttchyson.
     Executor: Dr. Mordecay Moore of Anne Arundel County.

William Spikeman   19.169   A   £8.16.0   #3530   Jul 15 1699
     Payments to: Henry Tompson, Elisabeth Smith (dead, relict) and executrix of
          William Smith and Philip Hoskins (administrator of William Smith).
     Administratrix: wife (dead, unnamed) of James Kirke.

Thomas Fisher   19.169   A KI £50.11.1   £7.5.1   Jul 22 1699
     Payments to: John Cross, Edmond Storey, Dr. Lewis Derochbrune, Lawrence Everett.
     Mentions: 1 orphan (unnamed).
     Administratrix: Ann Fisher.

John Wright   19.170   A   £19.13.9   £15.1.3   Jul 20 1699
     Payments to: John Numan, Mr. Nicholas Lowe paid to Mr. Robert Grundee, Thomas
          Hopkins.
     Executor: Thomas Smithson.

William Willson   19.171   A PG £26.1.9   £24.18.6   Jul 1 1699
     Payments to: Peter Paggan & Co., John Marth & Co. paid to John Snelson, Joshua
          Cecill, Katherine Willson & Joshua Cecill (administrators of Jonathon
          Willson).
     Administratrix: Sarah Hill, wife of William Hill.

Edward Beadle   19.171 A BA   #5731   Sep 5 1699
    Payments to: Andrew Hicky, Henry Hazlewood, Mr. Goldsmith, Thomas Newsam, Roger
        Mathews, Mr. Hall, Peter Fusate, Oliver Freeman, Samuell Findall, Symon
        Jackson, Sam Browne.
    Administratrix: Martha Hall, wife of John Hall, by George Smith.

James Pargrave   19.172   A SM   £37.18.2   £37.18.2   Jun 2 1699
    Payments to: Dr. Burrey, Joshua Doyne.
    Distribution to: 1 orphan (unnamed).
    Administratrix: Margrett Farguson (widow), wife of Robert Farguson.

James Harrison   19.173   A AA   £7.13.0   £7.2.1   Aug 10 1699
    Mentions: wife of deceased (died just prior to husband), child (unnamed) of
        deceased.
    Administrator: John Hurse.

John Abington   19.174   A CA   £12.4.1   £17.5.0   Aug 5 1699
The amount of the inventory also included #621.
    Payments to: William Bladen for Capt. Langley, George Plater, Esq.
    Administrator: Mr. George Lingan.

Jarvis Morgan   19.174   A AA   £17.14.1   £2.10.0   Jul 13 1699
    Payments to: Thomas Roper.
    Legatees: Clement Davis.
    Mentions: no orphans.
    Executor: William Roper.

Thomas Edmondson   19.175   A PG   £50.17.5   £14.4.5   Jul 24 1699
    Payments to: William Burgess.
    Mentions: no orphans.
    Administrator: Richard Lancaster by his attorney Mr. Robert Tyler.

Edward Wood   19.176   A CA   £21.8.0   £28.6.4   Jul 24 1699
    Payments to: Dr. Kursted.
    Executrix: Sarah Fowler.

James Mouney   19.176   A CA   £22.18.9   £39.4.9   Jul 20 1699
    Payments to: Mr. Robert Bradley, William Cooke (carpenter).
    Administrator: Richard Marsham.

Henry King   19.177   A   £3.1.0   £4.10.0   Apr 26 1699
    Received from: Edward Collington, Edmond Sheington.
    Executor: Ambross Hogg

Cornelius Johnson   19.178   A SO   £51.16.3   £61.11.0   Jul 22 1699
    Payments to: Mr. Francis Jenkins.
    Executor: William Jones.

Robert Sly   19.178   A CH   £25.18.0   £28.10.0
    Payments to: Mr. Richard Clouds, Mr. Robert Mason.
    Executrix: Pricilla Sly.

Henry Jones   19.179   A   £5.9.9   £4.8.2   May 11 1699
    Payments to: Joshua Cecill, Phillip TatterShall.
    Administrator: Samuell Warren.

John Holland   19½A.1   I   £49.2.0   Jun 29 1699
    Appraisers: Benjamin Cottman, Sr., John Freakes.
    Administratrix: widow Holland.

Ellis Thomas   19½A.1   I DO   £75.19.9   Nov 29 1699
    Appraisers: Thomas Taylor, Thomas Gray.
    List of debts: James Thisslewood, Henry Potts, Patrick Canin, Francis Anderton,
        John Franke, Capt. George Cows, William Spencer, Johnathon Clifton.

William Woodgate   19½A.2   I DO   £38.9.4
    Appraisers: Henry Griffith, Anthony Shillcott (also Anthony Chillcott).
    List of debts: Peter Williams.
    Administrator: James Cannon.

Mr. Alexander Fisher   19½A.3   I DO   £388.12.5   Aug 9 1699
    Appraisers: William Meshew, John Lecoumpt.

Manus Stanley   19½A.6   I DO   £75.8.6   Sep 18 1699
    Appraisers: John Nicolls, Nicholas Narleland.

John Colleson   19½A.7   I DO   £9.9.-
The part of the inventory for Elisabeth Colleson is cited at £8.0.0.
    Appraisers: Michaell Todd, Edward Turner.

William Dean   19½A.8   I   £16.11.4   Mar 19 1698
      Appraisers: Timothy McNemara, Edward Turner.

Dr. Allexander Chappell   19½A.9   I AA   £41.7.0   Sep 8 1699
      Appraisers: John Freeman, Henry Heard.

Margaret Gill   19½A.10   I AA   £297.2.1   May 19 1699
The amount of the inventory also included #2122.
      Appraisers: Josias Twogood, Thomas Hughes.
         List of debts: John Ladford, William Low, Hannah Powell, John Thompson, Roger
            Roberts, Ed. Chubb, Robert Sallows, Daniell Robbinson, Joseph Saunders, John
            Pritchard, Zachariah Cadle.

Francis Hill   19½A.11   I   £43.8.6   Oct 23 1699
      Appraisers: William Grimes, Matthew Lewis.

Mr. Edward Sanders   19½A.12   I CH   Apr 17 1699
His date of death is cited as 14 November 1698.
      Administratrix/Executrix: Jane Sanders (widow).

Issabella Thompson   19½A.13   I CH   £23.17.7   Nov 11 1699
The amount of the inventory also included #3494.
      Appraisers: Matthew Sanders, Griffith Davis.
         List of debts: Timothy Hindes, Thomas Howe, Richard Cowes, Mr. John Stone to
            Michael Ashford to Henry Thompson (husband of deceased).

Ignatius Wheeler   19½A.15   I   £63.15.5
The amount of the inventory also included #1063.
      Appraisers: Thomas Wheeler, Matthew Barnes.
      List of debts: William Summers, Henry Kee, Henry Smith, Frances Clarber.

Thomas Hilleary   19½A.17   I CA   £162.12.0   Jun 11 1698
      Appraisers: George Cole, John Bowles.
      Next of kin: William Mills, Robert Lyle.

Thomas Hilleard   19½A.18   I CA   £12.2.0   Aug 3 1698
      Appraisers: George Cole, John Bowles.
      Next of kin: Robert Lyle, Benjamin Berry.

Thomas Hilleary   19½A.18   I   £309.1.0   Aug 12 1698
This inventory includes items formerly belonging to Baruch Williams now in the
possesion of William Berry. The amount of the inventory is the total for the estate.
      Appraisers: George Cole, John Bowles.
      Next of kin: Robert Lyle, Benjamin Berry.

Thomas Hilleary   19½A.19   I
      Approvers: Robert Lyle, William Mills.
         List of debts: Mr. George Lingan, John Lewis, John Barrett, Mr. Thomas Hollyday
            on assignment from William Tompson, John Cole, Phillip Gittings, Robert Jones,
            Robert Roberson, John Corey.

John Fry   19½A.20   I   £23.10.8   Jan 23 1698
      Appraisers: Michael Marten, James Adams.

Mr. Lawrence Vanderbash   19½A.20   I KE   Dec 9 1695   Oct 2 1699
(minister).
      Appraisers: Richard Lowder, Robert Perke.
      Items sold to: Mr. Thomas Joyce, John Lee, Mr. Michaell Miller, Sr., William
         Frisby, Robert Perke.

Robert Trevett   19½A.21   I AA   #1369   Jul 26 1698
      Appraisers: Robert Stone, Nicholas Roads (also Nicholas Rhodes).

Justinian Tenason   19½A.22   I   £13.18.2   Apr 14 1699
      Appraisers: John Brinnard (also John Brinn), Benjamin Reder (also Benjamin
         Redar).
      Approvers: Jeames Seamans, John Hopkins.

Robert Blades   19½A.23   I SO   £6.13.3   Jul 3 1699
      Appraisers: John Henderson, William Hickman.
      Administrator: Robert Blades (son).

Robert Hewett   19½A.24   A   #1369   #1325   Dec 7 1698
(also Robert Trevett)
      Payments to: Richard Beard.
      Administrator: Thomas Tench.

Anthony Evans   19½A.24   I SM   £54.13.2   May 6 1699
      Appraisers: William Aisquith, Benjamin Inman.

Robert Cooper   19½A.26   I SM   £23.6.11   Sep 28 1699
     Appraisers: John Evans, Samuell Wheelar.

John Robarts   19½A.27   I SM   £16.1.6   May 28 1698
     Appraisers: John Gillum, James Woods.

Mrs. Mary Yates   19½A.28   I   £221.10.11   Oct 30 1699
     Appraisers: James Sanders, Thomas Odell.
     List of debts: Mr. John Hyde.

Susannah Vaughan   19½A.29   I TA   £37.4.8   Jun 29 1699
     Appraisers: Thomas Robins, John Robinson.
     List of debts: John Stannard, Andrew Tonnard, widow Oakley.

Andrew Orem   19½A.30   I   £86.9.4   Aug 8 1699
     Appraisers: Thomas Bennett, Thomas Smith.

Sarah Ywell   19½A.32   I TA   £84.9.9
     Appraisers: William Clayton, John Pooly.

Thomas Purnell   19½A.33   I   £58.16.2   Oct 16 1699
     Appraisers: John Greves, Sr., William Marstone.
     List of debts: John Manning, Patience Skipper.

James Meende   19½A.34   I TA   £64.17.8   Aug 25 1699
     Appraisers: William Clayton, William Denton.

Samuell Scidmore   19½A.35   I AA   £164.18.7   Jun 17 1699
     Appraisers: Capt. Humphry Boone, Robert Eagle.

Mr. Robert Mackling   19½A.35   I TA   £332.4.10   Jun 15 1699
     Appraisers: John Emerson (also John Emerton), William Clayton,
     Mentions: Mr. Richard Mackling (brother).

Simon Fine   19½A.44   I   £7.10.6   Nov 6 1699
     Appraisers: John Jacob, William Disney.

William Hornby   19½A.44   I   £14.9.4   May 2 1699
     Appraisers: Mr. William Clayton, William Hatfield.
     List of debts: William Hacker.

Thomas Clemens   19½A.45   I TA   £18.17.4   Nov 24 1698
     Appraisers: William Bexley, Thomas Delahay.

Henry Snoden   19½A.46   I TA   £47.2.11   Aug 7 1699
     Appraisers: William Clayton, William Ringold.

David Blaney   19½A.47   I TA   £229.4.7   Jul 8 1698
     Appraisers: William Clayton, John King.

Robert Broadaway

Francis Chittam   19½A.56   I BA   £3.13.8   Jun 3 1699
     Appraisers: Richard Perkin, William Lofton.

John Armstrong   19½A.57   I BA   £11.19.3   Mar 11 1699
     Appraisers: Thomas Preston, John Boon.

John Robinson   19½A.57   I AA   £15.10.2   Jul 29 1699   Oct 2 1699
     Appraisers: John Solman, Richard Duckett.

William Ebden   19½A.58   I BA   £103.7.10   May 6 1699
The amount of the inventory also included #5704.
     Appraisers: Israel Skelton, Samuell Scillmore.
     List of debts: Nicholas Day, Abraham Detape, Michaell Judd, Jr., Michaell Judd,
        Sr., John Ells, Thomas Honis, John Armstrong.

Ambrose Prevett   19½A.60   I BA   £16.1.4
     Appraisers: Abraham Taylor, John Boon.
     List of debts: William Doson, Samuel Standford, John Watson.

Capt. John Ferry   19½A.61   I BA   £367.8.9   May 12 1699
The amount of the inventory also included #9666.
     Servants mentioned: William Goyne, Darby Wharton, Mary Jones, Thomas Dodmund,
        Phill. Washington.
     Appraisers: John Gay (also John Gray), John Hays.
     List of debts: Mr. Gouldsbury, Charles Merryman, Edward Collings, Mr. Jefery
        Gray, John Rowe, Mr. Boothby, Alice Skinner, Richard Langley, Francis
        Whitehead, Thomas Maris.

Francis Frampton   19½A.66   I CH £5.6.0   Apr 13 1699
The amount of the inventory also included #2887.
          Appraisers: Matthew Sanders, Sr., Matthew Sanders, Jr.
          List of debts: Mr. Thomas Cranson.

Col. George Robatham   19½A.66   I   Sep 28 1699
          Appraisers: John Emerson, William Clayton.
          Mentions: Thomas Fisher.
          List of debts: George Robotham, John Salter, Nicholas Lowe, John Emerson, John
             Jones (shoemaker), Richard Bennett, Richard Tilghman, William Wrench, Sr.,
             Col. Coursey, Robert Smith, Esq., William Wrench, Jr., William Jump, widow
             Silvester, John Hews, Thomas Rowe, Catherine Tinney, William Coursey, John
             Keeld, Thomas Emerson, widow Hadder, William Alderne, Walter Quinton, Nicolas
             Banks, William Troth, John Hacker, Edward Tomlin, John Brownwey, Col. Sayer,
             Francis Holmes, John Lane, Robert Ungle, Andrew Abinton (dead), Griffith
             Jones, William Harris, Jeffry Mattershaw, John Lewellin, Edward Pindar, James
             Clayland, John Davis of Dorchester County, John Greenway, James Sedwick, John
             Howell, Patrick Freeman, John Davis, Thomas King, John Woodward, John Johnson,
             Thomas Hutcheson, Elias Goddard, James Silvester, Daniell Wheatley, Edward
             Stockley.

Thomas Hall   19½A.69   I SM £10.2.10
          Appraisers: Raphad Haywood, George Keeth.

Thomas Kingcart   19½A.69   I CA £11.19.0   Aug 14 1699
          Appraisers: George Spicer, Nicholas Fountain.

Mr. Christopher Gregory   19½A.70   I AA £67.18.8   Aug 30 1699
          Appraisers: Orlando Greenslade, Henry Heard.

Richard Maston   19½A.71   I CH £52.7.0   Sep 28 1699
          Appraisers: Joseph Willson, Thomas Dixon.

Lazerus Pesher   19½A.72   I KI £17.16.8   1699
          Appraisers: Allexander Walter, Lewis Meredith.

Walter Carr, Sr.   19½A.73   I AA £45.3.0   Sep 11 1699
          Appraisers: John Gale, John Atwood.
          List of debts: John Mortimore.

James Penny   19½A.73   I CH £5.2.5   Aug 22 1699
          Appraisers: William Compton, Nicholas With.
          Mentions: Elisabeth Penny (relict).

Walter Carr, Jr.   19½A.74   I AA £61.8.6   Sep 11 1699
          Appraisers: John Atwood, John Gale.
          List of debts: John Ford.

John Trundle   19½A.75   I AA £198.14.2   Aug 3 ----
The amount of the inventory also included #7150.
          Appraisers: John Atwood, John Gale.
          List of debts: Job Evans, Benjamin Chew, Gerrard Hopkins, James Ford, John
             Turner, Allexander Chappell, William Smith.
          Mentions: widow (unnamed).

Nicholas Milburne   19½A.77   I TA £185.12.8   Jun 13 1699
          Appraisers: John Dawson, William Alderne.

Henry Loftus   19½A.80   I AA £3.7.4   Jun 2 1699   Aug 23 1699
The amount of the inventory also included #6501.
          Appraisers: Robert Handcock, Joell Hecap.
          List of debts: Kenelm Chysledyne, Mr. Edward Batson, Mr. Kenelm Chesledyne on
             Mr. William Tucker, judgment to Samuell Watkins (administrator of James
             Harper).
          Administrator/Executor: Thomas Hutchins.

Elisabeth Newton   19½A.81   I AA £32.11.6   Mar 31 1699   Aug 14 1699
widow of John Newton.
          Appraisers: Richard Jones, Sr., Robert Phillips (not present on 14 August 1699).
          List of debts: Mr. Jackson, James Starley, Mr. Phillip Lynes upon Henry Hawkins,
             William Stone, James Shurley, Sir Thomas Lawrence upon James Shurley.

William Coventry   19½A.84   I BA £23.10.2   May 21 1699
          Appraisers: William Lewis, Jonathon Neal.

Benjamin Scrivner   19½A.85   I   £19.0.0   Jun 25 1699
          Appraisers: Nicholas Rhodes (also Nicholas Rhods), Thomas Hughs.
          List of debts: Mr. James Reed.

William Horn, Jr.   19½A.85   I   AA   £114.6.3   Oct 28 1699   Aug 21 1699
    Appraisers: John Chappell, John Trundle (deceased by 21 August 1699).
    List of debts: Samuell Groome, Abraham Wilde, John Hyde.

Thomas Sedwick   19½A.86   I   CA   £5.12.6   Sep 27 1699
    Appraisers: George Young, Hezekiah Buford.

Florah Kyele   19½A.87   I   BA   £159.0.0   May 12 1699
    Appraisers: William Lewis, Jonathon Neal.

John Goutey, Jr.   19½A.88   I   £19.5.1   Sep 4 1699
    Appraisers: Arthur Hart, Michael Todd.

Andrew Insley   19½A.89   I   £91.16.0   Sep 4 1699
    Appraisers: Edward Turner, Richard Peason.
    List of debts: Michael Todd.

Richard Rawlins   19½A.91   I   DO   Aug 29 1699
    Appraisers: Amos Pierpoint, Theophilus Kitten.
    List of debts: John Toiler.

John Trouton   19½A.92   I   CH   £50.5.0   Jan 1 1689
    Appraisers: Thomas Hughs, Richard Tucker.

William Selby   19½A.92   I   PG   £437.13.11   May 23 1699
    Appraisers: R. Bradly, Samuell Magruder.

William Brown   19½A.94   I   BA   £31.4.6   Nov 21 1699
    Appraisers: Leonard Wayman, Richard Duckett.

Dr. Woolfran Hunt   19½A.95   I   £45.9.4   Nov 11 1699
    Appraisers: Richard Warfield, John Gaither.

Robert Hancock   19½A.96   I   AA   £21.1.0   Jan 27 1699
    Appraisers: Daniell Canning, Benjamin Dickinson.

Thomas Taylor   19½A.97   A   CH   £91.8.2   #2123   Feb 3 1699
    Payments to: Col. John Courts, Capt. John Bayne, Kenelm Chesledyne, Mr. John
        Gouge, Mr. William Hewton, Mr. Robert Yates.
    Administratrix: Ann Taylor.

William Marshall   19½A.97   A   CH   £106.16.0   £3.6.8   Feb 23 1699
    Received from: Joyce Garrett.
    Payments to: Dr. Phillip Biscoe, Mr. Tubman (minister).
    Executrix: Elisabeth Marshall.

Clement Haley   19½A.98   A   £131.13.8   £52.15.3   Jan 2 1699
    Payments to: James Herris, Henry Witcholy, Justinian Tennison, William Taylor,
        Col. Blackiston, Michael Walles, Botherick Loyd, Abraham Price, John Cladge,
        John Cesar, John Noe, James Latimor, Samuell Chamberlaine, Abraham Hennison,
        James Williams, Daniel, Thomas Badger, Henry Ward, George Bery, Joseph Peters,
        William Thompson, Francis Bowe, James Connell, Christopher Knight.
    Mentions: Mary Haley and Eliza Haley as daughters of the deceased.
    Administratrix/Executrix: Mrs. Eleannor Ares.

William Porter   19½A.99   A   SO   £131.13.8   £131.13.8   Aug 8 1692
    Distribution to: administratrix.
    Administratrix: Elizabeth Porter.

John Write   19½A.100   A   CH   £187.11.6   Dec 16 1699
    Payments to: Richard Wade, John Waugh (executor of Dr. Edward Maddocks), Notley
        Warren, Elisabeth Smith, George Andrews.
    Administrators: Richard Harrison, Richard Wade.

Thomas Kingcart   19½A.101   A   CA   £11.19.10   £9.19.5   Nov 30 1699
    Payments to: Mr. Walter Smith.
    Administratrix: Martha Kingcart.

Thomas Hutchinson   19½A.102   A   CH   £287.13.11   £259.8.6   Dec 7 1699
    Payments to: Mr. Paggan & Co. (merchants), John Hawkins, Mr. Trottman, Richard
        Boughton, Mr. John Sothoron, Richard Comes, William Smith, William Trottman,
        Robert Skinner, Thomas Brook.
    Executrix: Ann Magruder, wife of Allexander Magruder.

George Delahai   19½A.103   A   CH   Oct 26 1699
    Payments to: Edward Rookwood, Ri. Harrison.
    Administratrix: Susan Delahai.

John Swain   19½A.104 A SO   £51.4.6   £41.1.6   Jul 29 1699
     Payments to: John Webb, William Stevenson, William Mead, Allexander White,
         Richard Tull, John Pope, James Maynard, John West, Ambrose Archer, William
         Focitt, James Round, Robert Roth, Robert Johnson, Maj. Whittington.
     Mentions: 3 orphans (unnamed).
     Administratrix: Ann Swain. The accounts are signed by Mary Swaine the
         administratrix.

William Roberson   19½A.105 A SO   £46.6.6   £46.6.6   Jul 17 1699
     Payments to: John West, Mr. Jenkins, Maj. Whittington, Johne Pocam, Mr. Levin
         Denwood, William Phillips, Timothy Roads, Jone Pocum.
     Distribution to: administratrix (unnamed), 3 orphans (unnamed).
     Administrator: Benjamin Cottman, Jr.

Hope Taylor   19½A.105 A   £29.11.0   £29.11.0   Jul 18 1696
     Payments to: Mr. Francis Jenkins, Thomas Cullaine, George Willson, William
         Rosey, Maj. Whittinton, Allexander Stone, Allexander Kill, Richard Tull,
         Samuell Hopkins.
     Distribution: widow (unnamed), 6 orphans (unnamed).
     Administrator/Executor: Dunnock Dennis.

John Hammon   19½A.106 A   £47.13.0   £47.13.0   Jul 15 1699
     Payments to: Maj. William Whittington, Dr. Davis, George Truit, Thomas Purnel,
         Francis Heap, William Richardson, James Remond, Edward Hammon, William Day,
         Henry Walker, Samuell Wothington, John Taylor, John West.
     Distribution: administratrix, 6 orphans (unnamed).
     Administratrix:, wife (unnamed) of Owen Maclamy.

Edward Wood   19½A.106 A CA   £21.8.0   £28.6.4   Jul 15 1699
     Payments to: Dr. Queasteed (?).
     Executrix: Sarah Fowler.

Ignatius Mathews   19½A.107 A CH   £166.15.10   £1.10.10   Dec 9 1699
     Payments to: John Clement.
     Administratrix/Executrix: wife (unnamed, relict of deceased), of Thomas Jameson.

James Price   19½A.107 A   #10236   £42.13.0   Jul 22 1699
The amount of the accounts is equivalent to #10236.
     Payments to: Maj. Whittington, Cornelius Ward, Benjamin Summers.
     Distribution to: grandson (unnamed) of husband of administratrix, administratrix.
     Administratrix: Jane Price (relict).

Robert Broadway   19½A.108 A TA   £20.14.8   Aug 17 1699
     Payments to: Mr. Charles Blake (executor of Col. Peter Sayer), Capt. Nicholas
         Lowe, Ann More (executrix of Daniell Glover).
     Administrator: Vincent Hemsley.

Samuell Newton   19½A.109 A TA   £33.11.1   £4.15.0
     Payments to: Mr. Mathew Ward, Mr. Thomas Emerson, Mr. Mr. Richard Bennett.
     Administrator: John Salter.

Mortough Horney   19½A.109 A TA   £24.5.10   £22.4.9   Jun 26 1699
     Payments to: Richard Macklin, Benjamin Peck, Samuell Hambleton.
     Mentions: John Nunam.
     Administratrix: Elisabeth Hopkins, wife of Thomas Hopkins.

Thomas Plummer   19½A.110 A AA   £110.15.0   #21348
The amount of the inventory also included #8434 and #1600.
     Payments to: George Bruice, William Goodman, Capt. Henry Hanslap, estate of
         Richard Tull, Gabriel Parrott, Capt. Abraham Wild & Co., Benjamin Scrivener,
         Capt. Nicholas Gassaway, Robert Kerkland, David Pool, Henry Bonner, Dr. M.
         Moore, John Edwards, John Beecher formerly administrator of Joseph Williams
         and paid to Benjamin Williams, Benjamin Williams (cooper), George Burgess,
         Capt. William Holland, John Larkins, William Cotter.
     Executrix: Elisabeth Plumer.

Johannah Hudson   19½A.111 A CH   £12.10.0   Aug 3 1699
A second inventory was cited for £5.15.5.
     Payments to: Mr. George Tubman, Philip Hoskins, Maj. William Dent.
     Mentions: William Hudson (son, dead).
     Administrator: Mathew Barnes.

Francis Robinson   19½A.112 A BA   £59.18.6   £72.6.0   Sep 26 1699
     Received from: John Jackson, Jiles Stephens.
     Payments to: John Taylor, John Gay, administratrix of Moses Groom, James Philips,
         William Hicks, Paggan & Co., Ed. Felks, Mr. Thomas Hedge, James Todd, William
         Barker.
     Administrator: Joseph Peak.

Richard Thompson   19½A.113 A BA £50.18.2   #5865   Aug 8 1699
     Payments to: Nicholas Hide, Edward Stephenson, Col. John Thomas, John Ferry,
        Josias Stanbrough, John Broad, Thomas Hedge, Mr. Roger Newman.
     Mentions: estate of the orphan (unnamed) of Richard Rutter in the amount of
        £18.6.8.
     Executor: John Rouse.

Richard Thompson   19½A.114 A BA £50.18.2   £32.11.7   Sep 6 1699
     Payments to: Michael Judd, Nicholas Hide, John Hall.
     Executor: John Rouse.

Flora Kyle   19½A.114 A   £159.0.0
     Payments to: Mr. Morton, Robert Hopper.
     Executors: Ralph Hawkins, Margarett Downs.

John Sharp   19½A.115 A DO £19.12.3   £25.10.7   Aug 2 1699
     Payments to: widow Ladimore, Mr. Eccleston, Jacob Lockerman.
     Executor: John Nichols.

Edward Fitzgerrett   19½A.115 A CH £7.5.3   #2228   Aug 11 1699
     Payments to: Capt. Randolph Brandt (father of accountant), Maj. William Dent by
        accountant's father.
     Administrator: Randolph Brandt.

Thomas Baker (taylor)   19½A.116 A AA £7.2.8   Aug 19 1699
     Administrator: Ebenezar Blakiston.

Ann Neal   19½A.117 A CH £154.2.6   £154.2.6
     Legatees: Henry Neal (son of James Neal), Mary Neal, Elisabeth Neal, James Neal,
        Elisabeth wife of James Neal, children (unnamed) of William Boorman, wife
        (unnamed) of the accountant, children (unnamed) of the accountant.
     Distribution to: James Neal, accountant.
     Executor: Anthony Neal.

Isaack Marshall   19½A.118 A BA £117.10.6   £21.0.5   Aug 2 1699
     Payments to: Edward Shephardson on account of Mr. Paggan, John Robinson, Thomas
        Handcock, Daniel Swendell, Joseph Peak, John Hall.
     Administratrix: Joyce Marshall.

James George   19½A.118 A TA £10.9.6   £12.12.0   Sep 18 1699
     Payments to: Edward Brown, William White, Anthony Workman.
     Administratrix: Dorothy George.

William Powell   19½A.119 A AA £144.4.3
     Payments to: Capt. William Holland of Thomas Shington (hireling), Capt. William
        Holland per William Powell (taylor), Dr. Alexander Chapell, Edward Reynolds,
        William Harry.
     Administratrix: Anna Mary Powell.

Thomas Cofer   19½A.119 A CH £20.7.8   #6193   Jul 28 1699
The amount of the inventory is equivalent to #5142.
     List of debts: Henry Hawkins, Jr., Cleb. Lomax, Thomas Chapman, John Clerk
        (dead), Edward Milsted.
     Payments to: Philip Hoskins, Francis Bannister, Henry Hawkins, Sr., Capt. John
        Bayne, John Contee, Mary Miller.
     Administrator: Francis Coffer.

Edward Edwards   19½A.121 A TA £2.16.0   £8.15.0   Oct 6 1699
     Payments to: Benjamin Peck, Edward Man.
     Administrator: William Thomas.

Robert Fisher   19½A.121 A CA £35.0.0   £13.10.0   Aug 2 1699
     Payments to: John Howell, Ignatius Sewell, William Bradley.
     Administrator: George Wade.

Philip Jones   19½A.122 A CH £2.18.6   #1868   Aug 3 1699
     Payments to: Benoni Thomas.
     Administrator: Mathew Barns.

John Pickett   19½A.123 A   £11.18.7   £15.7.9   Mar 3 1699
     Appraisers: John Serjant, Edward Tomlin.
     Payments to: John King, James Mason.
     Administrator: Nathan Scott.

Ann Leafe   19½A.124 A CA £42.1.8   £42.1.8   Sep 27 ----
     Payments to: Mr. Wilkinson, Capt. Henry Munday, Ann Bowen, Thomas Emms, Thomas
        Tasker, Esq., Mr. Edward Carlton & Co., Dr. George Cole, Dr. Kingsbery, John
        Hall, Edward Ball, George Henderson, Abraham Bird, Thomas Harvy.
     Executor: Francis Leafe.

William Read   19½A.125 A DO   £19.0.0   £12.4.3   Nov 21 1699
     Payments to: Walter Campbell, Capt. Goute, Robert Gouldsborrough, Hugh Eccleston
          per Walter Campbell.
     Executrix: Jane Read.

John Wells   19½A.126 A BA   £13.13.6   #3317   Sep 6 1699
The amount of the inventory also included #1500.
     Payments to: John Lekins, Richard Samson, Edward Stevenson, Col. Thomas, Joseph
          Wells.
     Administratrix: Elenor Wells.

David Rogers   19½A.126 A TA   £117.10.0   £11.15.0
     Payments to: Mr. Nicholas Low, Mr. Robert Grundy, Mr. John Pooly, Richard
          Carter.
     Executrix: Elisabeth Rogers.

Robert Noble   19½A.127 A   £224.4.6   £120.12.11 May 22 1705
     Payments to: Peter Sides, Richard Lamb, Capt. Sybery, David Johnson, John Pitt,
          John Serjant, Anthony Mail, Isaack Sheppard, Mr. Thomas Maxem, Capt. Richard
          Sweatnam, Richard Jones (smith), Griffith Jones, Edward Stephenson, James
          Downs, John Edmondson, Symon Stephenson, Mr. Clayland, John Pooly, John
          Davies, Col. Robotham.
     Distribution to: widow (unnamed), orphans (unnamed).

John Mercer   19½A.128 A AA   £57.18.10   #3466
     Appraisers: John Baldwyn, Edward Rumney.
     Payments to: Mr. Amos Garrett, Mr. Thomas Blackwell, Mr. Philip Howard for use
          of Mr. John Brice, John Mitchell per Mr. John Gerrard for use of Mr. Peter
          Paggen.
     Administratrix: Margarett Mercer.

Henry Francis   19½A.129 A AA   £21.0.6   £24.18.0   Mar 25 1700
     Payments to: Mr. Roger Newman, William Lewis, Blanch Staunton, Edward Fuller,
          Benjamin Scrivener, Catherine Rowser.
     Administrator: John Harebottle.

John Rockhold   19½A.130 I   £29.7.0   Mar 21 1699
     Legatees: Stephen White, William Hawkins.
     List of debts: John Smith, Thomas Rogers, John Pettet (merchant in London), Dean
          Cock, John Baldwyn.
     Executrix: Mary Rockhold.

John Rockhold   19½A.130 A AA   £227.2.6   £5.12.0   Mar 21 1699
The amount of the inventory also included #2810.
     Payments to: George Long, William Sladen, Mr. Christopher Vernon, James Duffe,
          Mr. Richard Beard.
     Executrix: Mary Rockhold.

Thomas Heifford   19½A.131 I AA   Dec 2 1699
     Appraisers: Thomas Hughes, John Beecher.
     List of debts: John Stomford, Walter Powell, John Radford, James Wise.

William Sharp   19½A.132 I TA   £646.4.3   Sep 25 1699 Feb-10 1699
     Servants mentioned: William Bell.
     Appraisers: Nicholas Lowe, Robert Ungle.

John Bennett   19½A.139 I AA   £83.0.0
     Appraisers: Humfrey Boone, Robert Eagle.
     Legatees: Mary Harbert (cousin).

Samuel Skidmore   19½A.140 A AA   £164.18.7   £6.7.0
     Payments to: John Rock & Co.
     Administratrix: Ann Skidmore.

William Brown   19½A.140 A   £31.4.6
     Payments to: Richard Kirkland, George Man, Daniell Wells.
     Administrator/Executor: Col. Henry Ridgley.

Henry Haslewood   19½A.140 I BA   £81.19.11   Jul 1 1699   Nov 15 1699
     Appraisers: Thomas Greenfield, Thomas Cord.

Mr. Thomas Hedge   19½A.142 A   £40.5.4   Jan 10 1699
The amount of the inventory also included #190264.
     Payments to: Charles Simmons, Edward Fuller, Thomas Preston, Paggen & Co.,
          Samuell Siklmore, Richard Colegate, John Hall, administrator as a factor for
          Richard Bell & Co., John Brood, Hugh Jones, Jonas Bowen, John Bennett, John
          Taylor, James Murry, Hedge Henry, Mr. George Ashman, John Philips, Col. John
          Thomas, Samuell Fendall (runaway, dead), John Weaver, Joseph Sanders, William
          Fuley (runaway), Thomas Butteras, John Roberts (runaway), Michael Judd
          (runaway), Michael Conworth (dead), Isaack Marshall (dead), Henry Inlons,

Thomas Darbin (dead), Joseph Wells, George Merritt (can't find), Nathaniel Anderson (dead), John Royston (dead), Isaack Jackson, Christopher Shaco, Thomas Preston, Samuell Brown, James Mason (dead), Francis Robins (dead), Robert Gardner, William Gugin (dead), Ambros Hogg (dead), Edward Waters (can not be found), George English (runaway), Edward Harsley (runaway), Col. Thomas Richardson, Mr. James Philips, William Horne, Richard Askins (dead), James Glasly (dead), Mr. Peregrine Brown, Robert Benger, Florine Hendrickson (runaway), Thomas Yowman (not to be found), Thomas Jones (piper, runaway).
    Administrator: Mr. Thomas Hedge (son).

Alexander Lumly   19½A.145 I BA   £101.7.2   Jan 29 1699
    Appraisers: Thomas Hammond, Nathaniel Stinchcombe.
    Mentions: "Madam Lumley's mother to Madam Lumley's daughter".

John Royston   19½A.147 I BA   £16.13.10   Sep 22 1699
    Appraisers: John Thomas, William Wilkison.

John Coopis   19½A.148 I   £25.7.0   Aug 17 1699
    Appraisers: Anthony Johnson, Robert Parker.

Richard Askew   19½A.149 I   Jun 22 1699
    Appraisers: Samuell Bain, George Smith.

Jane Price   19½A.150 I SO   £12.10.0   Dec 12 1699
    Appraisers: Capt. William Colbourne, John Taylor.

William Mickin   19½A.150 A BA   £20.8.0   #5584
    Payments to: John Merritt, George Lapthorne & Co. (merchants), Mr. William
      Hunter, Mr. Robert Mason, Joseph Heath, Mary Peters, Thomas Jenkins, Richard
      Vowells.
    Mentions: orphans (unnamed).
    Administrator: James French of St. Mary's County.

Andrew Magraw   19½A.151 I SM   £24.15.2   Jun 15 1699
    Appraisers: William Herbert, James Mason.

John Cossens   19½A.152 A AA   £13.0.3   £5.4.0   Apr 1 1700
    Payments to: Morris Baker.
    Executrix: Mary Cosens.

John North   19½A.152 A   £46.15.3   £16.9.0   Apr 1 1700
    Payments to: Mr. Roger Newman.
    Executrix: Elisabeth North.

Bartholomew Mackmorry 19½A.153 B SM   £1.18.6   Apr 23 1700
    Payments to: Mr. William Husband.
    Administrator: ------ (unnamed).

Solomon Rutte   19½A.153 A SM   #5968   Jul 24 1699
    Payments to: Mr. Charles Egerton, John Dunbar, Thomas Grunwyn, John Relay,
      William Herbert, Thomas Haddock, James Briscoe, John Manning, Mr. Robert
      Mason, Owen Guither, Mr. Carvill, Solomon Jakes, Isaack Paine.
    Mentions: 1 orphan (unnamed).
    Executrix: Ann Nowell, wife of Henry Nowell.

Daniel Richman   19½A.154 I   £4.15.0   Oct 11 1698
    Appraisers: Mich Rely, Peter Joye.
    Mentions: Thomas Blackman.

Charles Watts   19½A.154 I   £9.0.6   May 17 1698
    Appraisers: Capt. Thomas Hatoway, Mr. Henry Poulter.

Charles Watts   19½A.155 A   #1930   #1930
    Payments to: Mr. Ralph Rimer, William Legg, Thomas Green, James Seamans, William
      Watts.
    Administratrix/Executrix: ------ (widow, unnamed).

Wilmott Hill   19½A.155 I SO   £15.11.9   Sep 13 1699
    Appraisers: Walter Evans, John Webb.

William Knight   19½A.156 I SM
    List of debts: William Weydon, Samuell Chamberlain, John William Coxen, Edward
      Farr, Capt. Richard Clouds, Joseph Chantery, Jethro Merritt, Elisabeth Watts,
      Nicholas Geulich, John Batt. Carbery, Richard Glover, Bartholomew Sheppard,
      Lewis Watkins, Francis Bower, Mathew Tennison, James Capling, Edward Merritt,
      James Glass, Joshuah Guibert, Thomas Cissell, Lewis Tapper.

Mr. Walter Taylor   19½A.157 A   #1156
    Payments to: William Lowre paid by Mr. John Willmer, Mr. Chiseldyne, John Horne.
      Administratrix/Executrix: Margarett Taylor (widow).

Willmott Hill   19½A.157 A   £29.19.2   #18786   Sep 5 1699
A second inventory was cited in the amount of £15.11.9.
        Received from: Richard Warren, William Greer, Robert Sympson, Edward Green,
    William Round (?), Matthew Howard.
        Payments to: executors of Col. Brown, John Hendry, Robert Perrie, Edward Green,
    John Edgar (merchant), James Round, Esq., John Cavinar, John Edmunds, Samuell
    Hopkins, Sr., William Whittington, Dr. Davies, Fra. Heap, John Redwood
    (merchant).
        Distribution to: administrator.
        Administrator: William Wouldhave.

Howell Francis   19½A.158 A SO   £22.15.11   #5621   Aug 2 1699
        Received from: William Wouldhave, Warren Hadder.
        Payments to: Richard Warren, Mr. Dent, Mr. John Webb, Mr. Thomas Jones, Maj.
    William Whittington, Mr. John Henry, Mr. Worthington, Mr. Samuell Hopkins.
        Administrator/Executor: James Round.

William Garrey   19½A.159 I TA   £222.18.4   May 2 1699
        Appraisers: John Emerson, Sr., William Scott.
        Mentions: Richard Austin, Charles Neal.
        List of debts: Robert Munday, Philip Massey, Robert Hogthaw, William Mitchell,
    Charles Neal, John Jones (brazier), John Griffin, Dr. Jolly, Benjamin Peck,
    John Jones (carpenter), John Tarr, Capt. James Meires, Robert Grundy, John
    Eldrige, Jacob Price (runaway), John Neale (runaway), Edward Overing
    (runaway), Thomas Wallis, Thomas Allen, William Evans.
        Administrators: Edward Lloyd, Richard Tilghman, Thomas Thomas.

Mr. James Clayland   19½A.165 I   £70.7.8   Nov 13 1699
        Appraisers: Mr. William Hatfield, Mr. Moses Harris.

Peter Hutchinson (carpenter) 19½A.166 I TA   £5.1.10   Nov 14 1699   Jan 4 1699
        Appraisers: Oliver Millinton, Thomas McClanachan.
        Administrator: Henry Burt.

Peter Hutchinson (carpenter) 19½A.167 A TA   £5.1.10   #2315   Jan 4 1699
        Payments to: John Wooters.
        Mentions: orphan girl (unnamed) of administrator which the testator shot.
        Administrator: Henry Burt.

John Mogayer   19½A.168 A TA   £8.2.10   #3199   Feb 10 1699
        Payments to: Mr. Kenelm Cheseldyn, administrator of William Gary, William Scott,
    Anthony Rumball, Benjamin Peck.
        Administrator: John Jones (brazier).

Mr. John Marshall   19½A.169 I TA   £133.6.6   Jun 4 1699   Jan 16 1699
        Appraisers: Lawrence Swarbrocke, Robert Wade.
        Administrator: William Bickosleth (?).

John Dine   19½A.170 A TA   £48.19.0   £72.18.0   Jan 4 1699
        Payments to: Robert Grundy, Edmond Goodman, Benjamin Dubbs, Henry Land, Michael,
    Benjamin Peck, William Aaeron, William Ramming.
        Administratrix: Mary Smith, wife of Mathew Smith.

Thomas Skillington   19½A.171 I   £216.13.6   Aug 22 1699   Oct 20 1699
        Appraisers: Fra. Chaplin, John Preston.
        Mentions: Mary Skillington.

Ann Cosden (widow)   19½A.173 I PG   £17.16.6   Mar 6 1699
The amount of the inventory also included #3200.
        Appraisers: Francis Potts, John Deakens.
        List of debts: Charles Bean.

Mortaugh Horney   19½A.174 A TA   £24.5.10   £24.5.10   Nov 14 1699
        Payments to: Mr. Salter.
        Administratrix: Elisabeth Hopkins, wife of Thomas Hopkins.

Mr. Thomas Hillery   19½A.174 A   £389.4.7   Dec 6 1699
        Payments to: George Plater, Esq., Mr. George Lingham, Mr. William Dent, Mr.
    George Cole, Mr. Inmet Cranford, Daniel Robinson, Elisha Hall, James Moore,
    Capt. Francis Harbin.

Edward Wheelock   19½A.175 A BA   £46.14.0   £15.2.0   Apr 11 1700
        Payments to: James Homewood, Edward Smith, John Peasly.
        Executrix: Ann Wheelock.

Charles Bevan   19½B.1   I PG   £123.18.0   Sep 2 1699
        Appraisers: Thomas Greenfield, Robert Orme.

Richard Brightwell   19½B.1   I   PG   £52.0.5   Sep 5 1699
(gentleman).
          Appraisers: David Small, Edward Willett.

John Joyce   19½B.3   I   £41.1.8   Nov 28 1699
          Appraisers: John Pottenger, Christopher Tomson.

Thomas Hill   19½B.4   A   PG   £49.12.3   £4.18.8   May 29 1699
          Payments to: Mr. James Brook, Hugh Jones, Mr. Marsham.
          Executrix: Hannah Goff, wife of Thomas Goff.

Charles Hays   19½B.5   A   PG   £21.7.2   £30.4.3   Nov 28 1699
The amount of the inventory also included #5991.
          Payments to: William Wayford, William Moore, John Short for use of ------
          Carelson, Thomas Greenfield, James Beale, John Battee per William Young,
          Daniell Danielson, Thomas Box, John Battee, John Bennett, Samuell Peters for
          use of ------ Carlton per Alexander Beale, Josias Twogood on account of John
          Jackson & Co., Col. Darnall.
          Administratrix: Mary Johnson (late Mary Hays), wife of Thomas Johnson.

William Hutchison   19½B.6   I   £12.11.0   Jan 21 1698
          Appraisers: Daniel Ellet, William Tanyhill.

George Prater   19½B.6   I   £35.12.11   Jul 29 1698
          Appraisers: Joseph West, John Hallen.

Michael Kersey   19½B.7   A   PG   £5.15.10   £2.4.2   May 15 1699
          Administrator: John Lennam.

Jonathon Willson   19½B.8   I   £4.10.0   Jul 5 1699
          Appraisers: Robert Bradly, James Stoddart.

Joseph Lockworth   19½B.8   I   PG   £16.6.6   Dec 14 1699
          Appraisers: George Nayler, William Watson (also William Mosten).

Thomas Dixon   19½B.8   A   CA   £30.1.7   £14.5.0   Dec 28 1699
          Payments to: Capt. Thomas Ems, Mr. Robert Skinner.
          Executrix: Elisabeth Hunton.

Robert Brothers   19½B.9   I   CA   £244.4.2   Jun 6 1699
          Appraisers: Robert Wood, Daniel Brown.

Peter Hill (taylor)   19½B.10   I   CA   £26.10.6   Feb 11 1699
          Appraisers: George Spicer, John Floyd.

Henry Tomks   19½B.11   I   CA   £8.10.0   Dec 19 1699
          Appraisers: Thomas Atterbery, Charles Richardson.

Elisabeth How   19½B.11   I   £26.7.6   Dec 29 1699
          Appraisers: William Braban, Henry Heugh.

Henry Tomks   19½B.11   A   CA   £8.10.0   £15.17.0 Dec 19 1699
          Administrator: Darby Hernley.

Timothy Hunton   19½B.12   A   CA   £47.7.0   £13.9.1   Dec 28 1699
          Payments to: Capt. Thomas Ems.
          Executor: Elisabeth Hunton.

Joseph Stenet   19½B.13   A   CA   £8.7.6   £6.0.0   Feb 3 1699
          Administratrix: Sarah Stenett.

Mr. Samuell Scott   19½B.13   I   £112.14.7   Feb 10 1698
          Appraisers: Thomas Johnson, John Bradhurst.

John Cornelius   19½B.16   A   CA   £21.3.6   £20.11.0 Dec 19 1699
The amount of the inventory also included #1710.
          Payments to: Mr. Hugh Jones, Samuell Scott (merchant), Joseph Dawkins, David
          Hallen.
          Administrator: Thomas Atterbury.

Edward Armstrong   19½B.17   A   CA   £25.6.0   £21.5.0   Dec 20 1699
          Payments to: ------ Bradhurst (merchant), James Duke, Christopher Bateman, James
          Dawkins.
          Administrator: Darby Hernley.

John Hanie   19½B.18   A   CA   £43.16.6   £57.0.0   Apr 23 1700
          Payments to: William Derumple, Clark Skinner, Edward Butler, Thomas Hunter, Henry
          Fernley, Thomas Nickols, Abraham Clark, John Elsey, John Deaver, Walter
          Gilburn, William Nicholls.
          Executrix: Hermlas Hanie (?).

Thomas Mudd   19½B.19   A CA   £501.14.2   £298.10.0   Apr 19 1700
    Payments to: Robert Carvill, Samuell Watkins, Thomas Clark, William Wilkinson,
        Maj. William Boreman, Sr., Thomas Couth (?), Jeremy Snell.
    Executrix: Ann Hoskins, wife of Philip Hoskins.

Elisabeth Young   19½B.20   A CA   £10.2.0   £49.0.0   Apr 19 1700
The amount of the inventory also included #8806.
    Payments to: Mr. Thomas Hussey.
    Legatees: Boules Tire, James Tire, Mr. Richard Hubbart, Robert Yates, William
        Hunter, Richard Hubbart.
    Executor: William Boreman.

Mr. Philip Clark   19½B.21   I
    Appraisers: William Watts, Peter Watts.

Jonas Bowen   19½B.23   A BA
    Payments to: Fran. Alexander, John Heyman for use of John Rock, James Maxwell,
        John Hall, Col. John Thomas, Richard Colegate for use of Robert Benger,
        orphan (unnamed) of James Robartson.
    Legatees: Martha Bowen (daughter).
    Administratrix: Martha Bowen.

Capt. William Rycroft   19½B.24   I   £107.9.9   Feb 14 1699
    Appraisers: Mr. Thomas Greenfield, Mr. Richard Marsham.
    List of debts: Capt. Thomas Hurst, Capt. Charles Cook, Alexander Beal, Thomas
        Padget.

John Sides   19½B.25   A TA   £24.13.6   £80.2.11   Apr 20 1700
    Payments to: Mr. Robert Gouldsborrough, William Wrench, Benjamin Peck, John
        Swift, Laurence Draper, Esq. Lawrence, Robert Grundy, Sir Thomas Laurence,
        widow Serjant, ------ Creugh (merchant).
    Executrix: Bridgett Salter (relict), wife of John Salter.

Humphrey Jarvis   19½B.26   A CA   £8.5.4   Apr 22 1700
    Payments to: Gabriell Parrott, Henry Hanslap, George Burgess.
    Administratrix: Mary Jarvis.

John Smith   19½B.27   A CA   £243.4.11   £20.14.4   Apr 18 1700
The amount of the inventory also included #8499.
    Payments to: John Dawkins, Thomas Brickenden, David Hellen, Mr. Hugh Jones,
        James Beachum.
    Executrix: Joan Atterbery, wife of Thomas Atterbery.

Samuell Newton   19½B.28   A TA   £33.11.1   £37.3.4   Apr 20 1700
The amount of inventory also included #17500.
    Payments to: John Valliant, executors of ------ Millbourne, Esq. Laurence, Mathew
        Tilghman.
    Administrator: John Salter.

Robert Crook   19½B.29   A   £414.7.0   £420.10.0   Apr 23 1700
    Payments to: Thomas Richardson, Ann Garish, Symon Whittwell, John Thompson,
        Nathaniel Sapinton, Henry Penninton, John Jones, ------ Vanderheyden, Edward
        Lapage, John Keys, Charles Bass, Kenelme Cheseldyne, Mary Stanley, Mathias
        Mathiason, William Pearce, Daniel Pearce, Mathew Hendrickson, Mr. Willmore.
    Legatees: Dorothy Jones, Elisabeth Jones, James Frisby, Sr., William Pearce, Sr.,
        Edward Becker.
    List of debts: Ebenezar Blakiston, John Deubart, John Waggitt, John Fossitt,
        Jeremiah Barracklough, Edward Lappage, Mathias Mathiason, William Pope, Thomas
        Crewest, James Smithson, Richard Gain, Daniel Macknell, Richard Barker, John
        Cox, widow Bran.
    Executors: Henry Eldesly and his wife Parnell, Elisabeth Ladmore.

Mr. James Cranford   19½B.31   I CA   £389.16.0   Aug 3 1699   Feb 9 1699
    Appraisers: George Cole, Henry Boteler.
    List of debts: Aron Hall, Daniel Sheredine.

Arthur Oneale   19½B.35   I CH   £18.15.6   Dec 1 1699
    Appraisers: Morris FitzGerald, William Glover.
    Administratrix: ------ (name not given, widow).

Mr. Cleborne Lomax, Sr.   19½B.37   I   £33.18.0   Dec 28 1699 Dec 29 1699
    Appraisers: John Theobalds, Michael Marten.

John Hunt   19½B.38   I CH   £28.13.8   Nov 18 1699
    Appraisers: William Smith, Richard Justept.

John Frye   19½B.39   A CH   £23.9.6   Oct 20 1699
    Payments to: Capt. John Bayne, Elisabeth Hawkins, Rand. Garland, Capt. Philips,
        Gillion Martin, Robert Gutherick.
    Administratrix: Constance Frye.

Jacob Jennifer/Jenifer   19½B.40   I DO   £2.13.0   Dec 16 1699
        Appraisers: Robert Don, William Harris.
        Administrator: Thomas Pattison, Sr.

Patrick Danily   19½B.41   I   £39.15.10
        Appraisers: David Jenkins, John Willis.
        List of debts: widow Frayser, John Haslewood.

Alexander Frayser   19½B.42   I DO   £70.18.0   Dec 20 1699
        Appraisers: John Nichols, Mathias Allford.

John Vincent   19½B.43   I DO   £13.13.0   Mar 12 1699
        Appraisers: William Michew, Peter Stawks.

William Dean   19½B.44   A DO   £15.8.6   £7.12.11   Jan 2 1699
        Payments to: Mr. Hooper, Timothy Mackmara, Edmund Turner, John Goute.
        Administratrix: Elisabeth Dean.

Giles Porter   19½B.45   I CE   £97.10.1   Jul 27 1699
        Appraisers: Richard Kenword, Humphry Tilton.

John James   19½B.46   I CE   £55.8.6   Jul 31 1699
        Appraisers: Richard Kinword, Darby Haily (also Darby Haly).

John Eldrige   19½B.47   I CE   Feb 27 1699
        Appraisers: Thomas Pierce, John Baninton.

Edward Johnson   19½B.49   A CE   £26.7.0   £32.10.3   Mar 15 1699
        Payments to: Kenelm Cheseldyn paid to Col. William Pearce, John Thompson, Col.
        William Pearce, Charles Crowe, Thomas Hitchcock, Richard Nosh (?), Thomas
        Yoeman, Math. Vanderheyden, Thomas Powell, David Perry, William Sherwill,
        Sampson George & Edward Newell, James Robinson, Peter Minardo, Thomas
        Hichnorck, John Thompson.
        Executor: Owen Hughes.

Edward Johnson   19½B.51   I CE   £26.7.0
        Appraisers: Samson George, Edward Nevell.
        List of debts: Madam Harmar, Abraham Hollings, John Haus (steelman, Pa.)

Peter Sesserson   19½B.52   A CE   £38.2.6   £34.4.0   Apr 10 1700
        Payments to: Kenelm Cheseldyne paid to Thomas Browning, John Thompson, William
        Vezey, James Coatts, Peregrine Brown paid to John Hynson, William Hard, John
        Ward, Matthias Vanderhayden, Charles Bass, Matthias Mathiason, Thomas Kellton,
        John Pierson, Thomas Nicholson paid to William Brookson who married Elisabeth
        (administratrix of said Thomas Nicholson), John Thompson.
        Legatees: Henry Rigg.
        Executrix: Mary Atkins (relict), wife of John Atkins.

Lyonel Copley, Esq.   19½B.54   A   £1132.19.10 £1009.5.6   May 8 1700
The amount of the inventory also included £520.15.4 and #90682. The amount of the
accounts also included #92238.
        Payments to: Dr. Arnold, Elisabeth Baker, Henry Loftus, George Duffam, Thomas
        Green, Robert Davies, James Whitford, John Duckwood, Mr. John Llewelyn, James
        Anderson, William Taylard, John Smith, Christopher Gwin, Edward Parsons, Roger
        Henley, James Brown, John Corberyn, Abraham Roads, Ester Deen, John Lowe,
        Charles Carroll, Charles Egerton, James Stoddart, Mr. Edward Chilton, John
        Crapp, Dr. Mare, Anthony Evans, Mr. Thomas Harpham, William Richardson,
        Benjamin James, Garrett Vanswaringen, Mrs. Talbutt Herbert, Col. William
        Diggs, James Brown, Henry Loftus, William Gringoe, Dr. Godfrey, Thomas
        Courthny, Henry Lewis, John Green, Thomas Price, Thomas Balfore, James Bland,
        Thomas Green, William Hathead, Mr. John Llewelyn, Michael Chivers,
        Christopher Gwinn, Edward Parsons, Robert Cooper, Daniel Berry, John Evans,
        William Asquith, Dr. William Lowry, William Bladen, Sarah Hamstead, John
        Thompson, Thomas Harding, Robert Philips, William Greengoe, Thomas Williams,
        Samuel Wheeler, Col. Diggs, per his attorney Mr. John Llewelyn, James Brown,
        Garret Vansweringen, John Large.
        Mentions: orphan children (unnamed), Mr. Mason & Mr. Lynes.
        Administrator: Thomas Tench.

Lyonel Copley, Esq.   19½B.58   A   £1132.19.10 £1867.7.6   May 8 1700
        Mentions: Mr. James Harper, Mr. John Edloe.
        Received from: Miles Burrows, Maj. Robert King, Robert Ungle, Mrs. Ann
        Hopewell, John Pollard, William Harper, Benjamin Inman & Mr. Philip Lynes,
        William Bladen.
        Payments to: George Layfield, Col. Harman, Levin Denwood, Maj. Sewell, George
        Plater, David Todd, George Martin, Joseph Ferry, Robert Jones, Mr. Philip
        Lynes, Charles Beckworth, Mr. Henry Fernley for part of sum due Mr. Banckes,
        Mr. William Dent, Miles Burroughs, James Harper & Joseph Edloe, Madam
        Blakiston.
        Administrator: Thomas Tench.

Lyonel Copley, Esq.   19½B.60   A   #230213   May 9 1700
      List of debts: Miles Burrows, John Duckworth, Mr. William Harris, George Dufam,
      James Brown, Benjamin Scrivener, William Haines, Maj. Bele, Richard Benton,
      estate of Mr. John Llewelyn, Mr. William Taylard.
      Payments to: John Saner, Richard Benton, Francis Browning, Benjamin, John
      Cornelius, Mr. Robert Carvill by order of Mr. Batson, John Sanner, John
      Dibble, Mr. Robert Carvile, Richard Murrell, Gilbert Tubberfield, John Price
      (carpenter), Richard Benton, James Brown, John Large, William Harris, James
      Harper, Mr. Philip Lynes, Mr. Robert Mason, Sydrack Whitworth.
      Administrator: Thomas Tench.

Gov. Copley   19½B.62   A   £20.0.0   May 9 1700
      Payments to: Thomas Everard, John Edmondson.
      Administrator: Hon. Thomas Tench, Esq.

Col. George Robotham   19½B.63   A   £385.11.9   May 9 1700
      Payments to: Capt. Anthony Stratton by bill drawn by John Millard, Capt.
      Stratton by bill drawn by Richard Webb, Capt. Stratton paid to Thomas Smithson
      by bill drawn by John Hamilton and Laurence Swarbrook, Robert Smith, Esq.,
      Joseph Gregory, Charles Ferry, Ralph Moon (administrator of Katherine
      Katherson), Thomas Bruffe, Edward Lloyd, John Salter, William Haddon, Richard
      Hall, William Alderne.
      Executors: John Pemberton, Edward Lloyd, Thomas Smithson.

Henry Chapell   19½B.64   I AA   £39.2.0   May 1 1700
      Appraisers: Humphrey Boon, Robert Eagle.

Dr. Symon Wootton   19½B.66   A   £97.1.0   £38.9.5   May 8 1700
      Payments to: Hugh Ferguson per Col. John Bigger, Mr. George Plater, John Broom,
      William Stone, Mr. James Keech, James Leach, per Mr. Walter Smith.
      Administrator: John Fisher. Unadministered by Col. John Bigger.

Capt. Henry Johnson   19½B.67   A BA   £283.17.0   May 8 1700
      Payments to: Mathias Vanderheyden, James Fendall, Anthony Drew, George Utye,
      James Philips, Andrew Dalton, John Boulton, James Clark, Thomas Kersey, Ann
      Young, Philip Clark.
      Administratrix: Elisabeth Boothby, wife of Edward Boothby.

Christopher More   19½B.68   A CH   #7557   Jul 12 1699
      Payments to: Maj. William Dent, Edward Mong.
      Administrators: Samuel and Mary Mason.

Edward Beadle   19½B.69   A BA   £28.9.6   May 8 1700
      Payments to: Mr. William Hopkins, Samuell Groom, Col. Wells, Esq., James
      Fendall, Daniell Purnell (dead), Richard Green (dead), John Walster (dead),
      James Ives & Edward Harpley.
      Administratrix: Martha Hall, wife of John Hall.

George & Mary Utye   19½B.69   A BA   £256.4.5   £172.6.6   May 7 1700
The amount of the inventory also included: £40.14.06; £4.18.0 in the hands of John
Hall; £7.0.0. from the estate of Mr. Boothby; £12.0.0 in the hand of Peregrine Brown
(merchant in London).
      List of debts: William Askie.
      Payments to: William Polie, Thomas Smith, Robert Olie, Maj. Maxwell, Esq.
      Lawrence, Gibbard Perriott, George Smith, Ann Baker, Daniel Palmer, Lawrence
      Taylor, Benjamin Wells (executor of Col. George Wells), Mr. Hedge, James
      Philips for George Utye, Daniel Palmer, Henry Jackson, Thomas Morris, Mr.
      Robert Gouldsborrough, John Cobet, Robert Benger, Michael Judd, Loderick
      Morlame, Nathaniell Pew, John Hall for Col. Darnall, John Hall, Philip Clark,
      Mr. Cheseldyn.
      Paid in the deceased's lifetime: Thomas Pibel (?) per Mr. Hopkins, Samuell
      Fendall (dead), Thomas Harts (runaway), Charles Hall (runaway), Thomas
      Williams (runaway), William Abe (runaway to Pennsylvania), Mr. Richardson,
      Garett Garettson.
      Administrators: Mark Richardson, John Hall.

George Gouldsmith   19½B.72   A BA   #2659   May 7 1700
      Payments to: attorney of ------ Delagrange by assignment of George Agelsby.
      Executrix: Martha Hall (relict), wife of John Hall.

Nathaniel Dollen   19½B.73   A AA   £13.1.1   £13.13.0   May 7 1700
      Payments to: Charles Stephens, Thomas Brown, Capt. Philip Howard, Dr. Rigg,
      William Perkins, Robert Kitts, Esq. Cheseldyne, Edward Hall, widow Rockhold.
      Administrator: John Farthing.

John Towsey (merchant)   19½B.74   A AA   £7.4.0   £616.15.15   Feb 22 1699
The amount of the inventory also included debts amounting to £609.11.5.
      Payments to: Robert Lockwood, Dr. Thomas Hunter.
      Administrator: Stephen Cole.

John Towsey (merchant)   19½B.75   I AA   £609.11.5   Feb 22 1699
        List of debts: Capt. Gerrard Slye, Capt. James Waldie, Capt. John Read, Mr.
            Richard Wapplton, Mr. James Dunkin, Mr. Richard Evans, Maj. Walter Smith,
            Thomas Tench, Esq., Mr. William Cole, Sr., Mr. Samuell Chambers, Capt.
            Nicholas Humphreys, Mr. John Lambe, Capt. Stephen Cole.
        Administrator/Executor: Capt. Stephen Cole.

Mr. John Towsey   19½B.75   I   £54.1.6   Feb 22 1699
        Mentions: Capt. Slye, Mr. Nathan Smith.
        Administrator: Capt. Stephen Cole.

Mr. Clement Parks   19½B.76   I   £1.11.0   Jan 8 1699
        Appraisers: Joshua Guibert, James Hay.

Thomas Goult   19½B.77   A   May 7 1700
        Payments to: Thomas Fielder, Mr. Thomas Tucker.
        Administrator: John Wight.

Christopher Gregory   19½B.77   A   £61.18.8   £165.19.3   May 6 1700
        Received from: Henry Croft, William Wivell, Thomas Laurence, Esq., Richard Edgar.
        Payments to: Katherine Prout, Matthew Howard, Manus Devoran, Robert Philips, John
            Davies, Christopher Goodhand, Mr. John Freeman, Dr. Rottenbury, Mr.
            Secretary Laurence, Sir Thomas Laurence, Rachel Kilburne, George Jackson, Mrs.
            Hester Gross, Thomas Davies (taylor), Christopher Vernon, Richard Edgar,
            Abraham Claity (merchant), Col. Henry Jowls, Thomas Bale (merchant) Thomas
            Carpenter, William Harris, John Freeman, Orlando Greenslade.
        Legatees: Mrs. Ann Fowks, Thomas Lingan, Samuell Boughton, Rachell Thompson,
            Elizabeth Dent, Thomas Dent.
        Executor: William Dent.

Mr. John Leach   19½B.79   I   £321.19.2   Oct 14 1699
        Appraisers: James Heigh, Benjamin Ball.

Edward Evans,   19½B.80   I CA   £47.17.11   Apr 30 1700
        Appraisers: John Jenkins, William Williams, Sr.

John Fields   19½B.81   I CA   £7.3.0   Nov 29 1699
The amount of the inventory also included #1296.
        Appraisers: William Bradley, William Stennett.
        List of debts: Francis Mauldin, John Fisher, Richard Kent.

Robert Cattlyn   19½B.82   I   £48.9.3   Dec 30 1699
        Appraisers: James Curtis, George Lane.

Samuel Showell   19½B.83   A SO   £35.9.0   Feb 16 1699
        Payments to: Maj. Whittington, William Fausett, Charles Ratcliffe, Mr. James
            Rownd, Mr. Scarborrough, William Round, John Webb, Thomas Morris, John West,
            Thomas Powell, Henry Knight.
        Distribution to: Jonathon Showell (child), Armell Showell (child), their brother
            (unnamed), their sister (unnamed).
        Executors: Jonathon Showell, Armell Showell.

Richard Holland   19½B.84   A   £63.9.6   £3.12.6   Nov 13 1699
        Executors: Frances Holland, Nehemiah Holland.

Richard Wharton   19½B.84   A SO   #11694   #12901   Nov 16 1699
        Received from: William Henderson, Edward Gold, Ralph Millbourn.
        Payments to: James Sangster, Edward Gold, Richard Tull, Archibald Holines,
            William Faussett, Mr. James Beachim, Mr. Samuell Hopkins, Maj. Whittington,
            Mr. John West, Capt. John Cornish.
        Administrator: Francis Jenkins.

Robert Blades   19½B.85   A SO   £16.13.2   #5488   Jan 9 1699
        Payments to: Col. Francis Jenkins, William Mathews, Maj. Whittington, Samuell
            Hopkins, Sr.
        Administrator/Executor: Robert Blades (son).

John Holland   19½B.86   A SO   £49.2.0   £49.2.0   Mar 12 1699
        Payments to: George Febus, Mr. Denwood, John Bacon.
        Distribution to: administratrix, child (unnamed), 2 daughters (unnamed) of the
            administratrix.
        Administratrix: Ann Holland (relict).

John Williams   19½B.87   A SO   £43.3.3   £43.3.3   Dec 28 1699
        Payments to: Col. Jenkins, Mr. Cornish (merchant), William Bittingham, William
            White, Margarett Haggamore, Mr. Broadhaft (merchant), Dunnock Dennis, Jr.,
            Maj. Whittington.
        Distribution to: widow (unnamed), 6 orphans (unnamed).
        Administrator/Executor: Henry Rich who married the relict (unnamed) of the
            deceased.

Philip Adams   19½B.87   A SO £40.14.11   #10413   Nov 22 1699
The amount of the inventory is equivalent to #9779.
          Payments to: Mr. Jenkins, Peter Dikason, Thomas Thompson, Margarett Taylor, Mr.
          Dixon, Mr. Kyle, Maj. Whittington.
          Administrator: Thomas Adams.

John Townsend   19½B.88   A SO £32.18.0   £32.18.0   Dec 9 1699
          Payments to: Mr. Breechin (minister), Maj. Whittington, Francis Jones, Col.
          Jenkins, Alexander Maddox.
          Distribution to: widow (unnamed), 4 orphans (unnamed).
          Administratrix/Executrix: Elisabeth Holland.

Thomas Hutman   19½B.89   A SO £15.17.7   Nov 23 1699
          Payments to: George Hutchins, George Human, Katherine Lows (widow), John
          Thompson.
          Distribution to: administrator.
          Administrator: George Hutchins.

Ra. Smith   19½B.89   A CH £334.6.9   £22.3.8   Feb 24 1699
          Payments to: Mr. Richard Boughton, John Doughlass, Joseph Cole, Mr. Philip
          Briscoe.
          Mentions: no orphans.
          Executrix: Mrs. Sarah Smith (widow).

James Townsend   19½B.90   I AA £58.13.4   Jan 20 1699
          Appraisers: John Gale, John Blackmore.
          List of debts: Ann Bacon.

William Smith   19½B.91   I CH £23.10.0   Mar 6 1699
          Appraisers: John Booker, Lewis Jones.

Elisabeth Smith (widow)   19½B.93   I   £17.6.0   Mar 19 1699
wife of William Smith (dead) and Archibald Waughob (dead).
          Appraisers: John Booker (also John Brook), Lewis Jones.

Mary Hall   19½B.93   A   £11.17.0   £3.3.3
          Payments to: Maj. Dent.
          Executor: Philip Hoskins.

Jeremiah Eldridge   19½B.94   I CA £90.0.0   Feb 25 1698
          Appraisers: William Wadsworth, John Bowles.
          List of debts: John Bowing upon account of Richard Jackson, George Cole, Samuel
          Griffith, Aron Hall, Richard Evans, Thomas Kenistone, Caleb Chew, estate of
          Thomas Hillary, Edward Hall, Robert Lyles, John Fisher, Patrick Dew, William
          Mills, John Underwood, Jonathon Tench, William Rodery, Nicholas Sporne,
          Abraham Bird, John Attwell, Joseph Hall, John Bowles, Richard Perrin.

William Horne, Jr.   19½B.97   A AA £114.6.3   £9.5.0   Mar 7 1699
          Payments to: Thomas Tench, Esq., John Thompson, William Grey.
          Mentions: father (unnamed) of the deceased.
          Administratrix: Sarah Horne.

James George   19½B.98   I TA £10.9.6   Feb 17 1699
          Appraisers: Lewis Meredeth, John Oldson.

Mr. John Towsey   19½B.98   I   £7.4.0
          Appraisers: Richard Jones, Jr., John Willowby,

Edward Fowler   19½B.99   I   £55.10.7
          Appraisers: Thomas Horsman, Samuell Flewelyn.

James Stanfield   19½B.100 I SO £102.3.2   Nov 20 1699
          Appraisers: John Hendry, Edward Green.
          List of debts: John Gawdin, Mr. John West, Capt. Haman, Charles Ratcliff.

Mr. Erasmus Harrison   19½B.100 I SO £93.8.6   Mar 25 1700
          Appraisers: John Franklyn, Edward Green.

                           19½B.102 I   £37.0.0   Nov 20 1699
The inventory is for both James Stanfield and James Macoom.
          Appraisers: John Hendry, Edward Green.

Roger Philips   19½B.104 I   £90.1.10   Mar 8 1699
          Appraisers: Phil. Carr, Joseph Venabs.

Michael Harrison   19½B.106 I   £11.16.9   Dec 22 1699
          Appraisers: Richard Chainbard, Robert Carey.

Samuel Baker   19½B.107 I BA   £27.13.3   May 25 1699
The amount of the inventory also included #450.
    Appraisers: George Smith, Samuell Brown.
    List of debts: Robert Gard, Henry Jackson, Henry Haslwood, Thomas Bevans, estate
      of Mary Uty.

Samuel Baker   19½B.108 A BA   £27.13.3   #3656   Feb 20 1699
    Payments to: Roger Mathews, Maj. Maxwell, Robert Gard (runaway), John Hall,
      Samuell Brown & George Smith, Mr. Anthony Drew.
    Administratrix: Anne White, wife of William White.

John Mark   19½B.108 A BA   £39.18.0   #11447   Apr 13 1700
The amount of the inventory is equivalent to #7980. The amount of the inventory also
included #4552.
    Payments to: Mr. Staley, Moses Groome, James Philips, James Maxwell, John Ellis,
      Thomas Preston, John Hall, John Parker paid to John Hall, Samuell Browne paid
      to John Hall, John York (dead), John Evans, James Furell (dead), Joseph Gacion
      (dead), Abraham Taylor.
    Administratrix: Margarett Mark.

William Gary   19½B.110 A TA   £222.18.4   £101.1.9   May 9 1700
    Payments to: John Gary, Mr. Clayland, Robert Munday, Edward Lloyd, Dr. Imbert,
      John Jones (brazier), Richard Austin, Jr., John Jones (brazier) (administrator
      of John Magruder), Laurence Knowles, Daniell Walker, - Sr., Richard Macklyn,
      Nicholas Lowe, James Crowley, Thomas Jones (weaver), Philip Massey.
    Payments to (on account of Grace Gary (widow, dead)): John Edgar, Capt. Thomas
      Marshall, Ambros Kenimon, Edward Lloyd, John Grason, John Aldrige, Henry
      Jones, wife (unnamed) of John Jones (brazier), Laurence Knowles, John Jones
      (brazier), Jacob Gibson, Mr. Grundy.
    Legatees: Elisabeth Gary, Daniell Walker.
    List of debts: William Mitchell, Jacob Pride, Timothy Oneale, Edward Overing,
      Thomas Wallis, Thomas Allen, William Evans.
    Administrators: Edward Lloyd, Richard Tilghman, and Thomas Thomas during the
      minority of John Gary and George Gary.

Richard Hubart   19½B.112 A CH   £53.7.6   £10.6.0   May 6 1700
    Payments to: Kenelm Cheseldyne, Richard Boughton, Gerrard Slye.
    Executors: Benjamin Hall, William Boreman, Anthony Neale.

Thomas Tallor   19½B.113 A CH   Apr 25 1700
    Received from: John Loftin, Ann Hide, Samuel Burnham.
    Payments to: Joseph Venor, Ann Cox, Mrs. Sarah Smith.
    Administratrix/Executrix: widow (unnamed), wife of John Gwin.

Benjamin Scrivener,   19½B.113 A AA   £19.10.0   £49.14.6   May 9 1700
    Received from: James Kighe.
    Payments to: Maj. Edward Dorsey and John Taylor, John Merriton, Mrs. Rachell
      Kilburne, Kenelm Cheseldyn, Esq. paid to Mr. William Dent, Mr. Richard Beard
      per balance of judgment obtained by Mrs. Elisabeth Blakiston, Charles
      Carroll.
    Administrator: Thomas Tench, Esq.

Griffin Morley   19½B.114 I   £40.4.0   Feb 29 1699
The amount of the inventory also included #1200.
    Appraisers: Seaborne Tucker, Daniel Brown.
    List of debts: John Waters, John Emerton, Edward Ball.

William Medley   19½B.115 A SM   #682   Sep 20 1699
    Payments to: Mr. William Husbands.
    Administrator: Charles Deft.

Thomas Warren   19½B.116 A SM   Sep 7 1699
    Received from: James Blomfield, Mr. John Tant.
    Payments to: Rosana Cole, William Negale, Susannah Brewer, John Noble, Joseph
      Clark, Mr. Husbands, Mr. Robert Mason.
    Executor: Charles Daft.

John Roberts   19½B.117 A SM   #2844   Sep 6 1699
    Received from: Francis Grayham, Christopher Williamson.
    Payments to: Mr. Robert Mason, James Wood, Mr. Jacob Moreland, James Latch,
      John Gellum, John Duckett,
    Administrator: Joseph Edwards.

John Fordery   19½B.117 I SM
    Appraisers: John Jorboe, Cornelius Manley,

James Chesham   19½B.118 I SM   £15.13.0   Apr 22 1699
    Appraisers: Edward Parson, Thomas Haddock.

Daniel Moy   19½B.118 A SM   £10.18.0   #8141   Aug 20 1699
     Payments to: Mr. Aysquith, Ann Moy (the widow), Mr. Kenelm Cheseldyn, William
        Taylard, Mr. Peter Bodwyn, Mr. Philip Lynes, John Shanks.
     Administrator: Edward Miller.

Samuel Abell   19½B.119 A SM   #3394   Jul 17 1699
     Payments to: Mr. Thomas Hatton, Margarett Baley.
     Executrix: Ann Abell (relict).

Peter Jerboe   19½B.120 A SM   £20.19.7   #5590   Nov 8 1699
     Received from: Anthony Neale of Charles County.
     Payments to: William Husbands, Susanna Heard, John Nevett (son of administrator),
        Henry Spink, George Henderson (merchant), Thomas Low (shoemaker), Henry Jarboe
        (brother of deceased).
     Administrator: John Nevett for his daughter Ann Nevett (relict).

Benjamin Chew   19½B.122 I AA   £543.17.8   Jun 3 1700
     Appraisers: Abraham Birkhead, Thomas Hughes.

Abraham Naylor   19½B.125 I AA   £35.15.6   May 15 1700
     Appraisers: Josias Towgood, Thomas Hughes.

John Perry   19½B.126 A   £103.12.1   £149.1.10 Jun 9 1700
     Payments to: James Piller and William Salisbury, George Nicholson, David Jenkins,
        Mr. Charles Carroll, Thomas Wells, Lawrence Draper, Henry Carter, Mr. Croft,
        Solomon Thompson, Mr. John Rock, Mr. Thomas Grunwin, Elisabeth Newton, Maj.
        Dent, Thomas Harding, John Rock, William Jones, George Nicholson, Edward
        Dorsey.
     List of debts: James Cullen, ------ Kilburne.
     Administratrix: Sarah Evans, wife of Job Evans.

Christopher Bayne   19½B.127 A CA   #14803   Jun 8 1700
     Payments to: William Turner, Mr. Charles Carroll, William Creed, David Boule,
        Richard Keen, Henry Fernley, Thomas Tasker, James Duke, Christopher Pearl,
        Thomas How, William Parker, Jacob Moreland, John Turner, Elisabeth Wilkenson,
        Edward Butler.
     Executor: Christopher Bayne.

Daniel Macomas   19½B.128 I AA   £22.9.4   Apr 9 1700
     Appraisers: Nicholas Sheppard, John Marriott.

Joseph Sudler   19½B.129 I KI   £129.7.0   May 3 1700   May 29 1700
     Appraisers: Math. Eareckson, Thomas Baxter.

George Ashman   19½B.131 I BA   £415.6.2   Feb 27 1699
     Appraisers: Edward Dorsey, Thomas Hedge.

Thomas Wakefield   19½B.134 I CH   £44.0.1   Apr 2 1700
     Appraisers: John Barron, John Roby.

Robert Benjar   19½B.136 I CH   £208.2.3   Apr 3 ----   May 21 1700
     Appraisers: Thomas Chapman, Evan Jones.

Mr. Thomas Mitchell   19½B.139 I   £18.14.0   May 4 1700
     Appraisers: Francis Green, Andrew Simpson.

Ellin Steward   19½B.140 I   £10.2.0   Apr 13 1700
     Appraisers: Mathew Sander, Peter Mackmilon.

Richard Jones   19½B.141 I CH   £15.15.9   Apr 25 1700
     Appraisers: John Higgins, John Ford.

Charles Tracey   19½B.141 I PG   £45.0.0   Jun 26 1700
     Appraisers: James Stoddart, Joshuah Hill.
     Mentions: Mr. David Small, William Groom.

Mr. Richard Keen   19½B.142 I CA   £117.10.9   Jan 1699   Feb 5 1699
     Appraisers: William Williams, Jr., Jeremiah Sheredine.

William Roycroft   19½B.145 A   £107.9.9   £71.6.4   Jul 2 1700
     Payments to: Col. Thomas Holyday, Col. Thomas Tasker, Mrs. Bevan, Capt.
        Stephen Cole, Mrs. Greenfield, Thomas Bridges, Mr. Richard Marsham, John
        Fisher, Nicholas Sporne, Mr. Sheffield, Samuel Poler, Josh. Cecill, Richard
        Waplington.
     Administrator: Richard Waplington.

Richard Rawlings   19½B.146 A AA £86.8.9   £58.5.9   Jul 3 1700
A second inventory was cited in the amount of £8.7.6. A third inventory was cited in
the amount of £12.0.0. A fourth inventory was cited in the amount of £5.10.0.
     Received from: John Norwood.
     Payments to: Thomas Poland, Dr. Woolfran Hunt, Mr. John Taylor, Capt. Philip
        Howard, Edward Batson, Barbarah Broad.
     Mentions: suit by George Plater.
     Administratrix: Jane Griffin (relict), wife of Philip Griffin.

Robert Gover, Sr.   19½B.147 I AA £156.4.0   May 6 1700
The amount of the inventory also included #1200.
     Appraisers: Robert Wood, John Stephens.
     List of debts: Elisabeth Morley.

John Nicholson   19½B.149 A AA £130.0.0   £16.10.0   Apr 25 1700
     Payments to: Mr. Roger Newman, Mr. Charles Carroll, James Homewood.
     Executrix: Elisabeth Nicholson.

William Innis (widower)   19½B.150 A SO £53.3.6   £53.3.6   Jun 20 1700
     Payments to: Dr. Samuell Davies, James Stanfield, John Webb, Maj. Whittington,
        Andrew Whittington, Thomas Morris, John Robinson (merchant), Mr. James Round,
        John Hendry (merchant), David Richardson, Thomas Pointer, Samuell Hopkins,
        Samuell Wothrinton.
     Distribution to: orphan child (unnamed).
     Administrator/Executor: Cornelius Innis (brother).

William Tomkins   19½B.151 A SO £83.16.6   £25.12.1   Jun 12 1700
     Payments to: Dr. John Ronsalloe, William Fausett, Ellis Collman, Francis Heap,
        Mr. Samuell Davies, Richard Tull, Mathew Scarborrough, Thomas Fenwick.
     Legatees: George Wale, Bridgett Wale, Nathaniell Wale, Charles Wale, Rachell
        Wale.
     Executrix: Elisabeth Turvile, wife of William Turvile.

Leonard Camperson   19½B.152 I TA £58.14.4   Sep 15 1699
     Appraisers: George Vinson, Richard Knighton.

William Burgess   19½B.153 A   £390.8.2   Aug 15 1699
     Payments to: Mr. Samuell Chew, Mr. Charles Carroll, Capt. Bale, Ralph Bazell,
        Samuell Chew upon the account of Thomas Ely, Thomas Day, William Holland,
        Richard Harrison, Gabriel Parrott, Elisabeth Parrott, Christopher Vernon,
        William Bladen.
     Administratrix: Anne Jones, wife of Richard Jones.

Richard Gardner   19½B.154 A   Oct 6 1699
     Payments to: Mr. Thomas Turner, Mr. Thomas Brooke, Jeffrey Jeffrey (merchant in
        London).
     Executors: Clement Hall, Luke Gardiner.

William Brown,   19½B.155 A   £31.4.6   £33.7.10   Apr 17 1700
     Payments to: Richard Kirkland, George Man (servant), Daniel Wells (hireling).
     Administrator: Col. Henry Ridgley, Sr.

Thomas Johnson   19½B.156 A SO £16.10.8   £24.9.0   Jun 20 1700
The amount of the inventory also included #1900.
     Payments to: Levin Denwood, William Winright, William Haydon, Edward Coats,
        William Piper, Samuell Fluelyn, John Demorris, Robert Givin.
     Distribution to: relict (unnamed), 5 orphan children (unnamed).
     Administratrix/Executrix: relict (unnamed), wife of Charles Low (also Charles
        Lowe).

Mr. Notley Warren   19½B.157 I   £219.11.4   Apr 13 1700
     Appraisers: Thomas Whichaley, John Cage.

Mathew Selley   19½B.160 A   £58.5.0   Jun 20 1700
     Payments to: Samuell Hicks, Mr. William Paggan, Dr. Moore, Thomas Carpenter, Mr.
        Richard Beard, Mr. Richard Gallaway, widow of Gabriel Parrott, Jr., Edward
        Cox, Edward Parish, Henry Allchin, Samuell Chambers, Mr. Cheseldyn, John
        Roberts.
     Administrator: Benjamin Capell.

In the Inventories & Accounts is a list of the debts & payments for the estate of Thomas Hedge. The list is undated. This list can be found in Liber 16, Folios 211-216.

Edward Beedle
Joseph Saunders
Henry Hedge
Porter Norton
James Todd
Thomas Bytteras
Aucha Johnson Pagen & Co.,
John Durham
Thomas Freeborne
William Lewis
Michaell Judd
Hastwell & Co.
Joseph Peak
John Whitecar
Henry Mathews
William Harris
William Hicks
James Murry
Isack Marshall
Lawrence Taylor
Hendrick Enloe (?)
Robert Gardiner
Henry Ki---- (page is torn)
Joseph Wells
Sarah Teale
Marke Swift
Aquila Paca
Edward Wildey
Blanch Wells
John Watson
Nicholas Gassaway
Robert Parker
Simon Peirson
John Love
Nathaniel Anderson
George Hall
Dinah Nuthead
John Royston
John Hays
John Otton
John Gay
Thomas Hooker
Isack Jackson
Capt. Seaborne & Co.
Elisabeth Gibson
------ Palmer
George Morgan
Francis Smith
estate of Thomas Jones
Charles Jones
John Lockett
Ralph Gillion
Thomas Dadd
Thomas Litton
Gerrardus Wessells
Daniell Gasquaine

Christopher Shaw
Thomas Bevins
Thomas Rone
John Broad
Anthony Demondidier
Moses Groome
Robert Smith
Andrew Ceely
Robert Gibson
Nathaniell Hunchcombe
Benjamin Wells
Thomas Sheard
John Wright
Thomas Blackwell on Baltimore
John Merriton
John Robertson
Thomas Preston
John Debrula
William Lovey
Robert Love
John Camble
James Browne
Charles Smith
Thomas Reynolds
John Scott
John Anderson
John Smith
James Mazzard
Thomas Heath
Francis Robinson
Thomas Browne
Christopher Bembridge
John Copper
John Combest
John Parker
John Rowe
Robert Drydall
Daniell Dorney
Robert Gudgeon
William Farfar
Richolas Fitzsymons
Robert Gardiner
John Gray
William Gudgeon
William Jeff
Robert Gibson
Ralph Eves
Ambross Hogge
John Fuller
Giles Stevens
Edward Jones
John Leakins
Thomas Newsam
Michaell Canady
Edward Waters

Miles Hannis
Francis Dorrelhide
Cornelius Boyce
Joseph Strawbridge
Abraham Taylor
George Chancy
estate of George Utie
Andrew Anderson
Michaell Gorremon
William Hawkins
John Sollers
Capt. Richard Hill
William Lenox
Cornell Harrington
Thomas Gilbert
John Rawlins
Thomas Cannon
John Taylor
Maj. James Maxwell
James Sicklemore
William Love
John Hinson
Peter Bond
William Barker
Francis Watkins
Richard Kilburne
John Barranan
Richard Symson
Edward Hooke
Pattett & Co.
Jonas Bowen
John Webster
John Hurst
Patrick Dunkin
Edward Harpley
Edward Norris
Luke Raven
William Perkett
James Wrath
Charles Adams
executors of Col. George
   Wells
William Yorke
John Carvile
Col. John Thomas
Mr. Author Drew
Lt. Col. Thomas Richardson
Mr. Edward Boothby
Mr. James Phillips
George Smith
John Gould
William Horne
Francis Whitehead
Susannah Arnold
Capt. Peregrin Browne

John Copy
Robert Benjar
Manus Devorau
Richard Jones
Robert Olesse
George Ashman
Israell Skelton
Stephen Johnson
Mr. John Hall per Mr. James
   Maxwell
Mr. Marke Richardson
Edward Beedle & John Walston
   biestoes of ------ Fendall
Joseph Edloe
James Fendall
Symon Jackson
William Friley
John Roberts
George Norman
Michaell Cinnworth (?)
Richard Tylliard
Richard Brazier
Thomas Durbin
George Merritt
John Royston
George Morgan
Nathaniell Bevis
Edward Allelise
William Noble
Robert West
David Macklfish
Samuell Underwood
Robert Aynion
Capt. Abra. Wild
James Frisell
William Davis
James Growden
William Gayne
John Phillips
William Coventry
George English on Baltimore
John Tyllard
Thomas Morris
Thomas Kirkesey
George Hollinsworth
William Cockey
Edward Jordaine
James Shenon
Richard Asquew
James Glasbye
Flora Hendrickson
Thomas Yeoman
Thomas Jones (piper)
Thomas James
John Johnson

In the Inventories & Accounts is a list of the debts & payments for the estate of Col. Nehemiah Blackiston, Esq. The list is undated. This list can be found in Liber 18, Folios 164-170.

Edward Tipton
Samuell Cooksey
John Gillam
Capt. John Beane
Thomas Mattinley
John Cole, Esq.
Richard Screllman (?)
Richard BrightWell
Robert Doyne
Lawrence Young
Thomas Deacon
Thomas Chilmott
Francis Knott
Richard Chapman
Lewis Watkins
Thomas Witcheley
Thomas Clarke
Samuell Berry
Richard Clouds
James Bigger
Henry Bonner
Thomas Simpson
------ Camell
William Shirtleeft
Clemborne Lomax
Elisabeth Gardner
Caleb Osborne
Will Guyther
John Francis
John Evans
Phillip Willing
Col. Spencer
Charles Evans
Henry Fernley
Richard Hubbard
Peter Cordwaldyn
Abraham Price
David Parsons
Edward Cole
Thomas Beale
Edward Morgan
Humphrey Pope
John Grubb
William Smote
Robert Yates
Francis Johnson
William Knight
Jame Simond
William Symons
Edward Greenhoth
John Wilder
John Davis of Poplar Hill
John Wade up the bay
Robert Sly
Henry Browne

Roderick Loyd
James Findall
Thomas Grunwyn
Robert Simock
Luke
Henry Hawkins
Lewis Taper
John Polanie in England
Benjamin Whichcott
John Graves
John VanresWicke
Anthony Evans
Timothy Tracey
Thomas Oriole
John Boland (merchant in New England)
Thomas Edwards
Richard Gardner
William Farthing
William Guyther and John Baker
Elias Beech and John Baker
Arthur Tompson
Walter Jones
William Harper
James Ricketts
Thomas Williams
Richard Voules
Thomas Turner
Thomas Bincraft
Capt. John Addison
Edward Turner
Thomas Doyne
James Johnson
James Duke
Col. Richard Lowe
John Lambert in England
Jame Wells in England
John Bayley
Francis Harps in Virginia
Denis Sellyvent
Joseph Manneing
Francis Hill
John Barnes
Mathew Tennison
Thomas Michell
Joseph Peters
Edmond Payore
John Searbroff (?)
Ignatius Wheeler
John Noble
Garrett Vansweringen
Capt. Hugh Bedford
Chrimas Smith
Robert Williams

John Ellis
Samson Clarke
Robert Gooding
Charles Partis
Phineas Hyde
Ja. Sittle
Abra. Hooke
Alesander Daniell
Robert Lurtin
Nicholas Lynch
William Burd
William Waston
John Boreman
Joseph Cornish
John Long in England
S. Bartlet
William Nicholls
Thomas Evered
David Greenhill
Joseph Glover
William Hill
John Sinkler
Capt. Gasier
Edward Barecock
John Learch
Thomas Hinch
John Fisher
Capt. John Thomas
William Burnam
William Bascall
Cristopher Evetin
John Carne
William Jones of Bristoll
George Oldfeild
Thomas Ball
------ Bradley
William Black
Christopher Bunbridge
John Wahop
William Ball
Constant Daniell
William Thomas
Roger Ale
Thomas Jones of Somerset County
John Ceciele
John Garrett
John Aston
------ Kitchin of Kent
Bennett Seares of Kent
John Wilcokson of Kent
John Hinson of Kent
William French
Ralph Hutchyson of Delaware

William Thomas
Robert Noones
Robert Neele
Walter Davis
Justinian Brimson
John Burrost
Gilbert Turberfeild
Samuell Trumball
Elias Groome (alias Elias Potter)
Mary Pope of Calvert County
William Loveday
John Penry
John Redman
Robert John Dish
Emanuell Ratley
Thomas Coverill
Abraham Camaster
Thomas Smith
Owen Price
Robert Foster
Thomas Ranes
John Foster
Alexander Standish
John Noe
Col. William Diggs
Robert Edemes
John Larkin
Thomas Parsloe
Ralph Wormley, Esq.
Capt. Joseph Stevens
John Edwards
Capt. George Phillips
Cuthbett Sharpless
Col. Edward Pye
Thomas Burford
Thomas Thurston
Roger Ross
Col. Henry Jowles
William Taylor
Owen Brodie
Thomas Sikes
Daniell Hinley
Bartholomew Sheppard
Capt. Seather Lam
John Newman
Joseph Edloe
Maj. Ninian Beale
Col. Thomas Hollyday
Ralph Foster
John Hall
Justinian Tennison
William Dent
Roger Kemp

List of Debts & Payments for Samuel Withers

In the Inventories & Accounts is a list of the debts & payments for the estate of Samuel Withers. The list is dated 26 January 1698. This list can be found in Liber 18, Folios 173-179.

Other Debts

Sir Thomas Dil	William Robinson	John Richardson

Solvent Debts

William Moore	Richard Ratcliff	John Brachew	Peter Dod
John Palmer	Jaspar Hall	Moses Harris	Capt. James Murphey
Thomas Gerrard	Edward Latham	Christopher Spruy	Col. Peter Sayer
Richard Roberts	Nathaniell Graves	Johaniosa	

Desperate Debts

David Miles	Robert Betts	Henry Cosdin	David Rogers
James Scott	William Jones of Kent	William Warner	Samuell Farmer
Edgar Webb	George Smith	Robert Smith	Henry Sap
Samuell Stames (?)	Robert White	Robert Grundy	John Pursell, Jr.
Christopher Santee	Timothy Mounsser	William Wintersell	William Meares
William Robinson	Thomas Lister	John Downes	Abraham Sherring
Morris Nailer	James Wyatt	James Cullen	James Anderson
Margaret Covorwill	John Lawes of Kent	William Skinner	Richard Hamon
Israell Coleman	James Bonner	Robert Bradaway	Isaack Saserson
Elisabeth Smithson	John Murphey	John Clements	Henry Jones
Bryan Sene	John Burmant	Thomas Noeman	Daniell Redman
Loughling MackDaniell	Andrew Malpass	Edward Harris	Thomas Vaughan
John Bradshaw & Jobe Cane	widow Vickers	Christopher Goodhand	John Lawes
Richard Arrington, Jr.	Henry Ayler	William Camper	William Allen
Hannah Badson	Col. Perce	William Porter	Thomas Powers
Francis Anderson	William Hodges	William Prison	Henry Jones
Mathew Smith	Richard Arrington, Sr.	Robert Camper	Dennis Contey
William Scott	John Price	Michaell Earle	Lane & Clay
William Farrill	Thomas Thomson	Richard Clarke	John Evans
Ralph Fishburne	Pheby Bodwell	John Howes	John Mkey
John Richardson	William Troth	Johannes Dehoniosa	John Burden
John Lee & Ralph Elston, Jr.	Thomas Bruffe	Timothy Dunavan	Richard Dudley
Henry Wharton, Sr.	Peter Poley	Hinish Robinson (?)	James Laulten
Timothy Calves	John Wrightson	Clement Sayles	William Hodges
Nathaniell Grace	Robert Macklyn	William Harris	William Griffin
John Taylor	Andrew Plise	Abell Pride	John Wallsen (?)
Thomas Denman	John Wilson	Col. Peter Sayer	William Conell
Enian Williams	John Hill	Richard Carter	James Sandford
Thomas Beswicke	Garrett Dow	John Grason	Martha Robinson
Charles Wright	Lawrence Swarbeck	John Black	Robert Broadway
Isaack Saserson	James Clayland	William Evans	John Bayman
Thomas Wiler	Robert Ungell		

In the Inventories & Accounts is a list of the debts & payments for the estate of Benjamin Rosier and Edward Pye, Esq. The list is dated 28 June 1698. This list can be found in Liber 18, Folios 197-219.

Receipts

William Thompson to Col. Pye
Henry Bardy to Col. Pye
Robert Hatchyson
Thomas Burford
Richard Newman
Miles Gibson
William Booker
John Andrew
George Thoms
Richard Marshall
James Wild
Richard Newman
henry Bradley
Thomas Mattocks
Thomas Meeds
John Watken
William Bogle
Thomas Tofttan order to
    deliver to John Bowman
William Burley
Thomas Phillips
William Dent
Abraham Hooke
Thomas Orrell
William Diggs
Hugh Hamilton
Gilbert Clarke
Samuell Jefferson
Ab. Hoock
James Cullen
William Nicholas
Thomas Whichaley
James Mills
Thomas Whichaley
William Dent
Thomas Harper
Thomas Hussey
Andrew Fabister
Giles Blisard
John Talley
Gilbert Clarke
William Thompson
Giles Blizard
John Tryer
Lawrence Clay
Rand. Hinson
Col. FitzHugh
William Bushell
Thomas Orrell
William Dent
Henry Hardy
Anthony Neall
Henry Spinke
Thomas Whitchaley
William Leggs
Ralph Shaw
William Thompson
Richard Iles
Charles Brebrand
William Gore

Cornelius Maddox
George Thoms
Joseph Layton
James Mills
William Burrey
Cornelius Maddox
Charles Carroll
Thomas Whitchaley
Stephen Bayley
Thomas Mitchell
Thomas Whitchaley
Robert Thompson
Robert Sinclare
Charles Carless
William Thompson
William Barrell
Joseph Mohell (?)
William Dent
Gilbert Clarke
Thomas Richardson
Joseph Throgmorten
Thomas Mudd
William Leggs
Abraham Peters
William Tompson
Thomas Whitchaley
Gilbert Clarke
Phillip Fleacher
John Cornish
John Taylor
Edward Greenhath
Richard Helling
Marke Lampson
Patrick Innis
James Browne
William Wells
Robert Linten
Richard Hill
Thomas Whitchayley
an entry in what looks like
    Greek (Ed.)
James Bouling
Joshua Glover
Robert Yates
Cornelius Maddox
Abraham Gosly
Joseph Ungle
George Groves
John Dickman
George Thoms
Francis Harrison
Henry Hardy
Thomas Whichaley
John Gotwick
Thomas Pope
William Roe
Edward Lundell
Gilbert Clarke
Edward Grundy
Thomas Orrell

Charles Evans
Ignatius Wheeler
Richard Bankes
Stephen Mankin
Robert Thompson
Thomas Thompson
Henry Hardy
William Barrell
Anthony Neale
John Flanning
William Thompson
Archibald Ferguson
Isaack Jackson
Margarett Robins
Thomas Black
Charles Evans
George Lat
Ralph Shaw
William Stone
Gilbert Clarke
John Sanders
Phillip Hoskins
John Ellis
Francis Smith
William Thompson
Abram Bashfeild
William Tompson
Robert Thompson
William Nicholay
Sarah Swine
Edward Maddocks
Henry Martin
Thomas Orrell
Gilbert Clarke
John Ellis
William Diggs
William Nickoles
John Wilder
Thomas Hewtt
James Kingburry
John Flagwell
Thomas Orrell
Thomas Walmoth
James Semme
Charles Evans
Dennis Doyne
Thomas Clarke
Robert Thompson
George Combes
Robert Yates
Charles Porter
Henry Hardy
Thomas Whitchaley
William Dent
William Goodhouse
Ignatius Causeen
Phillip Clark
William Dent
George Thoms

John Bannister
Giles Blyzard
Benjamin Chew
William Diggs
Benjamin Chew
William Thompson
James Ewall
Randall Henson (?)
Elias Dolman
Thomas Jones
Richard Tregcan
Jacob Lewin
Gilbert Clarke
John Witch
Richard Tregcan
Jonathon Parkes
Stephen Bryan
Abraham Basford
Bartholomew Hooker
Thomas Whitchaley
John Newman
Henry Hardy
Arthur Garrett
Thomas Burford
Henry Bardy
John Anderson
Arthur Garrett
Edward Roockwood
WIlliam Simpson
Phillip Line
William Herbert
Robert Taylor
John Ellis
Walter Livrey
William Hall
Benjamin Chew
George Stanton
John Wincoln
Thomas Mattocks
Benjamin Chew
Charles Evans
Arthur Garrett
Arther Chew
Thomas Orrell
Arthur Garrett
Cornelius Mattocks
Thomas Askwick
John Wincolne
Stephen Mankin
William Tompson
John Galley
Benjamin Chew
Thomas Smoote
Henry Hardy
Cornelius Maddocks
Thomas Orrell
Henry Hawkins
Richard Henson
John Gallwick

Accompts

Walter Storey
John Cornwally
John Banks
George Comes
Col. Talbott
Mr. Hunter
Col. Pye
Roger Tayler
Hoockes
Col. Pye
Luke Gardiner
Clackson
Col. Pye
Nicholas Lowe
Col. Pye
William Dent
Charles Braband
Hamford
Col. Pye
Nicholas Lowe

Col. Pye
James Miller
Col. Pye
Thomas Burford
James Smallwood
Gilbert Clarke
John Wincolne
Col. Pye
Miles Gibson
William Hunter
Col. Chandler
Thomas Burford
Thomas Reynolds
John Cooper
William Blankington
Col. Pye
Sarpson Clarke
Col. Pye
Thomas Askwick
Josias Jenkins

Col. Pye
Capt. Burtray
Mashew Nicholas
Col. Pye
Rand. Henson
Col. Pye
Thomas Ellwayes
William Coursey
Thomas Phillips
Col. Pye
William Tompson
Col. Pye
John Betts
Giles Blyzard
Cornelius Buttwell
George Plater
George Thoms
John Wathen
Dr. Bourre
Col. Pye

Nicholas Lowe
Phillip Lynes
Henry Bradley
Capt. Watts
Col. Pye
William Chandler
John Cooper
John Bratcher
John Knitt
William Blankenstone
John Cooper
Col. Pye
Henry Mills
George Brent
Thomas Smith
------ Cooper
------ Ratclyff
Samuell Lockett
Col. Pye
Mary Griggs

George Plater   David Arbuthnott

Bill and Property belonging to estate of Col. Benjamin Roser

Dr. John Lemaire	Mickell Webb	Robert Goodrick	George Powell
John Gourley	George Athey	John Faulkner	Robert Goodrick
John Price	John Owens	Robert Thompson	Francis Evererd
John Bracher	James Rumsey	George Shenston	William Taylor
Robert Goodrick	William Lewis	Ja. Munkester	Thomas Chambers
Robert Massey	John Martin	Charles Cullises	Mathew Sanders
Thomas Jenkins	Thomas Beamond	John Flanning	Hugh French
John Cox	Edward Powell	Thomas OBryan	Kenelm Maglucklin
John Boyce	Thomas Helgar	Edmond Dennis	John Cornish
Thomas Bryant	Robert Sampson bill to Robert	John Lemare	John Miller
John Sheppard	Price	Francis Kilburne	Phillip Lines
William Taylor	Henry Exon	Thomas Witters	Charles Russell to John
John Owins	Richard Wright	Richard Clouters	Baylock

Letters relating to estate of Col. Pye

Mrs. Penellope Cornwallis	Mr. Nicholas Lowe	Mr. Samuell Groome	Mr. Nicholas Lowe to Col.
Mr. John Cornealius	Lord Baltimore	Mr. William Hickock	Rosier
Mr. Stephen Fondrick	Mr. Benjamin Whitchcott	Miles Gibson	Mr. Henry Meefe (?) to Col.
Mr. John Cooper	Col. George Talbott	Ann Burford	Rosier
Lord Baltimore	Col. Phillip Lightfoot	Mr. John Lancaster	Mr. Henry Meefe (?) to Col.
Mr. John Cooper	Lord Baltimore	Mr. David Arbuthnott	Rosier
Mr. Nicholas Lowe	Col. George Talbott	Lord Baltimore	Mrs. Penelope Cornwallis to
Mr. John Cooper	Lord Baltimore	Miles Gibson	Col. Rosier
Mr. John Lancaster	Mr. Phillip Lines	Mr. Benjamin Whitchcott	Mr. Nicholas Lowe to Col.
Col. George Talbott	Mr. Francis Pennington	Mr. Benjamin Whitchcott on	Rosier
Mr. Samuell Groome	Mr. Nicholas Lowe	account of sales from Mr.	Mr. Benjamin Whitchcott to
Mr. Benjamin Whitchcott	Mr. Samuell Groome	Lowe Lowe	Col. and Madam Ann Rosier
Mr. John Cooper	Mr. Thomas Dougan	Mr. Benjamin Whitchcott to	Col. Diggs to Mr. Nicholas
Mrs. Penelope Cornwallis	Col. Phillip Lightfoot	Mr. Rosier	Lowe
Mr. John Cooper	Mr. Robert Chaplin	Mr. Benjamin Whitchcott to	Mr. Fendrick
Mr. Henry Coursey	Col. George Talbott	Col. Rosier	Samuell Groome
Lady Baltimore	Mrs. Mary Butler	Mr. Benjamin Whitchcott	Mr. Benjamin Whitchcott
Mr. Benjamin Whitchcott	Mr. Robert Chaplin	Mr. Benjamin Whitchcott to	Mr. Robert Chaplin
Mr. Thomas Mackary	Col. William Diggs	Col. Rosier	Mr. John Cooper

from Col. Edward Pye

Mr. Samuell Groome	Lord Baltimore	James Jonsarf	John Cooper
Mr. William Hiccock	Mr. Samuell Groome	Mr. Nicholas	William Hiccock
William Griffin	Mr. Thomas Toft	Mr. Samuell Groome	Mr. Robert Chaplin
Mr. Nicholas Lowe	Lord Baltimore	Mr. Thomas Toft	Mr. John Cooper
Mr. Stephen Fendrick	Mr. Nicholas Lowe	Capt. William Whittington	Mrs. Penellopy Cornwallis
Mr. Benjamin Whitchcott	Mr. William Hiccock	Lord Baltimore	Lord Baltimore
Mr. John Cooper	Lord Baltimore	Mr. Miles Gibson	Mr. William Hiccock
Lord Baltimore	Mr. Henry Payne	Lord Baltimore	Mr. Thomas Toft
Mr. Cooper	Lord Baltimore		

Receipts pertaining to estate of Col. Rosier

Daniell Jennifer	Josep Boulett	Humphrey Warren	Henry Hawkins
Peter Sayer	John Hartwell	Mr. Edwards	James Eddennard
Joseph Pile	John Lunbray	Jacob Petterson	Kenelm Magclacklen
Francis Swinfen	Henry Hardy	James Winnard	Robert Massey
Henry Moore	Robert Thompson	Henry Hawkins	Thomas Wheeler
Jacob Peterson	Lord Baltimore	Elisabeth Green	John Lamare
Richard Wade	Arthur Taylor	Edward Dennis	

Papers returned by Jacob Peterson

Walter Jones	John Hamsteed	John Beale	William Merrill
Thomas Bradshaw	Robert Harman	John Smith	Alexander Gallant
John Crow	Robert Kadder	John Water	Col. Rosier
Allexander Gallant	Robert Criffett	Jacob Brewington	Col. Pye
Lewis Foster			

Receipts to Col. Rosier

John England	Lord Baltimore	Joseph Eason	John England
Archibald Vauhop	Barbary Crason	William Hawson	Charles Calvert

Papers concerning Mathew Paine

Col. Rosier	Col. Paine	Edmond Paine	Col. Rosier
Mathew Paine	Col. Rosier	Col. Rosier to Mathew Paine	Col. Pye to Mathew Paine
John Faning	Mathew Paine to Col. Pye	Mathew Paine	Col. Pye per Edmond Paine

Papers relating to Land

Madam Cornwallis indenture to	Madam Cornwallis indenture to	bond from ------	Thomas Cornwallis
Col. Pye	Col. Pye	Hollingsworth to ------	Thomas Ekins
Thomas Cornwallis indenture	Thomas Cornwallis to ------	Cornwallis	John CryCroft
to William Hollingsworth	Hollingsworth	Madam Cornwallis to Col. Pye	

Letters

John Knite	Col. Pye	Dennis Husenles	William Bourman

Page 61

William Dent   John Lambeth   William Ball   Capt. Hill
John Powell   John Martin   Col. Pye   James Brames
Col. Pye   John Lamaster

Several Bills and Bonds to Various Persons

bond of Col. Rosier and Mathew Paine

bond of Col. Rosier to Mrs. Penelope Cornwallis

Capt. William Nicholas to Col. Edward Pye

Col. Pye to Mr. George Plater

Col. Pye to David Jones of Baltimore County

William Nicholas to Col. Pye

Cleborne Lomax to Roger Foukes

Col. Pye bill of lading on John Harris to Benjamin Whitchcott

Cornelius Johnson to Robert Goodrig

Col Pye to Thomas Windrum

William Nicholas and Mathew Nicholas to Col. Pye assigned to Mr. Nicholas Lowe

Col. Pye bill of lading on Samuell Groome payable to Mr. George Plater

Mr. John Beanes to Mr. Thomas Hussey

Mr. James Neale to Mr. Samuell Brett

Col. Pye to George Slade

James Lee to Capt. John Allexander

Mr. Thomas Clipsam to Mr. Henry Bonner

Mathew Nicholas and William Nicholas to Col. Pye for Mr. William Hollingsworth bill to Thomas Cornwallis, Esq.

Kenelm Magloglin to Caleb Bickford assigned to Richard Roberts

Garrett Sinnett to William Wells

Richard Price to Caleb Megloglin assigned to Col. Rozier

Henry Johnson to Col. Edward Pye (executor of Col. Benjamin Rozier)

Lawrence Young to Col.

Edward Pye

Christopher Kirkley to John Butcher

Thomas Russell to Elisabeth Drechath (?)

Mr. Benjamin Rosier to Mr. Benjamin Whitchcot

Mr. John Lewellin to Edin Dennis

Col. Pye to Mr. James Cullens (executor of Marke Cordea) assigned James Browne and from him to John Toules

Col. Edward Pye to Edward Sweatnam

Thomas Craxon to James Cox

Col. Pye to Mr. Samuell Groome

James Wheeler to John Lemaire

John Faulkner to John Wood

Charles Evanes to Col. Edward Pye

Mr. Thomas Rosier to Col. Pye

John Cable to Richard Chandler

Robert Goodrick and William Standover to Francis Heyden

Col. Pye to Francis Butterey,

Col. Pye to Cornelius Maddocks

Ambross bill to William Wells

Mr. Phillip Lines his obligation to Col. Pye and Col. Talbott

Capt. George Thoms to Col. Pye

Thomas Kersey to Col. Pye

William Stockes to Christopher Wheeler

Mr. ------ Pires (?) to William Barrett

Col. Pye and John Wathens to Mr. Abraham Hooke

Ambross Bayley to Mr. Thomas Hussey

Mr. John Cornwallis to Col. Pye

Other Papers

Mr. Stephen Kendrick per Mr. Hiccock

Capt. Mathew Paine

Mr. Thomas Evins per account

between Col. Diggs and

Col. Pye

Companies
  Abraham Wild & Co. 43
  Capt. Abraham Wilde &
    Co. 24
  Capt. Peter Pagan & Co.
    23
  Choptico Indians 26
  Dean Cock & Co. 27
  Edward Carlton & Co. 27,
    44
  George Lapthorne & Co.
    46
  Jacob Mooreland & Co. 32
  John Helm & Co. 19
  John Jackson & Co. 48
  John Marth & Co. 37
  John Rock & Co. 45
  Joseph Jackson & Co. 30
  Micajah Perry & Co. 9,
    33, 34
  Paggan & Co. 42, 43
  Paggen & Co. 45
  Peter Pagan & Co. 30
  Peter Paggan & Co. 21,
    30, 37
  Peter Paggen & Co. 14
  Province of Maryland 24
  Richard Bell & Co. 45
  Robert Grason & Co. 27
  Thomas Harman & Co. 11
  Timothy Keysey & Co. 32
  Vestry of All Faith's
    Parish 3
  William Lurtin & Co. 28

Aaeron
  William 47
Abbot
  Samuell 19
Abbott
  William 28
Abell
  Anne 12
  Samuell 12
Abington
  John 17, 38
Abinton
  Andrew 41
Able
  Ann 2
Abrahams
  Elisabeth 11
  Isaac 11
  Jacob 11
Adams
  Elisha 23
  Francis 22, 31
  Grace 31
  James 39
  Peter 19
Adaneron
  Nehemiah 23
Adcock
  Henry 6
Addams
  Charles 30
Addison
  John 16, 27
  Joseph 8
  William 25
Adesley
  Henry 28
Affotts
  William 35
Agambre

Domingo 15
Aisquith
  William 22, 24, 29, 30,
    39
Aketh
  George 13
Alcock
  Thomas 6
Alderne
  William 41
Aldred
  Mary 2
Aldridge
  Henry 8
  Mary 8
  Nicholas 24
Alexander
  Fran. 49
Allen
  George 23, 27
  John 18, 31
  Phillip 22
  Thomas 47
  William Phillip 7
  Zachariah 11
Allerd
  John 25
Allexander
  Frances 6
Allford
  Mathias 50
  Matthyes 8
Allion
  Richard 29
Allison
  Charles 16
Anderson
  Andrew 35
  Francis 11
  Mary 11
  Nathaniel 46
  Nathaniell 35
  Rebecca 11
  Thomas 6, 11
  William 6, 18, 36
Anderton
  Francis 38
Andrew
  ------ 16
Andrews
  George 42
Anlley
  Capt. 3
Arackson
  Mathew 20
Archer
  Ambrose 43
Ares
  Eleannor 42
Arey
  David 12
  Jon 12
Armiger
  Daniell 22
Armstrong
  Edward 21, 48
  John 40
Arnall
  Thomas 36
Arnatt
  Benjamin 23
Arnol
  Col. 28
Arnold
  Benjamin 5
  Thomas 36

Arrington
  Cornelius 8
Arrundell
  Cornelius 29
  William 26
Arterby
  Thomas 21
Ashcombe
  Mary 37
Ashford
  Michael 39
  Michaell 22
Ashman
  Ann 16
  George 35, 45
  Richard 15, 16
  Thomas 32
Ashton
  Charles 15
  Robert 11
Askew
  Elisabeth 37
  Michaell 22, 37
  Richard 46
Askey
  John 37
Askin
  John 37
Askins
  John 18
  Richard 46
Astin
  John 17
Atchyson
  William 22
Atkison
  John 36
Attaway
  John 9
  Thomas 2
Atterbery
  Joan 49
  Thomas 48, 49
Atterbury
  Thomas 48
Attkins
  John 14
Attwood
  Richard 4, 12
Atwood
  John 41
Austin
  Richard 47
  Samuell 9

Badcock
  James 2, 15
Baddy
  Roger 6, 11
Badger
  Thomas 42
Bagg
  Mary 36
  Thomas 36
Bain
  Samuell 46
Baine
  John 25
Baker
  Isack 34
  James 15, 17
  Jane 14
  John 32
  Joseph 21
  Maurice 9

Morris 46
Samuell 30, 35
Thomas 3, 9, 21, 44
Baldwin
John 9, 34
Baldwyn
John 33, 45
Bale
Thomas 9
Ball
Edward 21, 22, 37, 44
John 36
Pricilla 37
Ballard
Charles 32
Baltimore
Lord 11
Baly
Richard 2, 5
Bambrick
Stephen 22
Bane
Capt. 25
Christopher 3
Banester
John 16
Bankes
Richard 28
Banks
Nicolas 41
Bannester
John 1
Bannister
Francis 44
William 13
Barber
James 16
Newman 21
William 23
Barbott
James 8
Bardo
William 3
Bareorgh
------ 36
Barker
------ 14
John 1
Mary 14, 32
Richard 28, 49
Roger 4
Thomas 13, 32
William 43
Barlow
Jeffery 6
Barnard
William 28
Barnes
Henry 18
Math. 16
Mathew 18, 43
Matthew 39
Barnet
Thomas 29
Barnett
Peter 24
Thomas 5
Barns
Job. 2
Mathew 44
Barracklough
Jeremiah 49
Barrett
John 3, 39
Barron
John 22
Barrop
Miles 26
Barrow
Thomas 1

Bartlett
John 11
Sarah 11
Barton
Maj. 3
William 2, 15, 23, 32, 35
Basboury
Edward 36
Basell
Ralph 5
Bass
Charles 9, 10, 11, 28, 49
Bateman
Christopher 21, 48
Bathurst
Edward 9
Batson
Edward 17, 32, 41
Battee
John 48
Battes
William 34
Battson
Edward 20
Batty
John 4
Baxter
Roger 35
Thomas 35
Bayard
Col. 11
Bayle
John 12
Bayley
Chr. 24
John 32
Margarett 25
Richard 28
Robert 25
Bayly
Richard 3
Robert 2
William 10
Baylye
Richard 2
Baynard
John 6, 11
Bayne
Christopher 7
John 6, 11, 23, 25, 31, 42, 44, 49
Baynes
John 27
Bays
John 33
Beach
Elias 2
Thomas 13
Beacher
John 24
Beachum
James 49
Beade
Nicholas 2
Beadle
Edward 38
Beal
Alexander 49
Beale
Alexander 48
Col. 3, 7
James 35, 48
Thomas 5, 25
Beall
Ninian 26, 27
Thomas 11, 27
Bealman
Christopher 27

Bean
Charles 47
Beane
John 25
BearCroft
John 15
Beard
Richard 24, 34, 39, 45
Beauman
Richard 3
Beaumount
Richard 7
Beaven
Charles 1
Beck
William 30
Becke
Edward 36
Becker
Edward 49
Beckles
Thomas 6
Beech
Elias 25
Beecher
John 43, 45
Bell
Daniell 13
Robert 10
William 45
Bellamie
Nicho. 15
Bellamy
Mathew 14, 17, 20
Bellman
Peter 16
Benger
Robert 46, 49
Bennet
John 34
Bennett
Edward 4
Elisabeth 24
John 11, 24, 25, 45, 48
Richard 11, 20, 27, 41, 43
Thomas 40
Benson
Dr. 11
James 11, 34
Robert 23, 31
Stephen 29
Benton
Elly 35
Richard 5, 12
William 30
Berry
Benjamin 39
Joseph 36
Naiomy 12
Richard 2
William 6, 39
Bery
George 42
Bess
Stephen 19
Beston
George 28
Betson
Christopher 29
Betts
George 18
Robert 6
Bettson
Christopher 19
Betty
Arthur 2
Bevan
Charles 47
Beven

Charles 1
Bevin
   Charles 28
Bexley
   William 40
Bickosleth
   William 47
Biddott
   William 9
Bigger
   James 13
   John 14, 15, 17, 26, 30,
     36
Biggs
   Robert 17
Bile
   James 22
Billary
   Francis 1
Billingsly
   ------ 7
   Thomas 7
Bird
   Abraham 22, 44
   George 2
Biscoe
   Phillip 42
Bishop
   Anne 6
   James 6
   Robert 6
   Roger 4, 5
   William 6
Bison
   Thomas 22
   William 23
Bittingham
   William 4
Biven
   John 30
Blackader
   Thomas 10
Blackbourne
   Edward 23
Blackister
   John 35
Blackiston
   Col. 4, 42
   Nehemia 36
   Nehemiah 24, 26, 27
Blacklock
   Robert 34
Blackman
   Thomas 32, 46
Blackmore
   John 9
Blackstone
   ------ 4
Blackwell
   Thomas 15, 30, 31, 33,
     34, 45
Bladen
   W. 25
   William 29, 36, 38
Blades
   Robert 39
   William 24
Blak
   John 6
Blake
   Charles 10, 43
   Thomas 24, 26, 29
Blakeston
   Nehemiah 23
Blakiston
   Col. 7, 17
   Ebenezar 44, 49
   Elisabeth 25, 29
   Nehemiah 26, 29
Bland

Thomas 6
Blaney
   Da. 33
   David 40
Blanford
   Thomas 8
Blany
   Danid 20
Blatchfoord
   Stephen 5
Blay
   Edward 9
Blinkhorne
   Robert 21
Blumfeild
   Elisabeth 12
Blunt
   Robert 27
Boarman
   William 16, 18
Boder
   John 16
Bodkin
   Peter 6
Bohary
   Francis 1
Bole
   David 21
Bond
   Benjamin 20, 32
Bonner
   Henry 2, 20, 24, 34, 43
Booker
   John 1, 2
   Thomas 3, 6
Boon
   John 40
Boone
   Humfrey 34, 45
   Humfry 17
   Humphrey 28, 32
   Humphry 3, 22, 40
   Jane 11
   John 11, 30
Boorman
   William 44
Booth
   Barett 23
   John 14, 18
Boothby
   Edward 14, 17
   Mr. 7, 23, 40
Boreman
   William 25, 34, 36, 49
Bornham
   Joseph 9
Boson
   ------ 16
Boston
   Henry 12
Boswell
   William 3, 24
Boteler
   Henry 36, 49
Boudle
   Phoebe 29
   Thomas 27, 29
Boughton
   Richard 25, 42
Boules
   James 16
   John 16
Bouling
   James 25
Boullon
   William 6
Bournam
   William 15
Bourne
   ------ 27

Elisabeth 7
   Madam 26
   Samuell 7
Bouton
   Sarah 25
Bouye
   John 8
Bowden
   Richard 9
Bowe
   Francis 42
Bowen
   Ann 44
   Jonas 35, 45, 49
   Martha 49
   widow 22
Bower
   Francis 46
Bowles
   Anthony 34
   John 39
Bowling
   John 18
   Thomas 31
Box
   Thomas 20, 48
Boy
   Jennett 23
   John 23
Boyce
   Cornelius 30
Boyden
   William 15
Boye
   John 26
Braban
   William 48
Braborne
   William 7
Bradbury
   William 7
Bradhurst
   ------ 48
   John 48
Bradley
   Isaack 37
   Robert 19, 20, 38
   William 30, 44
Bradly
   R. 42
   Robert 48
Braine
   James 9
Brame
   Benjamin 32
Bran
   widow 49
Brand
   Randolph 31
Brandt
   Rando. 15
   Randolph 44
Brannocke
   Cornelius 5
Brasseur
   John 5
Brawner
   Henry 22, 31
   Mary 31
Bray
   Peirce 18
Brayday
   William 12
Brazia
   John 17
Brecher
   Mr. 26
Breed
   William 23
Brent

George 25
Henry 20, 36, 37
Brett
George 22, 23
Joan 35
Brewer
John 23
Brice
Henry 31
John 45
Brickenden
Thomas 49
Bridge
Josias 30
Thomas 28
Bridges
Josias 29
Brigell
Thomas 28
Briggs
John 6
Bright
Richard 30
Brightwell
Richard 48
Brill
John 25
Brimmer
Elisabeth 12
James 12
Brinn
John 39
Brinnard
John 39
Briscoe
James 46
Mr. 25
Britt
George 34
John 2
Britte
John 2
Brittingham
William 7
Broad
John 44
Broadaway
Robert 40
Broadhurst
John 2, 7
Broadway
Robert 10, 43
Brockson
Bridget 28
Elisabeth 8
John 28
William 8
Brodaway
Robert 6
Samuell 6
Brood
John 45
Brook
Baker 1
James 48
Roger 25
Thomas 42
Brookbanke
Abraham 12
Brooke
Baker 37
Charles 22
Katherine 12
Brookes
John 15, 24
Brooks
Charles 5
Brothers
Robert 2, 48
Brown

Abell 34
Ann 1
Col. 47
Daniel 48
David 19
Edward 32, 44
Peregrine 46
Samuell 17, 46
William 6, 42, 45
Browne
Abel 34
Abell 27, 28
David 5, 14
James 7, 17, 25, 29, 30
John 20, 30
Sam 38
Thomas 17, 25, 28
Brownwey
John 41
Bruce
George 24, 30
Bruff
Richard 6
Thomas 4, 6, 10, 29
Bruice
George 43
Brumball
Anthony 29
Brumell
Robert 5
Brunnon
Cornelius 30
Bryant
Lidy 11
Buckmaster
Daniell 22, 36
Buford
Hezekiah 42
Bull
William 4
Burbett
Nehemiah 5
Burch
George 25
Burd
John 3, 21
Burdage
John 4
Burdin
Stephen 12
Burditt
Parthenia 1
Burfford
Edward 9
Burford
Thomas 1
Burges
Ann 24
Edward 20, 23
George 23, 24
William 9, 23, 24
Burgess
Edward 24
George 24, 43, 49
Mary 7
William 3, 38
Burgis
William 33
Burkett
Patience 25
Richard 1, 25
Burkhead
Abraham 2
Burnham
John 6
Burrell
Patience 25
Burrey
Dr. 38
Burrill

John 10
Burroughs
B. 15
John 13
Burt
Henry 47
Bussell
John 5
Bussey
Hezekiah 36
Buswell
John 28
Butcher
John 15
Butler
------ 4
Cecill 37
Edward 48
James 12
Butteras
Thomas 45
Butterworth
Michaell 29
Buttery
Francis 22, 23, 31
Buttler
Edward 26
Button
Nathaniell 15
Butwell
Cornelius 5
Byars
William 2

Cacill
Joseph 36
Cade
Robert 4, 6
Cadle
Zachariah 8, 39
Caldwell
James 14
Calvert
Jane 23
Madam 23
Cambell
Alexander 28
Walter 27
Cambridge
Oliver 2
Campbell
Alexander 4
Walter 1, 8, 45
Camper
Thomas 6
Camwell
Arthur 7
Canin
Patrick 38
Cannady
Michaell 30
Canning
Daniell 42
Cannon
James 28, 38
William 16
Cape
John 6
Caple
Benjamin 23
Capling
James 46
Carbery
John Batt. 46
Mr. 29
Carelson
------ 48
Carless
Charles 32

Carleton
  Dudley 33
  Edward 33
Carlton
  ------ 48
Carpent
  Henry 19
Carpenter
  William 10
Carr
  Walter 23, 41
  William 11
Carroll
  Charles 7, 21, 23, 26,
    33
  Mr. 6
Carsey
  William 33
Carter
  John 6
  Richard 10, 11, 45
  Valentine 26
  William 36
Carver
  John 11
Carvile
  John 9
  Mr. 16
  Robert 7, 11, 17, 24
Carvill
  John 36
  Mr. 46
  Robert 49
Carvort
  William 35
Caswell
  Robert 6
Catrop
  William 1
Catterson
  widow 11
Cattnell
  Benjamin 35
Cave
  John 29
Caves
  John 29
Cavinar
  John 47
Cecill
  Joshua 3, 5, 7, 17, 37,
    38
Cesar
  John 42
Chadburne
  Amos 16
Chaffee
  Richard 33
Chaiers
  John 10
Chaine
  Samuell 30
Chamberlain
  Samuell 13, 46
Chamberlaine
  Samuell 42
Chambers
  Richard 14, 34
Chandler
  John 2
  Richard 1
  Thomas 20
  William 22
Chantery
  Joseph 46
Chapell
  Alexander 44
  Henry 17
Chaplin
  Fra. 47

Chapman
  Edward 23
  John 19
  Thomas 31, 44
Chappell
  Allexander 20, 39, 41
  Dr. 2
  John 17, 20, 34, 42
Charbott
  James 28
Charles
  Richard 7
Charlett
  Richard 4, 27
Cheiffers
  James 6
Cheney
  Richard 23, 24
Cheseldyn
  Kenelm 8, 24, 28, 47
  Mr. 7
Cheseldyne
  Esq. 5
  Kenelm 7, 9
  Kenelme 9, 49
  Mr. 17
Chesher
  Richard 9
Chesledyne
  Kenelm 41, 42
Chessam
  Ann 25
Chesum
  William 2
Chew
  Benjamin 41
  Samuell 26, 34
  William 2
Childe
  Abraham 24
Chillcott
  Anthony 38
Chirne
  William 30
Chiseldyne
  Mr. 46
Chittam
  Francis 40
  John 1
Chittum
  John 1
Chubb
  Ed. 39
Chumble
  Fra. 15
Chyney
  Charles 27
Chysledyne
  Kenelm 41
Cissell
  Thomas 46
Cittor
  Theophilus 3
Cladge
  John 42
Claget
  Capt. 7
Clagett
  Thomas 20
Clarber
  Frances 39
Clark
  Abra. 15
  Abraham 48
  Andrew 18
  Edward 13
  Gilbert 7
  Peter 10
  Philip 49
  Phillip 17

  Thomas 7, 49
  William 6
Clarke
  Abraham 20
  Daniell 8, 28
  Gilbert 1, 3, 7, 25
  John 15, 22
  Mathew 20
  Mathias 26
  Philip 5
  Phillip 17, 21, 23, 25
  Richard 29
  Ro. 13
  Robert 3, 24, 31, 32, 37
  Thomas 5, 25
  William 28
Clayland
  James 41, 47
  Mr. 45
Clayton
  William 11, 40, 41
Cleggett
  Capt. 24
Clemence
  Rebecca 11
Clemens
  Thomas 40
Clement
  John 1, 15, 25, 43
Clements
  John 15
  Thomas 6
Clerk
  John 44
Clifton
  Johnathon 38
Clio
  Mary 33
Clouds
  Nicholas 10, 16
  Richard 24, 38, 46
Coale
  George 8
  John 14
  William 17
Coall
  John 14
Cobb
  James 7, 17
Cobreth
  Aron 15
Cobroth
  John 2
Cock
  Dean 34, 45
Cocke
  Sarah 8
Cocknell
  Edward 2
Cofer
  Thomas 44
Coffer
  Francis 44
  Thomas 18
Colbourne
  William 46
Cole
  Edward 5, 22, 25
  George 8, 21, 39, 44,
    47, 49
  John 39
  Nicholas 12
  Peter 28
  Thomas 25
  William 24, 26
Colegate
  Mr. 30
  Richard 45, 49
Colestack
  Edward 11

Colle
    John 2
Colleson
    Elisabeth 38
    John 38
Collier
    Alice 9
    Francis 20
    Robert 14
    Thomas 21, 27
Collings
    Edward 40
Collington
    Edward 38
Collman
    Benjamin 14
    Jos. 18
    Stephen 5
Collyer
    Francis 27
    Sarah 27
Comber
    John 33
Combes
    Edward 36
    William 24
Comebes
    William 12
Comegys
    Cornelius 16
Comes
    Enoch 24
    Richard 42
Compton
    Mary 21
    William 41
Conant
    John 26
    Robert 23
Connell
    James 42
Conner
    John 32
    Phillip 24
Connill
    Daniell 19
Connoway
    Joseph 21, 24, 25
Constable
    Katherine 22
    Mrs. 3
    Samuell 17
Contee
    John 44
Conworth
    Michael 45
Cood
    John 2
Cook
    Charles 49
Cooke
    John 16
    Morgan 17
    Thomas 12, 13
    William 38
Cooksey
    Phillip 6
    Sarah 6, 16
Cooley
    John 25
Coomes
    Robert 13
Cooney
    John 25
Cooper
    Joseph 15
    Nathaniell 2
    Robert 8, 27, 40
    Thomas 2
    William 7

Coopis
    John 46
Copedge
    John 8, 11
    Mary 11
    Phill. 8
Coper
    Gabriell 4
Copin
    John 29
Coppedge
    John 7
Cord
    Thomas 45
Corey
    John 39
Cormack
    Dennis 9
Cornelius
    John 27, 48
Cornish
    George 23
    John 7, 23, 26
    Martha 23
Cornwell
    Charles 25
    Thomas 17
Corrigan
    Dr. 19
Cosden
    Ann 47
Cosens
    Mary 46
Cossens
    John 46
Costin
    Comfort 4
    Stephen 4
Cotter
    William 43
Cottman
    Benjamin 38, 43
Cougley
    William 28
Coulbourne
    William 14
Councill
    Dennis 10
Counell
    Daniell 32
Courett
    James 31
Coursey
    Col. 41
    Henry 10
    William 10, 17, 29, 41
Courts
    John 42
Cousens
    John 2
Cousin
    George 28
Couth
    Thomas 49
Coventry
    William 5, 41
Covington
    Nehemiah 32
Cowes
    Richard 39
Cowley
    Bryan 29
Cowly
    John 13
Cows
    George 38
Cox
    Daniell 26
    Henry 8
    John 49

Coxen
    John William 46
Cozens
    John 9
Crabb
    Thomas 32, 37
Crackson
    John 25
Cracraaft
    John 3
Cracraft
    Ignatius 3, 4
Crandell
    Francis 35
Cranford 17
    Inmet 47
    James 2, 3, 7, 17, 37,
        49
    John 23
    Martha 30
    Nathan 30
    Nathaniell 21
Cranson
    Thomas 41
Craxon
    Thomas 1, 23, 31
Craxson
    Thomas 1
Craycroft
    Mr. 24
Creugh
    ------ 49
Crew
    Edward 9
Crewest
    Thomas 49
Crook
    Robert 49
Crooke
    James 4, 12, 13, 32
    John 12, 13, 37
    Mr. 1, 21
    Sarah 12
Cross
    John 37
Crouch
    Mary 9
Crumton
    Francis 35
Cullaine
    Thomas 43
Cullen
    James 30
Curry
    John 5
Curtis
    John 11
    Martin 6
    Mr. 29
    William 6
Cuson
    Isaack 30
Cussine
    Ignatius 4
Cutter
    John 29
Cuttler
    Gervas 8
Cæcill
    Joshua 5

Dacres
    William 12
Dail
    Thomas 1
Daish
    John 12
Daney
    Daniell 30

Daniell
    Christopher 21
Danielson
    Daniell 48
Danily
    Patrick 50
Danvas
    Thomas 8
Darbin
    Thomas 46
Dare
    Nathan 7
    Nathaniell 20, 26
Darnall
    Col. 6, 19, 23, 24, 37,
        48
    Henry 19, 25
    Mary 19
Dart
    Charles 13
Dasheill
    Ja. 32
    Thomas 32
Dashield
    Thomas 19
Dashiell
    George 14
    James 14
    Robert 14
    Thomas 14, 18
Davenish
    Robert 32
Daviden
    John 11
Davies
    Dr. 47
    John 45
Davis
    Andrew 6
    Clement 38
    Dr. 33, 43
    Griffith 39
    Henry 19, 33
    John 1, 4, 6, 11, 13,
        17, 19, 33, 41
    Mary 1, 4
    Morris 23
    Phillip 16
    Richard 19
    Thomas 1, 23
Davison
    Patrick 9, 30
Daviss
    John 2
    Thomas 2
Davy
    James 6
Dawkins
    James 17, 48
    John 49
    Joseph 48
    William 5, 23
Dawson
    Edward 8
    John 10, 20, 41
    Ralph 27
Day
    Edward 35
    Humphrey 30
    Nicholas 40
    Robert 20
    William 43
Deable
    Jeremiah 9
Deakens
    John 47
Deakins
    Thomas 21
Deal
    William 37

Dean
    Elisabeth 50
    William 39, 50
Deane
    Michaell 6
Deau
    David 10
Deaver
    John 48
Deavour
    John 2
Delahai
    George 42
    Susan 42
Delahay
    Arthur 12, 37
    George 31
    Jacob 23
    Thomas 3, 40
Delaroach
    Mrs. 15
Delaway
    Thomas 3
Delehay
    Thomas 11
Dellahide
    Graves 17
Demall
    John 19
Denner
    John 35
Denney
    Christopher 4
Dennis
    David 34
    Donock 6, 19
    Dunnock 43
Denny
    Christopher 10, 11, 17
Dent
    Maj. 7
    Mr. 29, 47
    Peter 4, 26, 32
    William 3, 7, 8, 11, 12,
        14, 20, 23, 24, 25,
        26, 28, 31, 36, 43,
        44, 47
Denton
    Edward 37
    Henry 17, 21, 23
    William 40
Denwood
    Levin 18, 32, 43
Dermot
    Charles 9
Derochbrune
    Lewis 37
DeRocheborne
    Lewis 7
Derow
    Isaac 11
Derrumple
    William 15
Derumple
    William 15, 48
Detape
    Abraham 40
Deubart
    John 49
Devall
    Maren 23
Devenish
    Robert 6
Devigh
    John 30
Devoren
    Mannus 34
Dickerson
    Edward 15
Dickingson

John 8
Dickinson
    Benjamin 42
    John 25
Dickson
    Thomas 21, 22
Diggs
    Col. 37
Dike
    Mathew 1
Dill
    Abraham 32
Dillon
    Thomas 25
Dimosa
    Alexander 30
Dinaho
    Eleanor 30
    Gillian 30
    John 30
Dine
    John 6, 47
Dinew
    Thomas 27
Disharoon
    Jone 4
    Michaell 4
Disney
    William 40
Divine
    Peter 3
Dixon
    Thomas 18, 41, 48
    William 34
Dixson
    Thomas 3
Dobbs
    John 35
Dodd
    Richard 1
Dodmund
    Thomas 40
Dodson
    John 2
Dolton
    Nathaniell 28
Don
    Robert 50
Donaldson
    John 8
Done
    Robert 19
Donellson
    Daniell 8
Dorington
    William 29
Dorman
    John 7
Doroline
    Benjamin 34
Dorrell
    Mr. 16
Dorrington
    William 1, 8
Dorsey
    Edward 34
Dorson
    John 11
Doson
    William 40
Douch
    Hugh 16
Douland
    William 32
Douse
    William 2
Dowlin
    Edward 37
Dowman
    Thomas 16

Downall
   James 3
Downes
   Francis 23
Downs
   James 10, 45
   Margarett 44
   Robert 4
Doxey
   John 18, 30
Doyne
   Dennis 16, 27
   Ethelbert 27
   Jese 21
   Joshua 16, 18, 25, 38
   Robert 5, 15
   William 27
Draper
   John 19
   Laurence 3, 49
   lawrence 24
Drew
   Anthony 35
Drewe
   Anthony 29
Drisdall
   Robert 29
Dryden
   John 6
Dubbs
   Benjamin 47
Ducker
   John 1
Duckett
   Richard 40, 42
Duckworth
   John 2, 6, 30
Dudlestone
   John 8, 24
Dudley
   Richard 6
Dueer
   David 27
Duffe
   James 45
Duglass
   Jo. 15
Duke
   James 48
Dukes
   Henry 37
Dunbar
   John 46
Dunbarr
   John 2, 25
Duncalfe
   Edmond 25
Duncells
   Richard 32
Dunevan
   Cornelius 15
Dunevas
   Cornelius 12
Dunkan
   Elisabeth 6
   James 6
Dunken
   John 3
Dunkin
   John 10
   Sarah 10
Dunnevant
   Timothy 6
Durbin
   Thomas 27
Duvall
   Mareen 27
   Merren 23
Duyer
   Edmond 15

Dyer
   Edward 11
Dyke
   Mathew 1
Dynes
   John 26

Eagle
   Robert 29, 34, 40, 45
Ealen
   William 18
Eareckson
   Mathew 10
   Matt. 35
Earle
   M. 11
   Michael 12
   Michaell 12
Eaton
   William 7
Ebden
   William 40
Eccleston
   Henry 36
   Hugh 45
   Mr. 44
Edelen
   Richard 18
Edgar
   John 6, 47
   Richard 35
Edger
   John 19
Edlin
   Richard 25
Edloe
   Joseph 7
Edmans
   Thomas 15
Edmonds
   Richard 5
Edmondson
   John 10, 11, 27, 34, 45
   Thomas 20, 38
   William 5, 11, 27, 33
Edmonson
   John 1
Edmunds
   John 47
Edmyfeild
   John 31
Edwards
   Edward 12, 44
   John 14, 24, 43
   Joseph 1, 4, 13, 14
   Thomas 24
Egerton
   Charles 25, 30, 31, 46
Elder
   William 30
Eldesly
   Henry 49
   Parnell 49
Eldor
   John 23
Eldridge
   Jeremiah 2, 36
Eldrige
   John 47
Ellet
   Daniel 48
Ellett
   Daniell 19
Elliott
   Col. 24
   Daniell 22
   William 8
Ellis
   Hugh 14, 15, 26

Elliston
   Mathew 24
   Matthias 34
Ellitt
   George 11
   William 22
Ells
   John 40
Elmes
   William 16
Elsey
   John 17, 23, 26, 48
Elvn
   William 24
Elzey
   Mr. 25
Emerson
   John 6, 11, 20, 40, 41,
      47
   Thomas 27, 33, 41, 43
Emerton
   John 40
Emery
   Arthur 6, 10
Emmes
   Capt. 1
Emmett
   John 19
Emms
   Thomas 20, 44
Emory
   Arthur 35
Ems
   Thomas 48
English
   George 46
Ennalls
   Elenor 29
   John 29
   Thomas 34
Ennis
   Ann 24
   Thomas 24
Ereckson
   Mathew 27
Erickson
   Mathew 26
Eriskin
   Mr. 4
Erner
   Nathaniell 22
Errickson
   Mathew 26
Errington
   John 11
Estall
   John 12
Esterlin
   Henry 15
Eston
   Ann 3
Eubanks
   Thomas 10
Evans
   Amos 30
   Anthony 39
   David 37
   Edward 7
   Job 23, 24, 41
   John 27, 30, 31, 40
   Nicholas 14, 33, 34
   Obadia 7
   Richard 8, 18
   Thomas 10, 29, 35
   Walter 19, 46
   William 47
Evenes
   Richard 6
Evens
   Anthony 1

Edmond 2
John 35
Richard 8
Walter 1
Everard
Thomas 23
Everett
Henry 10
Lawrence 37
Phillip 16
Eves
John 35
Ewbanks
Thomas 10
Ewebank
Richard 17
Ewings
John 29
Exon
Henry 23

Fairbrother
John 23
Fairfax
Thomas 2
Falkner
Martin 8
Fane
Augustin 27
Farfar
William 30
Farguson
Margrett 38
Robert 38
Farie
W. 17
Farmer
Samuell 10
Farr
Edward 46
Fater
George 36
Faucitt
William 6
Faulkner
John 6
Feesley
Francis 37
Feild
William 7
Feiles
William 20
Felks
Ed. 43
Fendall
Samuell 45
Fenley
James 2
Fenwick
John 1, 12, 13, 25
Fergason
Hugh 20
Fergeson
Hugh 31
Ferguson
Dr. 32
John 3
Fernely
Henry 7, 17, 37
Fernley
Henry 48
Fernly
Henry 7
Ferriell
Robert 1
Ferry
John 30, 33, 35, 40, 44
Joseph 7
Fidoe

Richard 34
Findall
Samuell 38
Fine
Simon 40
Finely
James 2
Fisbourne
William 29
Fish
Henry 2
Fishbourn
Ralph 34
Fisher
Alexander 38
Ann 37
Anne 18
John 26
Robert 15, 44
Thomas 8, 18, 37, 41
William 29
Fitzgarrett
John 36
FitzGerald
Morris 49
Fitzgerrald
Edmond 10
Edward 31
Fitzgerrett
Edward 44
Fitzsymond
Nicholas 3
Fitzsymons
Nicholas 14
Fletcher
John 24
Flewelling
Samuell 33
Floyd
David 5
John 48
Floydd
Mary 5
Flumbsteed
Mathew 27
Focitt
William 43
Follen
Andrew 6
Foorde
Christopher 1
Ford
Christopher 16
James 3, 41
John 2, 15, 41
Forde
Christopher 1
John 15
Forest
John 1
Forsler
John 10
Forubss
Alexander 29
Fossitt
John 49
Foster
Chr. 24
Edward 6
John 28
Ralph 22
Richard 1
Robert 22
William 3
Fouke
Anne 7
Fountain
Nicholas 41
Fountaine
Nicholas 21

Foutch
Hugh 28
Fowler
Charles 26
James 33
Sarah 38, 43
Fox
Henry 6
Foxen
William 4
Foxon
George 16
William 19
Foy
Andrew 24
Frampton
Francis 22, 23, 31, 41
Francis
Henry 17, 45
Howell 47
Jonathon 23
Stephen 33
Thomas 3
Franke
John 38
Franklin
Richard 9
Franklyn
Richard 16
Frayser
Alexander 50
widow 50
Freakes
John 38
Freeman
Francis 3
John 6, 33, 34, 39
Mathias 9
Mr. 36
Oliver 38
Patrick 41
Freman
William 24
French
D. 3
James 5, 13, 25, 46
Frisby
James 9, 11, 21, 49
William 39
Frith
Henry 33
Fry
John 39
Frye
Constance 49
John 49
Fucale
Peter 30
Fuillor
Edward 22
Fuley
William 45
Fulk
Harman 6
Fuller
Edward 17, 45
Furbey
Felex 16
Furley
Roger 36
Fusate
Peter 38

Gadesby
John 2
Gadsby
John 9
Gaile
John 17

Gain
  Richard 49
Gaither
  John 42
Gale
  John 41
Gallaway
  Richard 34
Gallion
  Joseph 30
Gamblin
  James 19
Gant
  Thomas 10, 27
Gardi
  John 3
Gardiner
  Ambros 7
Gardner
  Alce 25
  James 30
  Luke 25, 30
  Mathew 30
  Robert 46
Garey
  Laurence 26
  William 33
Garish
  Ann 49
Garland
  Rand. 49
  Samuell 24
Garman
  Lewis 17
Garner
  John 34
Garrett
  Amos 32, 45
  Joyce 42
  Richard 35
Garrey
  William 47
Garworth
  Richard 15
Gary
  William 47
Gassaway
  Ann 34
  John 17
  Maj. 24
  Nicholas 24, 34, 43
Gates
  Robert 4, 16
Gather
  John 30
Gawdard
  John 12, 13
Gawdred
  John 15
Gay
  Clew 29
  John 30, 40, 43
Gellett
  Walter 14
George
  Dorothy 44
  James 44
Gerrard
  John 45
Geulich
  Nicholas 46
Gibbs
  Edward 3, 5, 28, 29
Gibbson
  Robert 9
Gibson
  Elisabeth 30
  Jacob 6
  John 10
  Philip 17

Robert 9, 28
  William 10
Gilburn
  Walter 48
Gilders
  John 9
Gill
  Elisabeth 5
  John 10
  Margaret 39
  Roger 10
  William 5
Gillam
  John 13
GillCross
  Robert 35
Gillem
  John 1
Gilley
  William 21
Gillum
  John 3, 40
Gittings
  Phillip 39
Givan
  Robert 34
Glandenring
  John 6
Glanvill
  William 10
Glasly
  James 46
Glass
  James 46
  John 32
Glew
  Samuell 16
Glover
  Daniell 33, 43
  John 12
  Richard 46
  William 49
Gloves
  John 10
Goafe
  Daniell 15
Godard
  Peter 5
Godcross
  John 30
Goddard
  Elias 41
Godferry
  Charles 6
Godfrey
  George 16, 31
  John 16
Godfry
  George 22
Godin
  John 6
Godsgrace
  John 15
Godshall
  John 7, 15, 31
Goff
  Bartholomew 8
  Hannah 48
  Thomas 48
Goldsborough
  J. 2
  Mr. 36
  Robert 1
Goldsburrough
  Robert 27
Goldsmith
  Mr. 38
Gooch
  Jo. 15
Goodman

Edmond 47
  William 24, 43
Goosy
  Samuell 36
Goott
  Richard 9
Gore
  James 9
Goslin
  Thomas 18, 26
Gosling
  John 32
Gott
  Florence 20
  Rebecca 20
  Richard 23
  Robert 20, 24
Gouge
  John 42
Gough
  Stephen 2, 12, 13, 26
Gouldesboroug 11
  Mr. 11
Gouldesborough
  Mr. 11
  Robert 11
Gouldsborrough 43
  Robert 45, 49
Gouldsboury
  Mr. 40
Gouldsbrough
  Mr. 19
Gourley
  Barbary 23
  John 23
Goute
  Capt. 45
  John 50
Goutey
  John 42
  Joseph 28
Gover
  Robert 24
Goy
  Jacob 5
Goyne
  William 40
Grace
  Thomas 2, 25
Graf
  John 21
Grandy
  Capt. 1
Granger
  Christopher 35
Grason
  Mary 20, 23, 27
  Robert 20, 23, 27
Gray
  George 12, 21
  James 12
  Jefery 40
  John 14, 15, 16, 24, 40
  Samuell 24
  Thomas 33, 38
  William 33
Green
  Edward 1, 6, 47
  Francis 4, 18
  Henry 10
  John 2
  Thomas 46
Greenal
  James 1
Greenbery
  Nicholas 17
Greenbury
  Nicholas 32
Greene
  John 36

Page 72

Richard 10
Greenfeild
    Mr. 32
    Thomas 7, 31, 32
Greenfield
    Mr. 17
    Thomas 4, 26, 45, 47,
        48, 49
Greenhalf
    Capt. 30
Greenhalgh
    Edward 35
Greenslade
    Orlando 21, 41
Greenway
    John 41
Greenwell
    James 12, 13
Greenwood
    Samuell 32
Greer
    William 47
Greewell
    James 1
Gregory
    Christopher 41
Grenfeild
    Thomas 27
Gresham
    Mary 20
    Robert 20
Gressam
    John 20, 24
Greves
    John 40
Grey
    James 28
Grifeth
    Henry 5
Griffin
    Jane 6
    John 22, 24, 47
    Richard 25
    William 26
Griffith
    Henry 38
    Phillip 6
    William 10
Grifine
    John 2
Griggs
    John 7
Grimes
    William 39
Grinall
    William 21
Grissett
    ------ 24
Groom
    Moses 43
Groome
    Moses 29, 30
    Richard 34
    Samuell 3, 20, 21, 27,
        34, 42
    Sarah 20
    W. 21
    William 13
Grove
    William 9
Grover
    John 36
Groves
    John 5
    William 9, 26
Grubb
    John 18
Grundee
    Robert 37
Grundy

Robert 3, 12, 20, 45,
    47, 49
Grunwin
    Thomas 12, 21
Grunwyn
    Thomas 21, 46
Guardiner
    Luke 1
Gudgoon
    Michaell 29
    William 29
Gugin
    William 46
Guibert
    Joshua 13, 18, 28
    Joshuah 46
Guider
    William 12
Guile
    Edward 15
    John 24
Guillam
    John 21
    Ralph 29
Guillock
    Thomas 24
Guither
    Owen 46
    Thomas 2
    William 25
Gumey
    William 27
Gundry
    Gideon 9
Guntor
    Tymothy 8
Gutherick
    Robert 49
Gutridge
    Henry 5
Guyatt
    John 17
Guybert
    Joshua 23, 24
Guyther
    Will 58
    William 2
Gwinn
    Christopher 13
    Sarah 18
    William 18
Gwither
    Thomas 12
    William 12
Gwyn
    Sarah 36
    William 36
Gyard
    Francis 35
Gyles
    John 23

Hacker
    John 10, 11, 41
    William 40
Hadaway
    George 6, 10
Hadder
    Warren 47
    widow 41
Haddock
    Thomas 12, 25, 30, 31,
        37, 46
Haddocks
    Thomas 25
Hadock
    Richard 2
Hadway
    Peter 29

Haezlon
    Lewis 15
Hagan
    Thomas 22
Halerd
    Edward 13
Haley
    Clement 42
    Eliza 42
    Mary 42
Hall
    Aron 14, 49
    Benjamin 25
    Capt. 27
    Charles 19
    Edward 37
    Elisha 47
    John 14, 27, 29, 30, 32,
        33, 34, 35, 37, 38,
        44, 45, 49
    Joseph 3, 21
    Joshua 10
    Martha 38
    Mary 5, 7, 34
    Mr. 24, 34, 36, 38
    Sarah 37
    Thomas 13, 18, 41
    William 7
Hallen
    David 48
    John 48
Halock
    Walter 30
Haman
    Richard 6
Hambleton
    John 7
    Samuell 17, 43
Hamer
    John 33
Hamilton
    Gawin 22
    John 34
    Samuell 33
Hamlin
    John 4
Hammon
    Ann 5
    Benjamin 17
    Edward 43
    Elisabeth 33
    John 43
Hammond
    John 9
    Richard 10
    Thomas 46
    William 28
Hamon
    Capt. 33
    John 33
Hamond
    John 15
Hance
    John 32
Hancock
    Robert 9, 42
Handcock
    Robert 41
    Thomas 44
Hanford
    Richard 15
Hanie
    Hermlas 48
    John 48
Hanslap
    Capt. 24
    Henry 20, 24, 43, 49
Hanslapp
    Henry 27
Hansley

Edmond 17
Hanson
    Charles 15
    John 16, 22
Harberdine
    John 23
Harbert
    Alexander 32
    Mary 45
    William 37
Harbin
    Francis 47
Harbourne
    William 22
Harburt
    William 35
Hardage
    William 26
Hardidge
    Capt. 7
Hardin
    John 28
    William 2
Hardy
    Henry 1, 3
Harebottle
    John 45
Hargest
    Thomas 7
Harintun
    James 33
Harkin
    Cornelius 28
Harman
    Casparus 16, 28
    Katherine 28
    Thomas 33
Harmonson
    Christian 6
Harness
    Jacob 9
Harper
    James 41
Harrenson
    Joseph 35
Harrington
    Charles 17
    Cornelius 30
    Richard 6
Harris
    ------ 36
    Capt. 26
    Jacob 35
    John 2, 24
    Mary 4
    Moses 12, 47
    Mr. 16
    Peter 1, 4
    Richard 29
    William 14, 24, 26, 28,
        36, 37, 41, 50
Harrison
    Edward 2, 3, 9
    Francis 31
    James 38
    John 15
    Joseph 3, 31
    Ri. 42
    Richard 6, 16, 23, 31,
        42
    Robert 33
    Thomas 31
Harry
    William 9, 11, 44
Harsley
    Edward 46
Hart
    Arthur 42
Hartley
    Ann 18

Joseph 4, 18, 32
Harvey
    Murtah 6
    Thomas 36
    Winefred 8
Harvy
    Robert 20
    Thomas 44
Haselwood
    John 35
Haslewood
    Henry 45
    John 50
Hast
    Daniel 4
    John 34
Hatch
    William 7
Hatfeild
    William 6, 29, 33
Hatfield
    William 40, 47
Hatoway
    Thomas 46
Hatto
    Thomas 12
Hawkins
    Austin 24
    Elisabeth 28, 31, 35, 49
    Henry 7, 15, 23, 35, 41,
        44
    John 4, 6, 10, 11, 24,
        42
    Joseph 28
    Mathew 24
    Ralph 44
    William 45
Haws
    Mathias 23
Hawton
    William 31
Hay
    Charles 8
Hayes
    John 3
Hays
    Charles 48
    John 40
    Mary 48
Hayward
    Francis 29
Haywood
    Raphad 41
Hazelewood
    John 30
Hazelwood
    John 29
Hazlewood
    Henry 38
Hazlon
    Lewis 13
Head
    Adam 13, 32
    Ann 32
    William 14, 15
Heap
    Fra. 47
    Francis 6, 33, 43
Heard
    Henry 39, 41
    John 4
    Susan 4
Hearsly
    Joseph 6
Heartly
    James 8
Heast
    Daniell 18
Heatchoct
    John 24

Heath
    Joseph 46
    Thomas 10, 17, 29, 30
Heatham
    N. 26
Hebb
    Thomas 13
Hecap
    Joell 41
Hedge
    John 14
    Thomas 14, 17, 24, 29,
        30, 32, 43, 44, 45,
        46
Hedger
    John 36
Hedges
    John 15
    William 10
Heifford
    Thomas 26, 45
Heiger
    Samuell 15
Heigh
    James 5, 28
Heighes
    James 14
Hellen
    David 27, 49
    Davis 23
    William 13, 25
Hemesley
    William 33
Hemler
    John 1
Hemsley
    Charles 11
    Ja. 15
    Vincent 10, 29, 43
    William 4, 10, 11, 20
Hemsly
    Phill. 11
Henderson
    George 44
    John 6, 39
Hendrickson
    Florine 46
    Mathew 49
Hendrixson
    Mathias 9
Hendry
    John 47
Henery
    John 6
    William 6
Henington
    Henry 7
Henly
    Darby 7
Hennison
    Abraham 42
Henry
    Hedge 45
    John 6, 47
Hensley
    Sarah 30
Herbert
    William 30, 46
Herman
    Katherine 28
Hernley
    Darby 48
Herring
    William 7
Herris
    James 42
Hersley
    Edmund 35
Hetherington
    John 10

Heugh
   Henry 48
Heunton
   William 13
Hewes
   Owen 9, 16
Hewett
   Robert 39
Hewitt
   John 14
Hews
   John 41
Hewton
   William 42
Hexon
   Henry 15
Heyden
   William 32
Heyes
   George 10
Heyman
   John 49
Hick
   John 11
Hickman
   Timothy 2, 34
   William 39
Hicks
   Thomas 16
   William 43
Hicky
   Andrew 38
Hide
   Nicholas 44
Higgin
   Patrick 11
Higgons
   Michaell 17
Higham
   Francis 5
Higton
   John 18
Hiland
   Jane 28
Hill
   Ann 17
   Clement 28, 32
   Francis 39
   Peter 48
   Richard 3, 34
   Robert 23
   Sarah 37
   Thomas 15, 48
   William 37
   Willmott 1, 47
   Wilmott 46
Hilleard
   Thomas 39
Hilleary
   Thomas 39
Hillen
   David 21, 30
   John 18
Hillerd
   Edward 2
Hillery
   Thomas 47
Hillman
   Thomas 3, 4, 19
Hills
   Thomas 2
Hinderson
   William 6
Hindes
   Timothy 39
Hindsley
   Thomas 10
Hinett
   Joseph 36
Hinson

   Charles 16
   Hugh 4
   Randolph 31
Hinton
   Hugh 21
   Mordecai 26
   Thomas 2, 7, 15, 35
Hipison
   Charles 10
Hiring
   John 6
Hobart
   Richard 18
Hobbs
   Robert 26
Hodgson
   William 22
Hogg
   Ambros 46
   Ambross 38
Hogin
   John 29
Hogthaw
   Robert 47
Holdsworth
   Joshua 13
   Samuell 7
Holines
   Archbell 6
Holland
   Anthony 23
   Capt. 20, 26, 32, 36
   John 38
   Margarett 24
   Otho 9
   widow 38
   William 3, 15, 20, 43,
     44
Hollandworth
   Thomas 23
Holleger
   Phill. 36
Hollensworth
   Charles 6
Holliday
   Thomas 19
Hollingmead
   Joshua 37
Hollingsworth
   Charles 16
Hollins
   Abraham 9
Hollis
   William 35
Holloway
   John 14, 17
Hollyday
   Col. 22
   Thomas 39
   William 26
Holmes
   Fra. 11
   Francis 41
Homewood
   James 47
   Thomas 1
Honis
   Thomas 40
Hooke
   Thomas 35
Hooker
   Jacob 24
   Thomas 23
Hooper
   Henry 19
   Maurice 7
   Morris 11
   Mr. 50
   Robert 24
Hopham

   George 29
Hopkins
   Clement 12
   Elisabeth 11, 43, 47
   Gerd 24
   Gerrard 41
   James 12
   John 39
   Joseph 5
   Mary 12
   Richard 12
   Robert 12
   Samuell 4, 6, 18, 26,
     33, 43, 47
   Thomas 10, 11, 12, 37,
     43, 47
   William 12, 21
Hopper
   Robert 35, 44
   William 6
Horn
   William 42
Hornby
   William 40
Horne
   Edward 2
   John 22, 46
   William 46
Horney
   Mortaugh 47
   Mortogh 33
   Mortough 17, 43
Horrell
   Christopher 32
Horseman
   Thomas 14, 34, 35
Horsley
   Isaac 19
Horsman
   Thomas 14
Hosier
   Henry 16
Hoskins
   Ann 25, 49
   Philip 15, 22, 37, 43,
     44, 49
   Phillip 23, 25, 31, 36
   William 20
How
   Elisabeth 48
   Thomas 5
Howard
   Cornelius 2
   John 23, 31
   Mary 31
   Mathew 8
   Matthew 34, 47
   Philip 45
   Samuell 34
   Thomas 31
   William 21
Howe
   Thomas 2, 17, 39
   William 17
Howell
   Charles 30
   John 5, 41, 44
   Nathaniel 5
   William 32
Howgood
   William 6
Hubbard
   Richard 15, 25, 34, 36
Hubbart
   Mr. 5
   Richard 49
Hubert
   Humphrey 29
Hudson
   Johanna 16

Johannah 43
William 43
Hues
Owen 28
Samuell 28
Hugh
Ann 4
John 4
Hughes
Thomas 39, 45
Hughs
George 12
Owen 16
Thomas 8, 9, 17, 35, 41, 42
Hume
John 28
Hune
Capt. 23
Hungerfoot
William 15
Hunt
Ann 19, 28
Anne 8
Benjamin 8, 28
Edward 32
John 8, 16, 33, 34, 49
Wolfran 23
Woolfran 42
Hunter
Mr. 34, 36
Thomas 48
William 22, 23, 46, 49
Hunton
Elisabeth 48
Elizabeth 14
Mordica 14
Timothy 48
Hurlock
Abraham 6
Hurse
John 38
Hurst
John 25
Thomas 49
Husband
William 25, 46
Huse
Thomas 2
Hussey
Thomas 25, 31, 49
Hust
Thomas 2
Hutcheson
Thomas 41
Hutchins
Elisabeth 15
Francis 20, 21
George 3, 4, 19
Mathew 14
Thomas 33, 41
William 5, 14, 15
Hutchinson
Peter 47
Thomas 6, 12, 23, 31, 42
William 7
Hutchison
George 6
Thomas 15
William 48
Hutchyson
Thomas 23
Huttchyson
William 37
Hyde
John 3, 8, 21, 34, 40, 42
Thomas 8
Hyndes
Thomas 33

Hynson
Richard 6
William 6, 33

Imbert
Andrew 10, 11
Dr. 11
Impey
George 17
Peter 23
Inchboard
widow 12
Ingerson
Daniell 28
Seth 28
Ingram
Daniell 28
Inlons
Henry 45
Inman
Benjamin 39
Innis
Nathaniel 4
Insley
Andrew 42
Ipling
Robert 26
Issaack
Allerton 25
Ive
James 35
Ivery
Thomas 23

Jackson
Ezeakeall 9
George 21
Henry 17, 35
Isaack 46
Jacob 3
James 3
John 43
Joseph 8
Mr. 41
Richard 15, 21
Samuell 29
Symon 17, 30, 38
Thomas 10
William 17
Jacob
John 40
Jacobs
John 23
Jaggard
William 37
Jakes
Solomon 46
James
Charles 9, 16
Edward 27
Elisha 28
Joseph 29
Michaell 36
William 23
Jameson
Thomas 30, 43
Jarvice
Humphrey 20
Jarvis
Humphrey 49
Humphry 9
Mary 49
Jefferson
Peter 28
Richard 4
Jelfes
William 26
Jenifer

Jacob 50
Jenkins
David 50
Francis 6, 7, 18, 38, 43
Mathew 6
Mr. 4, 19, 43
Obediah 20
Rachell 20
Thomas 25, 31, 46
widow 20
Jennifer
Jacob 50
Jinking
John 21
Joanes
Phillip 16
Joannes
John 15
Joans
Elisabeth 15
Joce
Thomas 11, 16
Johnings
Thomas 6
Johnson
Anthony 35, 46
Capt. 12
Cornelius 38
David 45
Edward 9
Francis 3
George 20
Henrick 6
Henry 12
John 21, 33, 41
Mary 48
Peter 18
Robert 17, 19, 43
Thomas 3, 33, 48
Will 22
William 3, 5
Jolly
Dr. 47
Jones
David 2
Dorothy 49
Edward 16, 29
Elisabeth 49
Griffith 41, 45
Henry 8, 38
Hugh 9, 20, 26, 45, 48, 49
John 3, 11, 12, 17, 33, 35, 41, 47, 49
Lewis 17
Mary 40
Mathew 24
Morgan 16, 26
Moses 25
Moyses 25
Mr. 26
Philip 44
Richard 9, 10, 26, 33, 41, 45
Robert 39
Sollomon 13, 30
Solomon 1, 6, 13
Thomas 4, 5, 6, 46, 47
William 6, 11, 12, 14, 31, 38
Jonnes
Richard 1
Solomon 2
Jonns
Lewis 1
Jonson
John 16
Jorboe
John 13
Peter 13

Josling
    John 8, 10, 22
Jowles
    Col. 7, 17, 29
    Henry 3, 15, 21
Joy
    Charles 2
Joyce
    John 19, 48
    Thomas 39
Joye
    Peter 46
Judd
    Michael 44, 45
    Michaell 40
Judkin
    Obadiah 6
Judkins
    Obadiah 10
Jump
    William 41
Jury
    Elisabeth 21
Justept
    Richard 49

Kary
    Michaell 22
Kee
    Henry 18, 31, 39
    Sarah 27, 31
Keech
    James 12, 13, 18, 21
Keefe
    Arthur 25
Keeld
    John 41
Keen
    Joshua 34
    Richard 3, 21, 26
Keene
    Richard 14
Keetch
    James 21, 32
Keeth
    George 13, 41
Keirkly
    Thomas 12
Keirsted
    Jochem 15
    Mrs. 15
Kellett
    Jacob 28
Kelley
    John 31
Kelly
    Daniell 16
    John 10
    Thomas 26
Kemp
    John 4
Kempston
    Richard 8
Kene
    Arthur 4
Kenerly
    Alice 27
    William 27
Kennard
    Richard 9
Kennerly
    Alice 28
    Allice 8
Kerkland
    Robert 43
Kerkley
    Thomas 13
Kerkly
    Thomas 12

Kerry
    Michaell 22
Kersey
    Michael 48
Kersted
    Jockem 17
    Margarett 15
Key
    Henry 31
Keys
    John 49
Keyser
    Capt. 27
    Timothy 21
Kilbourne
    Rachell 21
Kilburne
    Charles 8
    Richard 8, 11
Kill
    Allexander 43
Killen
    Thomas 16
Kinemont
    Andrew 29
King
    ------ 36
    Belitha 14
    Elias 16
    Henry 38
    James 11
    John 14, 15, 40, 44
    Obadiah 8, 36
    Robert 32
    Thomas 41
    widow 19
    William 20
Kingcart
    Martha 42
    Thomas 8, 21, 41, 42
Kingsbery
    Dr. 7, 44
Kingsbury
    Dr. 26
    James 36
Kiniston
    Thomas 2
Kinningston
    Thomas 32
Kinwood
    Richard 28
Kirk
    Martin 25
Kirke
    James 37
    John 8
Kirkland
    Richard 45
    Robert 24
Kirsteed
    Joakim 31
Kitten
    Theophilus 42
Knight
    Christopher 42
    John 23, 25
    William 2, 12, 32, 46
Knighton
    Thomas 23
Knightsmith
    Thomas 24
Knott
    Francis 5, 13, 22
Knowles
    Laurence 27
    Lawrence 6, 17
    Peter 30
Kursted
    Dr. 38
Kyele

    Florah 42
Kyle
    Flora 44

Ladford
    John 39
Ladimore
    widow 44
Ladmore
    Elisabeth 49
    George 8
Lallyvan
    Owen 29
Lamb
    Richard 45
Lampton
    Mark 15
Lancaster
    Richard 38
Land
    Henry 7, 47
Lane
    George 2
    John 6, 11, 12, 41
    Morris 10
    Thomas 34
    W. 19
    William 37
Langham
    George 15
Langley
    Capt. 17, 38
    Richard 40
Lanham
    Capt. 24
Lansly
    Ann 5
    Charles 5
Laott
    William 29
Lapage
    Edward 49
Lappage
    Edward 49
Laremore
    Edward 16
Large
    Robert 12
Larkin
    John 24
Larkins
    Elisabeth 23
    John 43
Lary
    Lawrence 22
Lashland
    John 14
Lates
    Francis 6
Latham
    Edward 3
Latimor
    James 42
Laurence
    Esq. 49
    Thomas 49
Lawes
    John 18
    Katherine 18
Lawrence
    Benjamin 23
    Esq. 49
    John 8, 16
    Thomas 7, 8, 11, 12, 27,
        28, 41
Laws
    Katherine 19
Lawson
    Thomas 15, 16

Layfield
    George 4
    Mr. 19
Layne
    Thomas 36
Layton
    Henry 18
    Margrett 18
Leach
    John 21
Leaf
    widow 22
Leafe
    Ann 44
    Francis 36, 44
Lecoumpt
    John 38
Lecount
    John 23
    Mr. 21
Lee
    John 6, 39
Leech
    John 14
    Joseph 5
Leek
    George 35
Legcam
    William 31
Legg
    William 46
Leigh
    John 19
Lekins
    John 45
Lennam
    John 48
Lenox
    William 30
Leverton
    John 4
Levin
    Phillip 19
Lewellin
    ------ 4
    Audrey 24
    John 1, 2, 24, 36, 41
Lewis
    Allexander 17
    Edward 16
    James 9, 23, 34
    John 39
    Matthew 39
    Thomas 10, 15, 32
    William 20, 33, 41, 42,
        45
Leyfeild
    George 6
Lild
    Isaack 27
Linch
    Henry 23
    Robuck 34
    Roebuck 30
Lineam
    John 23
Lines
    Philip 22
    Phillip 24, 31
Lingan
    George 2, 7, 17, 26, 38,
        39
    Mr. 30
Lingham
    George 47
Linllame
    Teague 4
Linsey
    Thomas 9
Linwcomb

Richard 23
Lisle
    Elisabeth 37
    Robert 37
    Samuell 37
    William 37
Little
    Margarett 4
Litton
    Richard 16
Liverley
    Gilbert 12
Llewellin
    Audry 1
    John 7
Lloyd
    Edward 10, 11, 47
Lock
    Richard 17
Lockerman
    Jacob 44
Lockwood
    Robert 23
Lockworth
    Joseph 48
Lofton
    Robert 1
    William 35, 40
Loftus
    Henry 41
Lomax
    Cleb. 44
    Cleborne 5, 23, 26, 31,
        35, 36, 49
    Clement 3
    Katherine 29
Long
    George 45
    Jane 14, 17
Longman
    Daniell 4
    John 23
Lorson
    Thomas 22
Lory
    John 35
Love
    William 9
Low
    Nicholas 4, 11, 45
    William 39
Lowder
    Richard 39
Lowe
    Henry 7, 13, 15, 29
    John 5, 6, 29
    Joseph 2
    Mr. 36
    Nicholas 10, 11, 18, 27,
        28, 29, 37, 41, 43,
        45
    Thomas 25, 36
    Vincent 6, 23
    William 36
Lowre
    William 46
Lowrey
    William 12
Loxton
    Robert 23
Loyd
    Botherick 42
    Edward 11
    Henrietta Maria 27
    John 6
    Phillomen 27
Loyde
    John 21
Luckett
    Samuell 4

Luddall
    Jane 20
    William 20
Luisey
    John 12
Luke
    John 30
Lumley
    George 32
Lumly
    Alexander 3, 46
Lunn
    Thomas 24
Lurkey
    Thomas 29
Lurting
    Francis 15
Lurtty
    Nicholas 1
Lushy
    Jacob 3
Lydiatt
    John 37
Lyle
    James 18
    John 16
    Robert 39
Lyles
    Samuell 22
Lynch
    Roebuck 32, 33
Lynes
    Henry 6
    Philip 3, 21
    Phillip 18, 23, 41

Maccall
    John 26
Macfarland
    Alexander 23
Macgregory
    Elisabeth 10
Mackall
    David 33
Mackdowell
    John 21
Mackeall
    David 35
Mackeill
    William 8
Mackelfish
    David 9
Macklane
    Hector 3
Macklin
    Richard 11, 43
    Robert 10
Mackling
    Richard 40
    Robert 40
Mackmara
    Timothy 50
Mackmillion
    Peter 16, 23
Mackmorry
    Bartholomew 46
Macknell
    Daniel 49
MacKnitt
    John 19
Maclamy
    Owen 43
Maclanell
    James 5
Macmamy
    John 7
Maddocks
    Edward 42
Maddox

Allexander 7
Notly 22
William 21
Madocks
   Col. 7
Magar
   Thomas 30
Magetee
   Patrick 7
Magraw
   Andrew 46
Magruder
   Allexander 42
   Ann 42
   Samuell 8, 42
Mail
   Anthony 45
Maingt
   Edward 15
Makensee
   John 29
Makey
   Hezekiah 36
Makneale
   Daniel 16
Maldin
   Francis 3
Man
   Edward 3, 5, 17, 44
   George 45
Maning
   John 2, 14, 15, 17
   Ruth 14
Mankin
   Stephen 22, 31
Manly
   Margarett 25
Mann
   Mr. 12
Mannatt
   John 11
Manning
   John 2, 4, 7, 18, 25,
     26, 30, 40, 46
   Ruth 26
Manson
   Jeremia 17
Manthorp
   Samuell 34
Maplington
   Richard 12
March
   Nicholas 23
Margent
   William 36
Maris
   Thomas 40
Marke
   Margarett 29
   William 20
Markerly
   Ann 26
Marley
   Robert 6
Marline
   James 3
Marow
   Anguish 35
Marry
   James 3
Marsh
   Thomas 8, 27
Marshall
   Elisabeth 42
   Isaack 44, 45
   John 47
   Joyce 44
   William 15, 16, 42
Marsham
   Ann 20, 36, 37

Mr. 48
Richard 20, 25, 36, 37,
   38, 49
Marston
   William 34
Marstone
   William 40
Marten
   Michael 39, 49
Martin
   George 10
   Gillion 49
   James 1, 5, 26, 30, 32
   John 24, 31
   Mary 31
   Michaell 31
   Thomas 2, 8, 11, 35
   William 21
Marting
   Ja. 15
Mashett
   Isaack 30
Mason
   Fra. 15
   James 44, 46
   John 32
   Mr. 4, 37
   Robert 5, 12, 22, 24,
     25, 29, 32, 33, 37,
     38, 46
   Sebaston 5
   Thomas 33
   William 13
Massey
   Philip 47
Master
   Robert 10
Maston
   Richard 41
Mathew
   Jonathon 15
Mathewes
   Morrice 8
Mathews
   Ignatius 21, 43
   Jonathon 12
   Roger 17, 38
Mathiason
   Mathias 28, 49
Mattershaw
   Jeffry 41
Maxem
   Thomas 45
Maxfeild
   James 24
Maxwell
   James 30, 32, 49
   Maj. 27
   Samuell 10
May
   John 2
Maynard
   James 4, 43
Mazzard
   James 30
McClanachan
   Thomas 47
McColluck
   Allexander 6
McNemara
   Timothy 39
Mead
   Frances 33, 34
   Francis 34
   William 43
Meade
   William 35
Meads
   John 36
Mears

William 20
Mecens
   William 13
Medly
   William 13
Meech
   Thomas 5
Meek
   Mary 6
Meeke
   Francis 6
Meekins
   Richard 28
Meende
   James 40
Meers
   William 20
Meires
   James 47
Meran
   Darby 10
Mercer
   John 45
   Margarett 45
Meredith
   Lewis 41
Merideth
   Lewis 10
Meriken
   Joshua 5
Meriton
   John 5
Merrikin
   Hugh 24
   Joshua 24
Merriton
   Hugh 1
   John 2, 9, 20, 23
Merritt
   Edward 46
   George 46
   Jethro 46
   John 46
Merry
   Bartholomew 13
Merryday
   Henry 20
Merryman
   Charles 40
   Mr. 35
Merue
   James 10
Meryman
   Charles 35
Meshew
   William 35, 38
Messer
   Thomas 16
Methven
   James 2
Mettley
   Chr. 23
Michew
   William 50
Mickin
   William 46
Micollum
   Dunkin 30
Milbourne
   Nicholas 11
Milburne
   Nicholas 10, 11, 41
Milby
   Christopher 34
Miles
   John 2, 13, 30
   Susannah 24
   Thomas 24
Millbourne
   ------ 49

Miller
    Edward 12, 37
    George 15, 37
    John 13
    Mary 44
    Michaell 8, 10, 11, 16,
        39
Millington
    Ollivar 6
Millinton
    Oliver 47
Millner
    Isaack 14, 32
Mills
    David 6, 10, 18
    James 24
    John 2
    William 39
Millson
    Samuell 12
Millstead
    Edward 31
Milner
    Isaac 33
Milsted
    Edward 44
Minckin
    Richard 34
Minges
    Edward 23
Minooke
    Michell 15
Mirex
    Richard 6
Mitchell
    Henry 7, 26
    John 45
    Thomas 7, 25
    William 5, 47
Mitchew
    William 19
Moate
    Chr. 23
Mockdell
    William 28
Mockguyer
    John 33
Mockyfelt
    Daniell 35
Mogayer
    John 47
Mograh
    Andrew 2
Mohoone
    Timothy 13
Molls
    John 21
Moone
    Ralph 11
Mooney
    Rose 25
    Thomas 25
Moony
    James 6
Moore
    Allexander 6
    Dr. 5, 9, 14, 17, 24
    Hannah 19
    Henry 15
    James 5, 47
    M. 43
    Mordecay 24, 37
    Mordica 9
    Richard 29
    Thomas 16, 28
    Ursula 24
    William 15, 19, 48
Moorland
    Jacob 27, 32
More

Ann 43
Moreland
    Jacob 4, 7, 12, 13, 23,
        25, 37
Morely
    Patrick 2
Morgan
    Abraham 10, 34
    David 30
    Edward 18
    Elisabeth 12
    George 29, 30
    Israell 7
    James 16
    Jarvis 23, 38
    John 24
    Martin 26
    Thomas 3, 14
    William 12, 13, 16
Moriot
    William 30
Morison
    James 3
Morland
    Mr. 1
Morley
    Joseph 8
Morray
    James 3
Morris
    Daniell 10
    Francis 10
    John 9
    Thomas 35
    William 4
Morrison
    William 6
Morrow
    Anguish 29
Mort
    William 28
Mortemore
    John 2
Mortimore
    John 41
Mortin
    James 21
Morton
    John 20
    Mr. 44
    Robert 6
Moss
    Ralph 25
    Richard 8, 21
    William 7, 26
Mosten
    William 48
Mote
    William 3
Mouall
    John 5
Mounce
    Lawrence 9
Mouney
    James 38
Moy
    Daniell 2, 22, 26
Mudd
    Thomas 25, 49
Mullakin
    Daniell 11
Mullikin
    James 19
Munday
    Henry 44
    Robert 47
Murphey
    David 31
    James 29
    John 13

Murphy
    Charles 20
    James 6
    John 2
Murry
    Bartholomew 13
    James 45
Musgrave
    Cuth. 15
Musgrove
    Dorothy 18

Nailer
    Joseph 24
Narleland
    Nicholas 38
Natler
    George 19
Nayler
    George 48
Neal
    Ann 44
    Anthony 44
    Charles 47
    Elisabeth 44
    Henry 44
    James 44
    Jonathon 41, 42
    Mary 44
Neale
    Ann 1
    Anne 7
    Anthony 1, 3, 31, 32
    Elisabeth 1
    Henry 1
    James 1, 7, 10, 23
    John 47
    Jonathon 1, 33
    Madam 15
    Mary 1
Neales
    John 28
Neall
    Anthony 29
    Jonathon 29
Nellson
    Thomas 8
Nelson
    John 18, 31
    Richard 34
Nensley
    Benjamin 30
Newgatte
    Edward 25
Newgent
    Edward 25
Newman
    Daniell 17
    George 15
    John 18, 20, 33
    Richard 12, 13, 32
    Roger 17, 22, 27, 32,
        44, 45, 46
Newnham
    John 6
Newsam
    Thomas 38
Newton
    Elisabeth 41
    John 41
    Samuell 6, 20, 43, 49
Nicholes
    Thomas 21
Nicholls
    John 16
    Thomas 5
    William 15, 24, 48
Nichols
    John 44, 50

Thomas 7
Nicholson
    Gou. 26
    John 2, 17, 22, 23
    Mary 17
    Nicholas 23
    Thomas 8
Nickols
    Thomas 48
Nicolls
    John 8, 38
Noble
    George 6
    John 21, 25
    Robert 4, 45
    William 6
Noe
    John 42
Norman
    Elisabeth 3
    George 30
Norrest
    John 33
    Robert 4, 10
Norrington
    John 15
Norris
    Edmund 6
    Henry 13
    John 2
    William 16, 32
North
    Elisabeth 46
    John 24, 46
Norton
    Peter 29
Norwood
    Andrew 34
    John 6, 33, 34
    Philip 34
    Samuell 34
Nowell
    Ann 46
    Henry 46
Nuckin
    Cornelius 9
Nueman
    Henry 37
Nugent
    Edmond 16
Numan
    George 19
    John 37
Nunam
    John 10, 43
Nurn
    John 24
Nutthall
    John 3, 13, 24
Nutwell
    Elias 10

O'Bryan
    Patrick 6
O'Delly
    Daniell 6
Oakley
    widow 40
Obryan
    Patricke 4
Ocford
    Thomas 6
Odaham
    George 21
Odell
    Thomas 9, 40
Ogbey
    Mathew 19
Ogden

Andrew 15
Elisabeth 15
Ogg
    George 24
Ogleby
    John 37
Oldfeild
    William 9
Olesee
    Robert 17
Omaley
    Bryan 34
Omely
    Bryan 34
Oneale
    Arthur 49
Onsby
    Stephen 28
Orem
    Andrew 40
Orme
    Robert 2, 32, 47
Orrell
    Thomas 15
Orton
    Henry 37
Osborn
    Hannah 10
    William 10
Osburne
    William 35
Oulden
    John 26
Overing
    Edward 47
Owan
    Edward 10
Owen
    Nathaniel 18
    Richard 26, 27
    Rudolph 20
Owens
    William 19, 34
Ownbey
    Stephen 27
Ozen
    Francis 10

Pace
    Thomas 13
Padget
    Thomas 49
Padgett
    Henry 2
Pagan
    Peter 26
Paggan
    Mr. 44
Paggen
    Peter 32, 33, 45
Paine
    Isaack 25, 46
    John 22, 31
Palmer
    Daniell 4, 5, 17, 35
Panter
    John 3, 35
Parce
    William 16
Pargdan
    John 29
Pargrave
    James 38
Parke
    George 15
Parker
    Andrew 19
    Elisabeth 6
    George 23, 24

Jonas 6
Mr. 30
Richard 35
Robert 3, 17, 30, 35, 46
Thomas 9, 28, 35, 37
widow 24
William 7, 15, 17, 25,
    30
Parks
    William 7
Parnes
    Richard 6
Parrett
    Gabriell 9
    Mathew 15
Parrott
    Gabriel 43
    Gabriell 3, 49
Parslow
    Ellinor 7
Parsly
    Peter 18
Parsons
    Amos 19
    David 13
Pashell
    James 2
Pattee
    Francis 7
Patten
    Morgan 6
Pattison
    James 2
    John 6, 18
    Thomas 24, 50
Pattisson
    Gillburt 35
Paultry
    William 32
Paxton
    Hugh 10
Peace
    Thomas 13
Peack
    Joseph 35
Peacke
    Aquila 35
Peak
    Joseph 43, 44
Peake
    Catherine 14
    George 14
    Jane 14, 17
    Joseph 14, 17, 33
    Peter 13
Pearce
    Daniel 49
    John 30
    Mary 30
    William 8, 9, 28, 49
Pearch
    Symon 4
Pearl
    Bryan 6
Pearll
    James 19
Pears
    Cornelius 9
Peasly
    John 21, 47
Peason
    Richard 42
Peck
    Benjamin 11, 26, 43, 44,
        47, 49
Pecke
    Benjamin 12, 20
Peckett
    William 30
Peerce

William 9
Pemberton
    John 11, 12
    Margrett 11
Penington
    William 17
Pennington
    Henry 16
    Thomas 25
Penninton
    Henry 49
Penny
    Elisabeth 41
    James 41
Pent
    Michaell 37
Perce
    Edward 2
Percifull
    John 10
Perke
    Robert 39
Perkin
    Richard 40
Perrie
    Robert 6, 47
Perry
    John 21, 33
    Micajah 3, 34
    Richard 21
    Sarah 33
Persons
    Amos 7
Pesher
    Lazerus 41
Peters
    Joseph 42
    Mary 46
    Samuell 48
Peterson
    Jeffry 9
Pettet
    John 45
Pettibone
    Joseph 5
Pettybone
    Joseph 34
Pew
    David 1, 7
Phelps
    Walter 20, 23
Philips
    Capt. 49
    James 43, 46
    John 45
Phillips
    Anthony 30
    Elisabeth 32
    John 18, 19
    Nicholas 8
    Robert 8, 26, 41
    Thomas 2
    William 4, 18, 43
Phillman
    Thomas 3
Philmore
    William 26
Philpot
    Edward 16
Philpott
    Edward 16
Pickett
    John 44
    William 29, 30
Pierpoint
    Amos 42
Pilkton
    Mary 16
Pindar
    Edward 41

Pinder
    Christopher 6
    Edward 5
Pindor
    widow 32
Pinner
    Thomas 35, 37
Piper
    William 4
Pitt
    Ann 35
    John 12, 45
    Phillip 8, 29
Pitts
    John 11
Plater
    Ann 5
    George 1, 3, 5, 7, 8,
        11, 25, 26, 29, 32,
        34, 37, 38, 47
Plowden
    George 37
Plumer
    Elisabeth 24, 43
    Thomas 24
Plummer
    Thomas 24, 43
Plunkett
    Thomas 22
Pocam
    Johne 43
Pocum
    Jone 43
Pointer
    Thomas 19
Polk
    Robert 18
Pollard
    Mary 7
Pond
    Edward 6
Pool
    David 43
Poole
    David 24
Pooley
    John 6
Pooly
    John 40, 45
Poore
    Nicholas 24
Pope
    Daniell 5
    John 5, 6, 11, 43
    Mary 5
    William 49
Porish
    Philip 4
Port
    John 9
Porter
    Elizabeth 42
    Giles 50
    Hugh 19
    John 19
    Robert 10
    William 42
Pott
    Henry 2
    Richard 29
Pottenger
    John 8, 48
Potts
    Francis 47
    Henry 38
Poulter
    Henry 46
Poultery
    Henry 2
Powell

Anna Mary 44
Charles 8, 19, 26, 28
Guillian 25
Hannah 39
James 23
John 12, 13, 32
Mr. 16
Thomas 35
Walter 26, 45
William 20, 35, 44
Power
    Geoffery 16
    Jeffrey 16
    Nicholas 18
Prater
    George 48
Prather
    Jonathon 31
Pratt
    Henry 28
    Thomas 23
Preist
    Prooke 27
Preston
    John 47
    Thomas 30, 40, 45, 46
Prevett
    Ambrose 40
Price
    Abraham 42
    Alexander 34
    Andrew 6
    Jacob 47
    James 43
    Jane 43, 46
    John 11
    Richard 10, 15
    Robert 7
    Thomas 15, 16
    William 32
Prichard
    William 35
Primrose
    John 11
Prise
    Thomas 16
Pritchard
    John 29, 39
Proctor
    Rachell 21
    Robert 21, 23
Prois
    Ph. 1
Prosser
    William 10
Proutt
    John 2
Pullin
    Richard 11
Purdey
    John 24
Purnel
    Thomas 43
Purnell
    Richard 6
    Thomas 7, 33, 40
Pursivall
    Arthur 4
Pursor
    Symon 29
Pye
    Col. 23
    Edward 23, 25, 28, 37

Queasteed
    Dr. 43
Quincy
    Sutton 36
Quinton

Walter 11, 41

Rabitts
    William 26
Radford
    John 2, 45
Rake
    Richard 2
Rallow
    John 25
Ramming
    William 47
Ramsheire
    Nathaniell 18
Ramstopp
    Hugh 31
Randall
    Robert 16
Rappe
    Capt. 28
Ratchford
    Law 15
Ratcliff
    Emanuell 31
    Michaell 22
Ratcliffe
    Robert 6
Ratford
    John 22
Raven
    Luke 14, 17
Rawlegh
    Walter 28
Rawling
    Jane 6
    Richard 6
Rawlings
    Jane 6
    John 8, 29
    Richard 6
Rawlins
    Richard 42
Rayle
    James 11
Read
    Jane 45
    Robert 17
    William 45
Reade
    John 16
Redar
    Benjamin 39
Reder
    Benjamin 39
Redgrave
    Abraham 9
    Margarett 9
Redle
    Robert 34
Redman
    Dennis 10
    John 32
Redwood
    John 47
Reed
    James 41
Reeves
    June 4
    Thomas 12
    Ugatt 4
Regon
    James 15
    Joan 15
Relay
    John 46
Rely
    Mich 46
Remond
    James 43

Restall
    William 21
Revell
    Randoll 19
Reynolds
    Edward 44
    John 32
    Robert 26
Rhodes
    Nicholas 39, 41
Rhods
    Nicholas 41
Rice
    Evan 15
Rich
    Henry 7
    Stephen 4
Richards
    John 6
Richardson
    Charles 48
    Daniell 36
    David 19
    Dr. 2, 24, 25
    Elisabeth 36
    John 29
    Joseph 36
    Mark 23, 24
    Marke 17, 33, 35
    Sophia 36
    Thomas 30, 46, 49
    William 19, 20, 33, 36,
        43
Richman
    Daniel 46
Rickards
    John 8
    William 11
Ricketts
    John 36
    William 26
Rickward
    John 26
Rider
    Thomas 17
Ridgely
    Henry 21
Ridgley
    Henry 21, 23, 27, 45
    Mary 27
Ridgly
    Henry 6
Ridle
    Robert 34
Ridley
    James 12
Rigbey
    James 33
Rigg
    Thomas 15
Right
    Henry 9
Rimer
    Ralph 46
Ringgold
    James 35
Ringold
    James 35
    William 40
Roach
    John 14
Roades
    Nicholas 9
Roads
    John 6
    Nicholas 39
    Timothy 43
    William 2
Robarts
    John 40

Robartson
    James 49
Robatham
    George 41
Robbinson
    Daniell 39
Roberson
    Robert 39
    William 43
Roberts
    John 30, 45
    Robert 7, 34
    Roger 26, 39
    Sarah 7
    Thomas 6
Robertson
    Robert 6
    Susannah 17
    William 30
Robeson
    John 10
Robins
    Francis 46
    George 11
    John 6, 18
    Robert 15
    Thomas 6, 11, 18, 20, 40
Robinson
    Daniel 47
    Francis 30, 43
    George 2, 29
    Henage 33
    Hennage 11
    John 24, 40, 44
    Max 16
    Robert 10
    Susannah 14
Robison
    William 6
Robotham
    Col. 45
    George 6, 11, 41
Robson
    William 33, 35
Roce
    John 10
Rock
    John 49
Rockhold
    John 31, 45
    Mary 45
Rogers
    David 6, 33, 45
    Elisabeth 45
    Robert 31
    Thomas 45
Roockwood
    Edward 31
Rookewood
    Edward 15
Rookwood
    Edward 42
Roper
    Phillip 30
    Thomas 38
    William 38
Rose
    John 10
    Robert 22
    Thomas 2
Rosewell
    Mr. 2
Rosey
    William 43
Rosier
    Ann 37
    Benjamin 28, 37
    Notley 25, 37
Ross
    Allen 6

Mabell 19
Ruben 19
Rubian 28
Roth
  Robert 43
Rottee
  Sollomon 12
Round
  James 6, 33, 43, 47
  William 47
Rouse
  John 44
Rowe
  John 40
  Thomas 41
Rowell
  John 5
Rowles
  Christopher 28
Rowser
  Catherine 45
Royston
  Anne 7
  John 7, 46
  Mary 6
  Richard 24
Rumball
  Anthony 1, 6, 20, 33, 47
Rumbly
  Edward 2
Rumney
  Edward 45
Russell
  John 2, 29
  Jos. 15
  Mary 36
  widow 29
Ruth
  Edward 11, 37
Rutledge
  Edward 35
Rutte
  Solomon 46
Rutter
  Richard 44
Rycroft
  William 49
Rymer
  Elisabeth 36
  John 25
  Ralph 29, 36

Sadler
  Robert 11
Sallows
  Robert 39
Salter
  Bridgett 49
  John 10, 11, 12, 16, 18,
    20, 33, 41, 43, 49
  Mr. 47
Samson
  Richard 45
Samuell
  Richard 18
Sander
  William 28
Sanders
  Edward 39
  James 40
  Jane 39
  John 21
  Joseph 45
  Matthew 39, 41
Sandford
  James 11
Sandifer
  Richard 24
Sandland

Thomas 6
Sandry
  Francis 24
Sands
  Richard 2, 7
  Thomas 33
Sandsberry
  Richard 21, 22
Sandy
  Richard 3
Sandys
  Richard 15
Sannds
  Math. 15
Sapinton
  Nathaniel 49
Sapsole
  Abra. 15
Sargent
  John 10
  William 10
Satterfatt
  Edward 11
Saunders
  Edward 5, 15
  James 20
  John 1
  Joseph 2, 39
  Mathew 22, 31
Savoy
  Susannah 23
Sawell
  John 3
Sawyer
  Peter 23
Sayer
  Col. 41
  Peter 10, 17, 43
Sayles
  Clement 12
Scantey
  John 26
Scidmore
  Samuell 40
Scillmore
  Samuell 40
Scot
  Samuell 34
Scott
  John 3, 26, 28, 30
  Nathan 44
  Samuell 14, 48
  Thomas 6
  Walter 28
  William 10, 20, 29, 33,
    47
Scrivener
  Benjamin 9, 26, 43, 45
Scrivner
  Benjamin 41
Scrivneright
  Robert 28
Seamans
  James 46
  Jeames 39
Searth
  Jonathon 34
Searylen
  Isack 1
Sedgwick
  Thomas 36
Sedwick
  James 41
  Thomas 42
Seiffin
  John 24
Selby
  Daniell 6
  Mathew 34
  Parker 6

William 42
Sergeant
  William 31
Sergent
  John 29
Serjant
  John 44, 45
  widow 49
  William 31
Sessill
  John 13
Seth
  Jacob 6, 10
  Jacobus 10
Sewall
  Nicholas 3
Seward
  James 6
Sewell
  Ignatius 26, 32, 44
  James 32
  John 32
  Maj. 24
  Nicholas 23
  Peter 14, 15
  Timothy 22
Shaco
  Christopher 46
Shankes
  John 22
  Thomas 13
Shanks
  Margarett 24
  Thomas 24
Shanland
  William 6
Sharp
  John 33, 44
  William 8, 10, 18, 45
Sharpe
  William 20, 34
Shaw
  John 16
  Ralph 7, 22
Shayl
  John 1
Sheapeard
  John 2
Shearbutt
  John 2
Sheers
  Elisabeth 16
  Thomas 16
Sheild
  William 37
Sheington
  Edmond 38
Sheircliffe
  William 13
Shepard
  John 12
  Thomas 35
Shephard
  Robert 15
Shephardson
  Edward 44
Sheppard
  Bartholomew 46
  Isaack 45
Sherdue
  Daniel 21
Sheredine
  Daniel 49
Sherrevan
  Darby 22
  Derby 22
Sherriff
  John 31
Sherry
  Moses 6

Sherwood
    Daniell 5, 6, 11, 30, 34
    John 5
    Luce 5
Shettell
    William 17
Shettle
    William 20
Shillcott
    Anthony 38
Shington
    Thomas 44
Shippard
    Robert 20
Shofell
    Mr. 1
Shores
    William 27
Short
    Christopher 8
    George 25
    John 21, 48
Showell
    Samuell 35
Shrine
    William 30
Shurley
    James 41
    John 25
Sicklemore
    Daniell 14
    Samuell 30
Sidell
    Richard 2
Sides
    John 6, 10, 33, 49
    Peter 45
Siennett
    John 26
Siklmore
    Samuell 45
Silvester
    James 41
    widow 41
Simmons
    Charles 45
    John 35
    William 7
Simms
    Anthony 25
Simons
    John 35
Simpson
    John 23
    Thomas 3
Simson
    Thomas 25
Sinett
    Ignatius 21
Sinnett
    Garrett 18
Sirelson
    John 25
Sissary
    Edward 18
Sissell
    John 13
Skelton
    Israel 40
Skidmore
    Ann 45
    Pennellophia 14
    Samuel 45
Skillington
    Mary 47
    Thomas 47
Skinner
    Alice 40
    Clark 48
    Clarke 14, 36

    Richard 10
    Robert 14, 15, 21, 42,
      48
Skipper
    Patience 40
Slacom
    George 34
Slacomb
    George 34
Slacum
    George 34
Slade
    William 30
Sladen
    William 45
Slatton
    Anthony 6
Slaughter
    William 32
Sly
    Pricilla 38
    Robert 22, 38
Slye
    Gerrard 27
    John 18
Small
    David 5, 18, 19, 20, 26,
      48
Smallpage
    Robert 22
Smallwood
    James 7, 21, 22, 23, 25,
      31
    Thomas 4
Smart
    John 28
Smith
    Alice 8, 20
    Allan 11
    Anthony 3
    Benjamin 11
    Charles 2, 32, 34
    Daniell 9
    Dennis 5
    Edward 4, 47
    Elisabeth 36, 37, 42
    Esq. 4
    Francis 30
    George 6, 10, 17, 29,
      30, 33, 37, 38, 46
    Henry 2, 25, 26, 35, 39
    James 4, 10, 11, 12, 19,
      32, 33
    John 2, 13, 14, 17, 22,
      23, 24, 25, 27, 29,
      31, 45, 49
    Mary 47
    Mathew 47
    Nathaniell 22
    Ralph 26
    Richard 8, 14, 24, 28,
      30
    Robert 6, 9, 10, 11, 17,
      26, 28, 33, 41
    Samuell 29, 35
    Sarah 26
    Thomas 2, 14, 29, 40
    Walter 17, 26, 42
    William 1, 3, 5, 10, 16,
      20, 29, 32, 36, 37,
      41, 42, 49
Smithick
    Thomas 2
Smithson
    James 49
    Maj. 11
    Thomas 6, 10, 11, 19,
      20, 27, 37
Smoote
    Thomas 25

Snell
    Jeremy 49
Snelling
    William 6
Snelson
    John 8, 37
Sneyon
    John 26
Snoden
    Henry 40
Snowden
    Richard 23
Sollers
    John 20
Solman
    John 40
Sorrell
    Richard 2
Sorrill
    Christopher 12
Sothern
    John 32
Sotheron
    John 23
    Valentine 26
Sothoron
    John 42
    Richard 3, 13, 15
Southerland
    David 35
Southern
    Ann 20
    Henry 20
Southerne
    Richard 21
Southeron
    Richard 1
Southey
    John 29
Southorn
    Richard 13
Sparrow
    Thomas 24, 36
Spell
    Joseph 6
Spence
    Adam 6
    James 18
Spencer
    John 24
    William 38
Spicer
    George 8, 21, 41, 48
    John 23
Spikeman
    William 37
Spink
    Henry 13
    John 7
Spinke
    Henry 13
    William 13
Sporne
    Nicholas 3, 37
Spourne
    Richard 19
Sprigg
    Thomas 8, 35
Spry
    Christopher 6
Stafford
    James 24
Staley
    Thomas 17, 29
Stanbrough
    Josias 44
    Recampens 33
Standbank
    Thomas 24
Standefer

Samuell 30
Standford
  Samuel 40
Standifor
  Samuell 29
Stanfeild
  James 6
Stanford
  John 2
Stanley
  Manus 38
  Mary 49
Stannard
  John 40
Starley
  James 41
Starter
  William 27
Staunton
  Blanch 45
Stavies
  Samuell 11
Stawks
  Peter 50
Stayley
  Thomas 34
Stayly
  Thomas 35
Steevens
  Thomas 16
Stenet
  Joseph 48
Stenett
  Sarah 48
Stephens
  Charles 26, 28
  Francis 26, 27
  Jiles 43
  William 8
Stephenson
  Edward 44, 45
  Symon 45
Stevens
  Charles 26
  Edward 29
  Joseph 24
  William 16
Stevenson
  Edward 45
  William 43
Steward
  David 9
  Margarett 9
Stewart
  Mary 10
Stinchcombe
  Nathaniel 46
Stinchcome
  Nath. 3
Stoakes
  Peter 29
Stockley
  Edward 41
Stoddard
  James 18, 19
Stoddart
  James 10, 48
Stoddert
  James 34
Stokes
  Petter 35
Stomford
  John 45
Stone
  Allexander 43
  Dorothy 23, 31
  John 16, 23, 24, 39
  Matthew 18
  Robert 2, 39
  Thomas 21, 30

William 1, 3, 5, 7, 21,
  25, 31, 41
Stoop
  John 28
Storey
  Edmond 37
  Joseph 23
  Walter 25, 26
Story
  Walter 1, 3, 16
Stourton
  Robert 12
Stratton
  Robert 7
Strawbridge
  Joseph 14, 34
  Sarah 34
Strottan
  Capt. 3
Strutton
  Anthony 34
Stuart
  John 19
Suckpale
  Gregory 37
Sumer
  Benjamin 30
Summers
  Benjamin 43
  Robert 2, 36
  William 31, 39
Sumner
  Margaret 17
  Robert 17
Sumy
  Richard 28
Sunderland
  John 17
Sutton
  Alic 14
  Anne 16
  Francis 11
  Henry 33
  Philip 16
  Thomas 23
  William 9
Swailes
  Francis 13, 18
Swain
  Ann 43
  John 43
Swaine
  John 11
  Mary 43
Swallow
  John 1, 10
Swan
  James 22
Swarbrocke
  Lawrence 47
Swatewell
  John 37
Sweatnam
  Edward 11, 16, 24
  Richard 10, 11, 24, 45
Swendell
  Daniel 44
Swetman
  Edward 4
Swift
  John 49
  Margarett 31
  William 17
Swindall
  Daniell 30
Swine
  Dennis 33
Swoins
  John 28
Sybery

Capt. 45
Sykes
  Robert 22
Symons
  Daniell 15
  Thomas 26
Sympson
  Robert 47

Tailor
  Lawrence 33
  Magdalene 15
  Robert 31
  William 15
Talbot
  John 24
Talbott
  Edward 36
  Elisabeth 36
  John 36
Taney
  John 15
  Michaell 7, 27
  Mr. 1
  Thomas 4, 21
Tannehill
  William 22
Tanner
  Ann 35
Tanny
  Mr. 18
Tannyhill
  William 19
Tant
  John 1, 13, 18
Tanyhill
  William 48
Tapper
  Lewis 46
Tarr
  John 47
Tarry
  Thomas 14
Tasker
  Thomas 3, 37, 44
Tattersall
  Phillip 22
TatterShall
  Phillip 38
Tattershoall
  Lawrence 21
Tauney
  Michaell 37
Taylard
  William 12, 24
Tayler
  John 4
  William 1
Taylor
  Abraham 29, 40
  Ann 18, 42
  Col. 24
  Edward 34
  Francis 8
  Hope 6, 43
  James 9, 28
  Jane 28
  John 1, 8, 21, 26, 30,
    34, 43, 45, 46
  Lawrence 33
  Margarett 46
  Mary 30
  Michaell 26
  Richard 6, 10
  Thomas 15, 18, 20, 38,
    42
  Walter 13, 46
  William 2, 13, 27, 42
Teale

Sarah 30
Telley
    Charles 9
Temple
    Michaell 9
Tenason
    Justinian 39
Tench
    Edward 35
    Esq. 26
    Jonathon 3
    Mr. 36
    Thomas 7, 17, 24, 26, 39
Tenesse
    Thomas 9
Tennison
    Justinian 42
    Mathew 46
Tenniston
    John 25
Terrett
    Nicholas 20
Terry
    Thomas 9
Tetersham
    Lawrence 25
Tettersall
    Lawrence 25
Thackston
    Thomas 11
Thackstone
    Thomas 9, 11
Thaxton
    Thomas 28
Theobalds
    John 49
Thisslewood
    James 38
Thomas
    Benoni 44
    Benony 31
    Col. 45
    Ellis 38
    John 29, 44, 45, 46, 49
    Thomas 10, 27, 47
    William 15, 19, 44
Thompson
    Anthony 8, 29
    Arthur 4, 32
    Christopher 18
    Henry 39
    Issabella 39
    James 22, 30, 37
    John 2, 8, 9, 16, 26,
        28, 39, 49
    Richard 44
    William 15, 16, 22, 42
Thoms
    William 9
Thomson
    Ann 14
    John 9
    Richard 14
Thopson
    John 35
Thorley
    Samuell 3
Thornbourgh
    Rouland 7
Thornton
    Richard 28
Thorowgood
    Francis 18
Tiers
    James 34
Tilden
    Charles 16, 37
Tiley
    Ann 11
Tilghman

Mathew 49
Richard 10, 11, 41, 47
Till
    Edward 23, 31
    Sarah 22, 23, 31
Tillotson
    John 4
Timms
    Peter 2
Timothy
    William 15, 18
Tinney
    Catherine 41
Tinsly
    Thomas 3
Tippon
    John 35
Tipton
    Jonathon 3
Tire
    Boules 49
    James 49
Toads
    Daniell 4
Toas
    Daniell 11
Tod
    Lancelot 34
Todd
    ------ 35
    James 17, 33, 43
    Lancelot 34
    Michael 42
    Michaell 38
    Richard 3, 5
Toiler
    John 42
Tole
    Thomas 13
Toley
    Walter 10
Toll
    Henry 13
Tolley
    Thomas 32
    Walter 10
Tomco
    Thomas 1
Tomks
    Henry 48
Tomlin
    Edward 41, 44
Tomlinson
    Katherine 7
Tommy
    Dennis 30
Tompson
    Christopher 19
    Henry 31, 37
    James 18
    John 19, 20, 32
    Mr. 24
    Robert 25
    William 18, 25, 39
Tomson
    Christopher 48
    James 34
Tonnard
    Andrew 6, 40
    Joseph 20
Toulson
    Alexander 27
Tourford
    Thomas 24
Tourlin
    Edward 29
Towers
    Jonathon 6
Towes
    Daniell 11

Towgood
    Joseph 19
Townsend
    John 19
Tracey
    Charles 3, 34
Tracy
    Charles 4, 10, 13
Trevett
    Robert 39
Tribell
    Thomas 35
Tripp
    Henry 1, 27
Trippe
    Henry 26
Troth
    William 20, 41
Trottman
    Mr. 42
    William 42
Troughton
    Elisabeth 19
Trougton
    Roger 19
Trouton
    John 42
Truckam
    Roger 19
Trueman
    Henry 3, 21
Truit
    George 43
Truitt
    George 33
Trulock
    Joseph 9
Truman
    ------ 14
    H. 20
    Henry 7, 17
    Jane 20
Trundle
    John 2, 9, 41, 42
Tubman
    George 27, 43
    Mr. 42
    Richard 19
Tucker
    Dorothy 17
    Richard 42
    Seaborne 17
    William 41
Tull
    Richard 4, 7, 24, 43
Tully
    Chr. 24
Turberfeild
    Payn 2
Turbett
    Michaell 11
Turling
    John 7
Turner
    Edmund 50
    Edward 38, 39, 42
    James 18
    John 7, 23, 27, 30, 31,
        41
    Samuell 35
    Thomas 12, 26
    William 23, 26, 30
Twisdeal
    Mrs. 25
Twogood
    Josias 39, 48
Tyers
    Bowles 34, 36
    James 36
Tyler

Page 87

Robert 38

Underwood
   Andrew 21
   Anthony 21
   John 36
Ungle
   Robert 41, 45
Upperdine
   James 16
Ureers
   Nathaniell 18

Valliant
   John 10, 11, 49
Vallient
   John 6
Vanderbash
   Lawrence 39
Vanderheyden
   ------ 49
Vanderhyden
   Mathias 9
Vanibles
   William 14
Vanswaringen
   Zacharia 2
Vanswearingen
   Mr. 2
Vansweringain
   Gerrard 23
Vansweringen
   Garrett 23
Vaughan
   David 30
   Johannas 1
   Susannah 40
Vauhop
   Archibald 36
Veitch
   Nathan 37
Vernon
   Christopher 20, 45
Vesey
   John 16, 28
Vestall
   George 5
Vickers
   Francis 12
   Joseph 6
   Thomas 29
Vickory
   John 1
Vigore
   Isack 9
Vincent
   George 8
   John 50
Viner
   John 6
Vinson
   George 8, 20, 35
Vivers
   Nathaniel 13
Vorson
   Thomas 33
Voss
   Robert 17
Vowell
   Richard 12
Vowells
   Richard 46
Vowles
   Richard 12
Vuderhay
   Samuell 16

Wad
   John 32
Wade
   George 44
   John 8, 16, 35, 37
   Richard 42
   Robert 23, 47
Wadsworth
   William 26
Wae
   Richard 15
Waggitt
   John 49
Wainewright
   Jossias 11
Waker
   Daniell 6
Walden
   John 16
Walker
   ------ 32
   Daniell 3, 17
   Henry 43
   Richard 13
Walkinson
   Cornelius 21
   Elisabeth 21
Wallace
   William 7
Wallase
   William 14
Walles
   Michael 42
Wallice
   J. 25
Wallis
   Richard 32
   Thomas 47
Walls
   John 9
Wallwin
   Edward 16
   Susannah 16
Wally
   Richard 17
Walson
   Charles 6
Walter
   Alexander 41
   Elisabeth 4
Walters
   Alexander 10
   Christopher 5
   Elisabeth 5
   John 2, 23
   Joseph 25
   Robert 10
Walton
   Stephen 30
Ward
   Cornelius 43
   Henry 42
   John 15, 31
   Mathew 43
   Thomas 10, 35
Warfield
   Richard 42
Warfoot
   Mary 17
Warner
   George 28
Warren
   Col. 7
   Hum. 23
   Humphrey 26
   Ignatius 18
   Notley 1, 42
   Richard 47
   Samuell 37, 38
   Sarah 37

Thomas 13
Washfeild
   Robert 8
Washfell
   Robert 8
Washington
   Phill. 40
Waters
   Edward 46
   John 26
   Robert 6
Wathen
   John 4
Watkins
   Anne 10
   Cornelius 3
   Elisabeth 3
   Francis 14
   John 4, 32
   Katherine 32
   Lewis 46
   Peter 6
   Samuel 4
   Samuell 7, 17, 21, 24,
      26, 32, 33, 41, 49
   Thomas 2
Watkinson
   Elisabeth 32
   widow 13
Watson
   Charles 31
   James 37
   John 23, 30, 40
   Mary 23
   William 48
Watters
   Edward 34
Wattkins
   Katherine 19
Watton
   John 31
Watts
   Charles 15, 46
   Charolus 2
   Elisabeth 27, 46
   James 27, 35
   John 6
   Peter 6, 49
   Robert 24
   William 6, 46, 49
Wattson
   William 8
Waugh
   John 42
Waughop
   Thomas 22
Wayford
   William 48
Wayman
   Lenerd 20
   Lennord 35
   Leonard 23, 30, 42
Wealdes
   Samuell 2
Weales
   Joseph 33
Weals
   John 33
Weasells
   Gerardus 37
Weathers
   Samuell 11
Weaver
   John 45
Webb
   Edgar 6
   John 4, 6, 43, 46, 47
   Michaell 3
   Richard 24
   Robert 12

William 29

Webster
  John 30
Wedge
  John 16
Weeb
  John 1
Weekes
  Thomas 7
Weeks
  John 30
Welch
  Henry 24
Wells
  Benjamin 17, 28, 30
  Daniell 45
  Elenor 45
  Jenkin 22
  John 11, 30, 32, 45
  Jonathon 12
  Joseph 14, 45, 46
  Osias 2
  Tobias 11
  William 25
  Zorobabell 10
Welsh
  James 30
  Silvester 3
Wenman
  Edward 15
Wersley
  Samuell 6
West
  John 14, 43
  Joseph 48
Wetherly
  James 4
Weydon
  William 46
Wharton
  Darby 40
  Thomas 32, 34
Whealock
  Edward 21
Wheatle
  William 34
Wheatley
  Daniell 41
Wheatly
  Arthur 19
Wheelar
  Samuell 40
Wheeler
  Alice 19
  Allice 8
  Ignatius 7, 16, 18, 27,
    31, 39
  John 15, 36
  Sarah 8
  Thomas 39
Wheelock
  Ann 47
  Edward 47
Wheelwright
  Stephen 17
Wheightler
  Alice 19
  John 19
Whetherell
  Jane 9
Whichaley
  Thomas 15
White
  Allexander 43
  David 25
  Guy 27
  John 18
  Josias 30
  Nicholas 2, 6
  Richard 21

Stephen 45
William 44
Whitehead
  Charles 3, 35
  Francis 29, 30, 40
  Wharles 24
Whitely
  Arthur 19
Whitle
  Mary 34
Whitom
  William 16
Whitter
  Susanna 32
  William 32
Whittherd
  Samuel 1
Whittington
  Maj. 4, 18, 19, 26, 33,
    43
  William 6, 7, 43, 47
Whittinton
  Maj. 43
Whittwell
  Symon 49
Whorton
  Richard 18
Wickam
  Nicholas 5
  Sabina 5
Wider
  Robert 15
Wiggott
  Joseph 11
Wight
  Ann 27
  Anne 10
  John 3, 10, 27, 37
Wild
  Abraham 9
Wilde
  Abraham 5, 42
  Isacc 9
Wilkeson
  John 7
Wilkinson
  John 14, 15
  Mr. 44
  William 31, 33, 35, 49
Wilkison
  John 22
  William 34, 46
Wilkisson
  William 35
Willeson
  John 22
Willett
  Abraham 28
  Edward 48
Williams
  Baruch 39
  Baruck 37
  Benjamin 24, 43
  Charles 4, 6
  Ester 2
  James 6, 19, 42
  John 7
  Joseph 24, 43
  Peter 38
  Thomas 2, 15
  William 7, 10, 21, 30
Williamson
  Christopher 15
Willis
  Francis 12
  John 36, 50
Willmare
  Charles 23
Willmer
  John 46

S. 11
Willmore
  Mr. 49
Willobey
  John 23
Willoughby
  John 26
Willson
  Ephraim 21, 32, 34
  George 6, 43
  Giles 16
  Jonathon 19, 26, 36, 37,
    48
  Joseph 3, 41
  Josiah 29
  Josias 4
  Katherine 36, 37
  Thomas 18
  William 22, 35, 37
Wilmer
  Simon 10
Wilson
  James 22
  Jonathon 3, 37
  Joseph 1
  Joshua 26
  Thomas 12
Winchester
  Isaack 27
  John 8
Windall
  Thomas 28
Winder
  John 32, 34
Windle
  Thomas 28
Winfeild
  Jonah 37
Winsmore
  John 29
Winsor
  John 4, 18
Wise
  James 45
  John 6
Wiseman
  John 30
Wissells
  Gerardus 29
Witcholy
  Henry 42
With
  Nicholas 41
Withers
  Samuel 27
  Samuell 6, 11, 24
Withington
  Ann 11
Wood
  Edward 38, 43
  James 26
  John 15, 18, 22, 31
  Robert 48
Woodgate
  William 38
Woods
  James 40
Woodward
  John 18, 41
  William 5
Wooland
  Edward 33, 35
  Jane 33
Woolfe
  John 11
Wooten
  Symon 26, 37
Wooters
  John 47
Wooton

Mr. 3
Workman
    Anthony 11, 44
Worley
    John 10
Worrell
    Ralph 37
Worthington
    Mr. 47
    Samuell 6, 14, 33
Wothington
    Samuell 43
Wothrinton
    Samuell 4
Wotton
    John 19
    Simon 17
Wouldhave
    William 1, 47
Wrench
    William 11, 41, 49
Wright
    Arthur 19
    John 10, 15, 29, 30, 35,
        37
    Sollomon 10
    Solomon 5
    William 35
Wriothsley
    Henry 30
Write
    John 42
Wroughton
    John 19
Wyles
    John 6

Yates
    George 23
    Martin 13
    Mary 40
    Robert 1, 34, 36, 42, 49
Yeildhall
    William 23
Yeoman
    Thomas 16
Yewell
    Thomas 29
Yoakeley
    Michaell 20
Yoodall
    Patrick 2
Yorke
    William 29
Young
    Arthur 37
    Elisabeth 34, 36, 49
    George 36, 42
    Mary 3
    Samuell 3
    William 48
Yowdall
    Patrick 2
Yowman
    Thomas 46
Ywell
    Sarah 40

Other Heritage Books by Vernon L. Skinner, Jr.:

Abstracts of the Administration Accounts of the Prerogative Court of Maryland, 1718–1724, Libers 1–5

Abstracts of the Administration Accounts of the Prerogative Court of Maryland, 1724–1731: Libers 6–10

Abstracts of the Administration Accounts of the Prerogative Court of Maryland, 1731–1737: Libers 11–15

Abstracts of the Administration Accounts of the Prerogative Court of Maryland, 1737–1744: Libers 16–20

Abstracts of the Administration Accounts of the Prerogative Court of Maryland, 1744–1750: Libers 21–28

Abstracts of the Administration Accounts of the Prerogative Court of Maryland, 1750–1754: Libers 29–36

Abstracts of the Administration Accounts of the Prerogative Court of Maryland, 1754–1760: Libers 37–45

Abstracts of the Administration Accounts of the Prerogative Court of Maryland, 1760–1764, Libers 46–51

Abstracts of the Administration Accounts of the Prerogative Court of Maryland, 1764–1768, Libers 52–58

Abstracts of the Administration Accounts of the Prerogative Court of Maryland, 1768–1771, Libers 59–66

Abstracts of the Administration Accounts of the Prerogative Court of Maryland, 1771–1777, Libers 67–74

Abstracts of the Balance Books of the Prerogative Court of Maryland: Libers 2 and 3, 1755–1763

Abstracts of the Balance Books of the Prerogative Court of Maryland: Libers 4 and 5, 1763–1770

Abstracts of the Balance Books of the Prerogative Court of Maryland: Libers 6 and 7, 1770–1777

Abstracts of the Inventories and Accounts of the Prerogative Court of Maryland, 1674–1678, 1699–1703

Abstracts of the Inventories and Accounts of the Prerogative Court of Maryland, 1679–1686

Abstracts of the Inventories and Accounts of the Prerogative Court of Maryland, 1685–1701

Abstracts of the Inventories and Accounts of the Prerogative Court of Maryland, 1688–1698

*Abstracts of the Inventories and Accounts of the Prerogative Court of Maryland, 1697–1700:
Libers 16, 17, 18, 19, 19½A, 19½B*

*Abstracts of the Inventories and Accounts of the Prerogative Court of Maryland, 1699–1704:
Libers 20–24*

*Abstracts of the Inventories and Accounts of the Prerogative Court of Maryland, 1708–1711:
Libers 29, 30, 31, 32A, 32B*

*Abstracts of the Inventories and Accounts of the Prerogative Court of Maryland, 1711–1713:
Libers 32C, 33A, 33B, 34*

*Abstracts of the Inventories and Accounts of the Prerogative Court of Maryland, 1712–1716:
Libers 35A, 35B, 36A, 36B, 36C*

*Abstracts of the Inventories and Accounts of the Prerogative Court of Maryland, 1715–1718:
Libers 37A, 37B, 37C, 38A, 38B, 39A, 39B, 39C*

*Abstracts of the Inventories and Accounts of the Prerogative Court of Maryland, 1699–1708:
Libers 25–28*

Abstracts of the Inventories of the Prerogative Court of Maryland, 1718–1720

Abstracts of the Inventories of the Prerogative Court of Maryland, 1720–1724

Abstracts of the Inventories of the Prerogative Court of Maryland, 1724–1727

Abstracts of the Inventories of the Prerogative Court of Maryland, 1726–1729

Abstracts of the Inventories of the Prerogative Court of Maryland, 1728–1734

Abstracts of the Inventories of the Prerogative Court of Maryland, 1733–1738

Abstracts of the Inventories of the Prerogative Court of Maryland, 1738–1744

Abstracts of the Inventories of the Prerogative Court of Maryland, 1744–1748

Abstracts of the Inventories of the Prerogative Court of Maryland, 1748–1751

Abstracts of the Inventories of the Prerogative Court of Maryland, 1751–1756

Abstracts of the Inventories of the Prerogative Court of Maryland, 1755–1760

Abstracts of the Inventories of the Prerogative Court of Maryland, 1760–1763

Abstracts of the Inventories of the Prerogative Court of Maryland, 1763–1766

Abstracts of the Inventories of the Prerogative Court of Maryland, 1766–1769

Abstracts of the Inventories of the Prerogative Court of Maryland, 1769–1772

Abstracts of the Inventories of the Prerogative Court of Maryland, 1772–1774

Abstracts of the Inventories of the Prerogative Court of Maryland, 1774–1777

Abstracts of the Proceedings of the Orphans' Court of Sussex County, Delaware: Libers 1, 2, 3, 4, A (1708–1709, 1728–1777)

Abstracts of the Proprietary Records of the Provincial Court of Maryland, 1637–1658

Abstracts, Worcester County, Maryland Estate Docket, 1742–1820

Other Wills in the Prerogative Court for Somerset and Worcester Counties, 1664–1775

Provincial Families of Maryland, Volume 1

Somerset County Will Books, 1750–1772

Somerset County Wills, 1667–1748: Liber EB9

Somerset County Wills, 1770–1777 and 1675–1710: Liber EB5

Supplement Abstracts Inventories and Accounts, Prerogative Court, 1691–1706

Worcester County Inventories and Accounts, 1694–1742: Inventory Book JW15

Worcester County Wills: Will Book MH3, 1666–1742